NATIONALISM AND WOMEN'S MOVEMENT IN SOUTH INDIA, 1917-1947

NATIONALISM AND WOMEN'S MOVEMENT IN SOUTH INDIA, 1917-1947

P.N. Premalatha

GYAN

GYAN PUBLISHING HOUSE
New Delhi-110002

NATIONALISM AND WOMEN'S MOVEMENT IN SOUTH INDIA, 1917-1947
(*Women*)

Rs. 690

ISBN: 81-212-0788-6

Published in 2003 in India by
Gyan Publishing House
5, Ansari Road
New Delhi 110 002
Phones: 3261060, 3282060, Fax: 3285914
e-mail: gyanbook@vsnl.com
visit our website at: http://www.gyanbooks.com

Laser Typeset at Alphabet, Delhi
Printed at Mehra Offset Printers, Delhi

Contents

Foreword

For sustainable development men and women should not only contribute equally but also be equally recognized for their contribution. Ignoring one section leaves out one half of humanity. It also leads to distortions of facts for the posterity.

This work is an attempt by Dr. P.N. Premalatha, Reader in Historical Studies, Mother Teresa Women's University to make Women in history visible. The casual linkage of the subjection of women with the subjecting of our country is an analysis to be appreciated and pondered over.

The books throws light on:

The status of women from the sangam age and the evolution of the same during various periods and the factors responsible.

The book forms an interesting reading and enriches the historians from Women's Studies perspective and the feminists from historical perspective.

I congratulate her for her endeavour.

Dr. (Mrs). Anandhavalli Mahadevan
Vice-Chancellor

Mother Teresa Women's University
Kodaikanal - 624102

An Appraisal

Women who form fifty per cent of the population everywhere have remained invisible and unnoticed in the past several hundreds of years. Their education was negligible; their economic conditions were not even noticed; their emotional pleas for betterment of the living conditions were mostly ignored. They were, on most occasions considered on par with property and products. Seldom were they considered as human beings, with equal intelligence or feelings. In the West, thanks to the Industrial Revolution, which provided opportunities for women to work in factories along with men, and hence opportunity for earning their bread, "Movements" for women's emancipations began their on ward march. Persecution of any sort against women was resented. There were protests and marches and much resentment was voiced against the "masculine gender".

In the East and especially in India, women's emancipation efforts were supported by the great sons of the nation, such as Raja Ram Mohun Roy, Swami Vivekananda, Rebindranath Tagore, Subramania Bharathiyar and others. The movements work towards women's development through education and economic independence and strive towards women - in - development.

In such a context, "Nationalism and Women's Movement", written by Dr. P.N. Premalatha, is acclaimed as laudable, since the focus is on women's status of Equality and Recognition during the Struggle for political independence of the nation. Efforts were maximised towards India's Independence. After independence of course and especially during the past three decades, women's movement has gathered tremendous momentum. Government and non-governmental organizations marched forward to voice their grievances and aspirations. The fight for equal status had begun. By the declaration of the International Decade for Woman (1975-1985) and other measures, the UNO voiced its concern and support for women.

In India, in Tamil Nadu, Women's Movements gathered momentum under its women - leaders.

Dr. Premalatha's work covers, besides the struggle for India's independence, the women's development in the Tamil speaking area of the Madras Presidency. The primary and the secondary sources throw much light on this area.

Her study is divided into five chapters, excluding introduction and conclusion. The study is a conscious attempt to focus on untrodden areas, in women's progress. The work of some of the great women, in the venture are referred to at the appropriate places.

The study has, hence contributed significantly to the existing fund of knowledge pertaining to women - study materials in Tamil Nadu. This book needs to be appreciated as a unique contribution to the field of women - study and development.

Dr. S. Lakshmi
M.A., (Eco), M.A., (Pol.Sc)., M.Ed., Ph.D.

(Former Vice-Chancellor,
Mother Teresa Women's University)
(Former Member - N.C.T.E.
Southern Regional Committee)
163-K, Sundarar Street, Fairlands, Salam - 636 016.

Preface

One of the objectives of the department of Historical Studies, Mother Teresa Women's University, where I am working, is to make women visible in history. Women's history has a dual purpose - to restore women to history and history to women. Accounting for the present situation of women involves scrutiny of the past. Our traditional historiography has been focussing upon areas of human activity in which males were predominant. Women figured chiefly as exceptions. Like other subordinate groups in society, women were also silent voices in history. Now the trend is changing.

The worldwide movement for the emancipation of women, the declaration of the International Decade for Women by the United Nations, the financial assistance made available by international agencies and research institutiions for research on women and the setting up of the National Committee on the Status of Women paved the way for a series of studies on different aspects of women from different strata of society throughout the globe. Social reforms and also women in India's freedom struggle attracted the attention of many scholars for specific study. But there are not much references regarding South Indian women especially Tamil Nadu. Hence this work "Nationalism and Women's Movement in South India 1917-1947" is taken up for investigation. This work was started in 1992 as minor project titled "Feminism and Nationalism in Tamil Nadu 1917-1947" sponsored by the Indian Council of Historical Research, New Delhi.

The status of women from the Sangam age and the factors

responsible for the awakening of women, formation of Women's India Association, its works in connection with the voting rights for women, the movement for social reform and women's education and the role of women in the nationalist movement are analysed in the study.

The study covers a span of thirty years i.e., from 1917 to 1947. Both these years are landmarks in the history of India. The year 1917 is a milestone in the history of women in Modern India. In that year for the first time a group of women officially led a delegation for women's franchise. The year also witnessed the formation of the Women's India Association in Madras. It was the first purely feminist organisation and became the pivot of the women's movement. In that year for the first time a woman became the President of the Indian National Congress. The terminal year of the study is also a momentous one. In that year India attained independence and a new era in the history of India began.

Variety of sources are utilised for this study mainly archival, preserved in the Tamilnadu Archives, Madras. Among these sources, the government orders of the various departments of the then Government of Madras, fortnightly reports from the Government of Madras to the Government of India, under secretary's safe files (secret) and the freedom movement files furnish information of extraordinary value especially on women's role in freedom struggle and their fight for voting rights. Besides, proceedings of the Madras legislative council, the annual administration reports and annual reports on public instruction have been found useful. Various commission reports provided useful documentation of women's demands for reforms and the official attitudes of the government and political elites towards these demands. In addition to these, Women's India Association's journal *Stri - Dharma* and *Indian Ladies Magazine,* provide a rich source of insights into the thinking of women leaders and are valuable in communicating a sense of the social context surrounding these women. Vernacular newspapers such as *Navasakti* and *Suthandira Sangha* preserved in the Marai Malai Adigal Library, Madras and English newspapers *New India* available in the Theosophical Society Library, Madras, *Young India* and *Harijan* kept in various libraries contain valuable information. The Madras native newspaper reports (1885-1935) compiled by the Government of Madras give an extensive extracts from both vernacular and English newspapers, most of them are not available in their original form are found useful. Apart from that the *Indian Annual Register* and *Indian Review* were also consulted. All these journals and newspapers provide pieces of information on women's movement. Annual reports of the Women's India Association supply vivid and coherent information about the multi-dimensional activities of the Women's India Association are widely utilized.

Finally there are extensive secondary sources preserved in various libraries are read. Of which biographies of Muthulakshmi Reddy and Ambujammal and Muthulakshmi Reddy's book *My Experience as a Legislature* serve as a source of useful information. Souvenirs, journals, pamphlets and articles published in various books and Journals, though they are not mainly pertaining to the present investigation have been read. Maximum care is taken to ensure the relevance and authenticity of the data. Inorder to ensure the validity of the government records, they are checked and cross-checked with other sources. All these sources provide pieces of valuable information and every bit of them, after proper analysis put together give a comprehensive picture of nationalism and women's movement in South India.

For writing this work, besides the library in the Mother Teresa Women's University, Kodaikanal, I have spent a considerable amount of time for data collection in the Tamilnadu Archives, Madras, libraries in Madras like Connemara Public Library, Theosophical Society Library, Madras University Library and Maraimalai Adigal Library.

Apart from that, libraries in Madurai Kamaraj University, Madurai, Gandhi Museum, Madurai, Kerala University Library, Trivandrum have also been utilised.

I am glad to record my sincere thanks to the respected Vice Chancellor, Registrar and the Professor and Head for permitting me to do this work. My deep sense of gratitude to Dr. M. Sundararaj, Tamilnadu Archives, for all his valuable assistance and encouragement during the progress of this work. I am always grateful to him for providing me with some of the valuable data that he had collected from the National Archives, New Delhi.

I thank all my colleagues who encouraged me in my humble effort towards writing this book. My special thanks are to my family members especially my husband Mr. R. Vijayakumar without whose help and encouragement, I would not have completed this work.

P.N. PREMALATHA

Introduction

Women's movement in India emerged as a part of the social reform movement of the nineteenth century when individual reformers and organisations initiated efforts towards social reform. It was a period of Enlightenment marked by intense social reform activities. It is natural that one of the many subjects, the reformers and thinkers of this period touched was the women's question. They focussed on the condition of women as reflecting the degenerate state of Indian Society as a whole and took conscious action to change the situation. It stimulated the movement for social reform. Raja Ram Mohan Roy's efforts for the abolition of the custom of *sati* marked the beginning of this movement. It was followed by a galaxy of reformers who raised their voices against various restrictions imposed on women.

It resulted in the enactment of laws abolishing *sati* and child marriage and permitting widow marriage and the Age of Consent Act. Soon they realised that these social evils could best be eliminated through education. Education creates motivation for change. Hence many reformers campaigned infavour of women's education. The most distinctive feature of this movement is that it was initiated by men and was later taken up by the educated middle class women.

The first off shoot of western system of education was the rise of nationalism. The disillusionment with British rule and the experiences of British timidity about reform, generated a desire for political reform and self rule. As the appeal of poliltical nationalism grew by leaps and bounds the essentiality of social reform became minimised. Infact many women came forward to join the nationalist movement. In India women's movement was not merely against conservatism, but also against imperialism which undoubtedly favoured in its own interest, the continuance of reactionary forces. Women's issues were closely associated with issues of India's subordination as a British colony and with the problem of how Indians could gain independence. They found that the women's question was not a purely Indian problem. The root cause of the evil lay not in customs but in political subjugation. Hence they devoted themselves to the cause of political freedom and believed that the achievement of freedom would automatically solve all the problems. The struggle for freedom brought about great changes in the intellectual, moral and social outlook of Hindu women. It united all the enlightened women and inspired them to constantly agitate for progressive social reforms. The appearance of Annie Besant on the Indian political arena was an important landmark in the development of public consciousness towards their rights and emancipation. Her vigorous campaign to redeem girls from illiteracy and to stop the pernicious practice of early marriage gave a fresh stimulus to the women's movement. Thinking that the social condition of India could not be changed unless the political slavery was overthrown, she started the Home Rule movement. By leading the nationalist movement Annie Besant not only opened the gates of politics to women, but also facilitated the acceptance of the women's cause by the nationalists. A founder president of the Women's India Association, Annie Besant also became the first woman President of the Indian National Congress. The national movement helped women in their struggle for liberation as nationalism and womens movement were closely interlinked.

This awakening manifested in the new women's organisations started by women themselves to voice their grievances and aspirations. The first purely feminist organisation to arise in India was the Women's India

Association, formed in 1917 at Madras. It was only after the formation of the Women's India Association, that women began to involve directly in their own affairs and women's movement as a serious movement against female condition began. Women began more and more to participate in the conferences where their advocacy of reform of evil social customs was more effective than that of the speeches of men in influencing the Hindu public opinion in favour of social reform. Women's India Association, demanded equal franchise and representation in legislatures for women as a necessary prerequisite for other female rights. These demands were supported by the Congress also. Thus Women's India Association became the pivot of the women's movement.

For the purpose of analysis, the study is divided into five chapters excluding introduction and conclusion. Chapter one concentrates on the status of women in the past. It also examines the efforts of the reformers and writers of the late nineteenth and the early twentieth centuries in the emancipation of women, and the organisations formed to work for the uplift of women. Chapter two explores the role of Women's India Association, in securing voting rights for women in general and women's role as voters and contestants in the elections in particular. It had two phases. In the first phase the issues were female enfranchisement and eligibility for the legislature, in the second phase the movement was for adult franchise. The role of women in freedom movement, starting from Home Rule movement to Indian National Army are taken up for a detailed discussion in the third chapter. In Madras, Home rule movement was started by Annie Besant. Sivakamu Ammal, a medical student had given up her studies and joined this movement. During salt satyagraha, Rukmini Lakshmipathi led the satyagraha and was the first woman to be arrested during the civil disobedience movement in India. This chapter brings to light the achievements of all these invisible women.

The fourth chapter is devoted to the discussion of the progress of girls and women education in Tamilnadu. Efforts of the missionaries, the government of Madras, the Women's India Association and the professional education for women form the substance of this chapter. Sister Subbulakshmi's efforts for widows' education and S. Muthulakshmi Reddy's contribution for girls education are also highlighted. The main focus of the fifth chapter is the activities of the Women's India Association towards social reforms pertaining to women, especially social legislations. It has three sections. The first section deals with the measures taken up for the eradication of the evil of child marriage. The other sections are respectively about the abolition of the *devadasi* system and the suppression of immoral traffic on women and children. They were the worst systems which ruined the life of the women in the state.

In the concluding part, a critical analysis of the study is presented.

Though a conscientious effort has been made in the present study to concentrate on the untrodden areas, for the sake of clarity and coherence, repetition of known facts seemed unavoidable. Only significant personalities are covered though a hundreds of women contributed their might for the freedom of women and the freedom of the country.

One

The Status of Women: An Overview

Ancient Period

Studies on the status of women in India indicate that there were distinct stages of rise and fall in her status. Scholars believe that in the pre historic period matriarchy existed in India. Women participated in the outdoor life and there was no prescribed position exclusively earmarked for men. Women gathered food for the family, did hunting and fishing. Since there was no marriage based family fatherhood was uncertain and mother was respected by the children.

The life of the people of Indus Valley Civilization was advanced. Women were given due respect and were not subjected to merciless laws. They were as busy as men. They made toys for their children. The clay figurines of women depict them in all their finery. They wore ornaments. They worshipped the Mother Goddess and also Pasupati, the Lord of animals. Between 2000 and 1500 B.C. Aryans came to India and settled here. Though the Aryan Society was a patriarchal one women had as much rights to enjoy life as men had. Women were friends, co-workers and never inferior to men. They respected and admired women that the most beautiful aspects of nature such as the dawn, the rivers, the earth were defied as goddesses.[1] *Rigveda*, the oldest religious text in the world shows that women enjoyed great respect in the society. Women had not only the right of offering sacrifices in their own names, but also that of composing hymns. Women were admitted to discussions on metaphysical subjects and great philosophical gathering. They had access to and capacity for the highest knowledge even the knowledge of the Absolute or Brahma.

The high ethical standard attained by the Aryan Society can best be seen in the wedding hymn in the *Rigveda*. Bride enjoyed the privilege of choosing from many suitors through *Svayamwara*. The Brahmanic literature, the epics and post epic literature are replete with illustrations.[2]

Between the Vedic and Brahmanical period came the transitory epoach, which witnessed the dawn of the separation of the spiritual from the temporal power. This epoch still retained a certain liberty of expression for women's religious aspirations.

In the south, the recorded history begins with the Sangam age. The status of women in ancient Tamil society is well described in the Tamil literature of the Sangam age and that is the only source of information. It praises the womanhood. Women enjoyed certain privileges and freedom during the ancient period.

Sangam Age

Women of the Sangam age had distinguished themselves in their cultural attainments and virtuous living. They were given a good training in domestic science, literature, music, and dance. The ancient Tamil poets stressed the value of education for all. "Learning is the true imperishable riches, all other things are not riches" says *Kural*.[3]

We come across more than thirty women poetesses who wrote very fine poems like Auvaiyar, Adimandi, Velliveediyar, Okkur Masathi, Kakkaipadiniyar Nachchellaiar, Perunkopendu, Parimagalir, Vennikkuyattiyar, Kuramagal Kuriyeyini, Kuramagal Illaveyini, etc. Poets hailed from all classes and strata of society, right from the royal family down to the common artisan class. Perunkopendu, Adimandi and Parimagalir belonged to royal families. Kuramagal Illaveyini and Kuramagal Kuriyeyini were from hunter class and Vennikkuyattiyar hailed from a potter family. Among them

Auvaiyar was the one who wrote more poems and outshines as the most distinguished one. She went as an ambassador to the court of a mighty monarch and prevented a war. Kakkaipatiniyar wrote two works on prosody namely *Kakkaipatiniyam* and *Sirukakkaippadiniyam*. A total of 154 of the 2,381 poems carry women's name. The most exquisite and social-stirring pieces contributed by the Tamil poetesses of Sangam period have been praised as the repositories of poetic excellence and fertile wisdom. It appears that the Tamils of those times were not averse to imparting education to such women as aspired to them and did not prevent their genius from flourishing. Madavi of *Manimekalai* excelled in all the three aspects of Tamil - *iyal, isai* and *natakam* (literature, music, and dance).

Sangam literature bears ample evidence to the fact that the education imparted to women was different from that of men. Young men were taught the art of warfare and other administrative training and various professions for earning a living. On the other hand the girls were given training for the good management of the home.[4] The difference which started in the education system continued throughout their life in all respects.

Women of that time were reputed to have fostered lofty ideals of military valour and heroism. We find from *Purananuru* interesting evidences regarding the extraordinary valour and intrepidity displayed by women during times of war. They felt happy if their husbands and sons sacrificed their lives in the battle for the sake of victory. It is apt to quote a poem from *Purananuru* :

> "In the battle the day before yesterday, her father attacked an elephant and died there on the field,
> In the battle yesterday, her husband faced a row of troops and fell,
> And today, she hears the battle drum and eager beyond reason, gives a spear in the hand of her only son,

Wraps a white garment around him, smears his dry
tuft with oil and having nothing but her only son,
'Go' she says sending him to the battle field."[5]

One mother stated that her duty was to give birth to a son and the father's duty was to educate him and the son's duty was to blossom out into a valiant hero killing even the fierce elephant that encountered him.[6] Once when a mother heard of the death of her beloved son in the battle field, she rushed to the spot inorder to see whether he had died of a wound at his back or chest taking a vow that if he had fallen with a wound on his back she would cut off her breasts which suckled him. She was delighted to find that her son had died in the battle only by a wound on his chest.[7] From the accounts of Megasthenes and Pliny, it is clear that Pandya kingdom was once ruled by a woman called Pandaia. Ancient Tamil poems also referred to a woman as the founder of the Pandyan Dynasty. She had been subsequently worshipped as the Goddess of Madurai. In the *Silappadikaram*, she was referred as Mathuraipathi or Queen of Madurai.[8] But there is no evidence that women went to the battle field to fight directly in the war. On occasions of war or other danger, women too like Brahmins, cows and aged persons were given special protection. At the same time there were instances of women having been captured in war, treated mercilessly as captives and subjected to humiliation and harassment by the victorious kings. They even went to the extent of making ropes from the hair of the widows of the slain for dragging the enemies and also to tie the elephants.

Women were glorified as the 'lamp of home'. *Nanmanikkadikai* laid down that a 'home is a void without a woman to run it'.[9] It also said 'a virtuous wife gives a good status to her house.[10] Thiru Valluvar described the wife as *'illal'* that is the person who runs the household. Women enjoyed freedom. They played games in the open, bathed in rivers and ponds, went to temples with their offerings and worshipped. Rich women took part in certain pastimes and amusements and participated freely in the amenities of life.[11] The inscriptions of the Chola period give many examples of women of the upper classes owning property in their own right and disposing of it if they so choose. Some of the princesses of the royal families also exerted influence over the ruling princes on the public policies.[12] In the later Pandyan period a woman sat on the council of *nyayattar* (court). Tyagavalli, the second wife of king Kulottunga I[st] enjoyed the right to equal authority with the king according to *Kalingathuparani*.[13] There was no reference to the dowry practice during that time, but the bride groom had to pay certain amount to the parents of the bride known as bride price.

There is no evidence to prove that child marriage existed during the Sangam age. Both loved and married. Young women born of *mullai* tract liked to marry only those heroes who came out successful in bull fighting games.[14] Women of talents wanted to marry those who won in the contests. Kantharvathathai of *Civaka Cintamani* was a gifted singer and a vina player. It was announced that any prince won in a contest with her in singing and *vina* play would be entitled to her hand in marriage. Many princes came with the hope of winning her in marriage. But they were not able to win in the contest with her. This shows that in those days at least few women were there in a position to challenge men in competition.

Marriage was a sacrament and not a contract. This meant that the condition of wedlock could not be ended by divorce. The best that could happen to a married woman was to predecease her husband for if she had survived him and had no courage to commit *sati*, she was consigned to widowhood. This was a rather unpleasant state for a woman. She had to live the life of an ascetic.[15] Widowhood was inevitable if she had children to bring upon. To look after the children she had to give up the luxury and social immolation and she became a *'kaimpen'*. (widow) Her life was miserable.[16] In order to escape the horrors of widowhood, women committed *sati*. When king

Bhuta Pandya died, his wife was dissuaded by others not to commit *sati*, she replied that it was better to become a *sati* rather than a *kaimpen*. A poem says,

> "It is better to jump into the fire rather than live without the beloved".[17]

But *sati* was not a widely prevalent custom. It was usually confined to royal families. It was a general practice to dissuade women who had lost their husbands from immolating themselves and *sati* was by no means encouraged. There were other forms of committing *sati* also. During war times wives of the heroic soldiers would go to the battle field in search of their husbands and if they saw them in a pool of blood and under the pangs of death, they would pull out the weapon from the body of the dying and thrust it into their own to escape widowhood. Some wives would go to the battle field embraced the head of their dying husbands closely and remained in that position till they themselves became dead.[18] To lead a life of religious devotion in widowhood was recognised as proper for all classes of women. Sembiyan Mahadevi, wife of Gandaraditya survived her husband and even her son Uttama Chola for many years and lived on till A.D. 1001. After the death of her husband, she devoted her life to religion and charity. She built a lot of stone temples for Lord Siva and also granted substantial endowments for their upkeep. However that the heroism and devotion of the *sati* was applauded. It was said that the true wife was the one who at the death of her husband would enter his burning pyre as if she was entering the cool water in a tank of bathing.[19] *Sati* stones were erected in memory of such women and were worshipped.

'Karpu' or absolute obedience to the husband was the quality expected of women. *Kural* says,

> "What is more excellent than a wife if she possesses the stability of chastity"[20]

Woman who came upto this difficult standard of conjugal behaviour was admired and praised and equated with Gods and Goddesses.

> "If she who does not worship God, but who worships her husband, say let it rain, it will rain"[21]
>
> "Virtuous wife never offer worship to God, but her husband"[22]

Modesty was considered as the highest among their graces. This meant that the ideal of a wife was the one dancing at the will and command of her husband. The housewife was spoken extremely high of and with great reverence if she was a perfectly obedient wife. But those who fell short of it were condemned. Theoretically the observance of a moral code in conjugal relationship was enjoined on men no less than on women. Connections with *'parathaiyar'* or prostitutes was looked down upon as unnatural and unbecoming of elegant man. Tholkappiar and Thiruvalluvar condemned this illicit relationship.[23]

> "A house holder who follows *dharma* is one who does not desire another's wife"

It was considered as the greatest sin if one wanted to have illicit relationship with another person's wife.[24] But there seemed to have existed a wide gulf between theory and practice. Men appeared to have often deviated from the lawful path. In practice prostitution had become a well established institution. But the wife never tolerated or agreed to it. It was but natural that when the wife came to know about that, she became furious.

The parents were disappointed when daughters were born. It was not out of hatred. It was best expressed by a poet "like the sandal, the pearls, the music of the harp etc. the daughters leave their birth place for aliens' home".[25] Though women did not enjoy equal status during the ancient period, they were neither unhappy nor their life miserable or ill treated. Definitely their status was better comparing to that of the later period. The very fact that girls could select their life partner is a proof positive for the large amount of freedom enjoyed by women.

Gradually they were relegated to an inferior position. The deterioration of their position was visible in the law regarding property rights, ban on female education, child marriage, *sati*, widowhood and the allied institutions of *devadasis* and prostitution. When the father of Tirunavukkarasu Nayanar died, his mother at once committed *sati*. According to Tiruvalankadu copper plates, the queen of Sundara Cholan Parantakan II (957-970) Vanavanma Deviyar committed *sati*.[26] This custom was found here and there even during the period of the East India Company. Abbe J.A. Dubois had written that in South India *sati* was not common. In the Bengal Presidency 706 women became *sati* in the year 1817. In the Madras Presidency in the same year not even thirty widows allowed themselves to be thus burnt. Tanjore was the worst district had twenty four cases of *sati* in eighteen months (1816 to 1817). But if a woman after a mature deliberation had once declared that she desired to be burnt alive with her deceased husband, her decision was considered irrevocable. She could not afterwards change, and if she refused to proceed on her own free will to the funeral pyre, she would be dragged to it by force.[27] When Ameer Singh, the deposed king of Tanjore died in 1802, inspite of the precautions taken by the company's official at Tanjore to dissuade the sacrifice, two wives of the deceased king devoted themselves to the flames at the funeral of that king. Not only among the royal families, it was frequently practiced particularly in Tanjore and its vicinity by the other people also. Within a few years, there were no less than hundred women had become victims to this inhuman practice there. This practice was neither encouraged by the persons of education nor influence or the king of Tanjore. In fact, Tanjore prohibited *sati* before the end of the eighteenth century. Even then there were incidence of *sati*. The Regulation of 1829 had immediate effect and the practice was almost completely stamped out. References indicate that there were some instances of private *sati* also. One such incident occurred in Tirunelveli district in 1876. The widow had shown extraordinary determination, dug a pit inside her house filled it with sandalwood and dressed herself as a bride, shut the doors, lit the pile and leapt in. This case was strange in Tirunelveli, it was not a district where *sati* lingered with any great presistance.[28]

Bhakti Movement

It is remarkable that one of the features of the Bhakti movement was the recognition of the equality of the sexes in religious matters. Andal, Karaikal Ammaiyar and Thilagavathiar were fitting examples to show the equality of status granted to women in the sphere of religion.

Andal and Karaikal Ammaiyar, the two poetesses of Tamilnadu, broke away from their social nests to pursue their individual spiritual pursuits. They composed a lot of hymns. Andal was counted among the Tamil saints as a jewel. She wrote *Thiruppaavai* and *Nacchiyar Thirumozhi*. She was one of the twelve Alvars of the Vaishnava religion. *Thiruppaavai* composed by her was so famous and popular that people in Tamilnadu celebrate the month of *markali* (Dec.-Jan.) as the most prayful month by singing *Thiruppaavai* and holding discourses on *Thiruppaavai*. In Srivilliputtur, the God would accept only those garlands first worn by Andal. Hence she was called *chutikkodutha nachiyar*'. It is significant to note that Karaikal Ammaiyar was the first saint composer among the sixty three Nayanmars. Her hymns were *Mootha Thiruppathikam Arputa Thiruvanthati* (100 songs) and *Thiru Irattai Manimalai*. Chekkilar, the author of *Periyapuranam* who recorded her biography said that she was a master in both literary and musical Tamil (*iyal* Tamil and *isai* Tamil). She was the pioneer in employing both music and poetry for the propagation of bhakti (devotion) and religion. She sacrificed her family life and took up the unearthly form to get rid of worldly fetters to reach the lord unencumbered.[29] The famous *Athichudi* was written by one Auvaiyar of medieval age. The Pandian queen Mangaiyarkkarasi converted her husband from Jainism, the royal religion to Saivism. She also brought Thiru Gnana Sambandhar, the Saiva saint to the Pandya court. Chekkilar and Thiru Gnana Sambandhar composed songs in praise of her.[30]

Rani Mangammal (1689 - 1704)

There were incidents of women ruling the country also. Rani Mangammal ruled Madurai for fifteen years. After the death of Ranga Krishna Muthu Virappa, the Nayak of Madurai,his mother Mangammal acted as queen regent on behalf of her grandson for fifteen years during his minority (1689-1704). She was a popular administrator and is remembered as a maker of roads and avenues and a builder of temples, tanks and choultries. She had a perfect estimate of her own calibre and the capacity of the Kingdom and submitted to Aurangazeb, the Mughal emperor. By sending tributes regularly she established friendship with the Mughals. Her war against the Setupatis of Ramnad was a failure. Madurai lost a major parts of its territory during her regency. But her campaign against Tanjore, Mysore and Travancore yielded remarkable success.[31] Prof. R. Sathianathaier said "Mangammal was a faminine politique. Her vigour and diplomacy gave the Nayak kingdom a longer tenure of life than it would have otherwise had. Her prudent administration in an age of storm and stress makes her out as a ruler of high repute." In religious matters she was very tolerant and was a liberal patron of arts.[32] Under her guidance the Nayak kingdom regained the proud position it had held in the days of Tirumala Nayak.

Queen Minakshi

Queen Minakshi (1732-36) succeeded her husband, Vijayaranga Chokkanatha who died with out heir to the throne. To settle the internal problem to the throne, Nawab of Arcot, Dost Ali sent Chanda Sahib to Madurai. Chanda Sahib after settling the question of the heir to the throne, violated the terms of amity and imprisoned the queen. Unable to bear the disgrace the queen committed suicide.[33]

Velu Nachiar (1780-90)

After reducing Ramnad in 1772, the East India company's forces under col. Smith marched towards Sivaganga. Muthuvaduganatha, the ruler of Sivaganga prepared for the defence of the Kalaiyarkoil headquarters. In his efforts, he was ably assisted by the Marudu brothers. In support of the company's forces, the forces of the Tondaiman also came in. The defenders heroically withstood the attack. The battle that ensued was made notable by the role played by Velu Nachiar W/o Muthuvaduganatha. She came out into the front and gallantly played the role of a defender. Muthuvaduganatha was shot dead in an engagement with the Nawab at Kalaiyarkoil. Evading capture Velu Nachiar fled to Dindugal along with Marudu brothers.[34] Marudu brothers with the help of the Hyder Ali's forces drove the Nawab's troops out of the territory of Sivaganga and usurped the country. The Nawab came to a compromise and made Velu Nachair as the ruler of Sivaganga in 1780 on condition of regular payment of ransom.[35] She died in 1790 and was succeeded by her daughter Vellachi alias Velu Nachiar, whose government was actually in the hands of the Marudus. Vellachi also died in 1793.

Mangalesvari Nachiar (1803 - 1807)

There were uprising in Ramnad. Soon the number of the insurgents reached unwieldy proportions. So the company's government decided to restore Mangaleswari Nachiar of the Sethupathi dynasty acknowledging her hereditary right. The company thought that it would win the support of the people and might help the company in posing as the guardian of individual interests. So Ramnad was converted into a *zamin* and Rani Mangaleswari Nachiar was re-instated on the throne of Ramnad in 1803 and the company deputed the Collector Mr. Parishes to inform the queen Mangaleswari the terms of the relationship between the *zamin* and the East India company. The queen accepted her position and agreed to pay an annual *peshkush* of Rs. 3,24,404. After a period of four years which was marked by Managaleswari's benefaction to temples and Brahmins she died in 1807.[36] During her reign she was ably assisted by her *pradani* Thiagarajapillai.

Parvathavardhani Nachiar (1846 - 1862)

In 1846, the company recognised Parvathavardhani as the successor of the Ramnad *zamin*. Various claimants to the *zamin* challenged her title and filed suits. But her title as the heir to the *zamin* was upheld in all the cases. She ruled for sixteen years and in the administrative field she was ably assisted by her brother Kottaisami Thevar who was appointed as the manager of the *zamin*.[37]

Reformers

The nineteenth century was a period in which the problems of women became the major concerns of the social reformers. The leaders of the social reform movement who raised women's issues were mostly men. Later on the movement was taken over by women. During that period in Tamilnadu reformers like St. Ramalinga Adigal, Mayuram Vedanayagam Pillai, G. Subramania Iyer, V.S. Srinivasa Sastri etc. spoke and wrote about women's rights.

St. Ramalinga Adigal's (1823-1874) *sutha sanmarga* movement of the nineteenth century was a spiritual movement with due emphasis on social problems. He supported female education and widow marriage.

As early as 1869 Mayuram Vedanayagam Pillai, in his book on *'pennkalvi'* (Women's Education) enumerated the advantages of educating women. He considered female education as essential as food.[38] He condemned child marriage, widowhood and dowry system.[39] The child marriage was described as puppet marriage and peppermint marriage.

Advocating the claim of women to a higher status, G.Subramania Iyer (1855-1916) stated,

> "It is self-love, narrow sympathy and a low standard of conduct that constitute the cause of the subordination of women to men..."

He pleaded that female education should be as high as scientific and as invigorating as the education of men. He said "how do you expect ignorant mothers to know their duties to their children, realise their responsibilities not only for the good breeding of their children, but also through their children for the well being of the country at large and to perform these duties satisfactorily". He spared no pain in convincing the people about the necessity of widow marriage. He not only advocated widow marriage, but himself set an example by conducting marriage for his own widowed daughter. The marriage took place on 31st December 1889, a Tuesday evening 5 p.m. considered to be inauspicious by the orthodox Hindus.[40]

V.S. Srinivasa Sastri (1869-1946) though a moderate in politics was an ardent social reformer of the Madras Presidency. He advocated post-puberty marriage of girls and wrote books on the status and rights of Indian women.[41] He also wanted female education with the same curriculum for boys and girls.

Two zealous western women were active in Tamil Nadu at that time. They were Annie Besant and Margaret E. Cousins. Both hailed from Ireland and adopted India as their second motherland. Annie Besant (1847 - 1933) asserted that in the ancient times, Hindu women were educated and moved freely in society. She urged to return to this golden age through education. She warned that India's fate would be sealed if women were not educated. Her famous series of lectures delivered in 1913-14 in the city of Madras under the title 'Wake up India' was a sharp, stimulating call to the people to begin working out their freedom by liberating their women from illiteracy and child marriage. Her approach to all these problems was through religion.[42] The lectures addressed to both men and women combined nationalism, women's issues and Hindu revivalism. She was the founder President of the Women's India Association. Margaret E. Cousins came to India to help Annie Besant in her works. In order to bring an ever widening circle of women into united action in matters relating to education, social and political reforms, she helped in opening numerous branches of the Women's India Association, all over India. Under her inspiration and guidance, the Women's India Association, opened many avenues of service to women such as maternal and child welfare, education of girls, abolition of purdah and child marriage, promotion of health and hygiene, and above all worked for the Home Rule for India.[43] Many women derived their inspiration from them, began to dominate the women's movement with ardent cries of reviving vedic past.

In all parts of India, there were Hindu men who longed to have their daughters educated and who were willing to face the disapproval of their families and friends inorder to make this possible. One such man was R.V. Subramania Iyer from Tanjore. His daughter Subbulakshmi (1886-1969) popularly known as "Sister Subbulakshmi" got married at the age of eleven and within seven weeks, her boy husband drowned in flood water and died. Contrary to the custom of those days himself a lecturer, he did not burden her with all restrictions normally placed on widows and instead taught her all subjects at home. She was given tuitions in music, violin, and veena. She expressed her desire to become a teacher and her parents agreed to that and sent her to school. Since it was vehemently opposed by their community, the family moved to Madras and she was sent to a convent school. After completing her matriculation, she joined the Presidency College, Madras. She was the first Hindu widow in Madras to pass the B.A. examination as early as 1911. Her concern was society's discarded child widows. She wanted to transform these unfortunate women into useful and valued members of society. She started many organisations such as a widow home, Sri Sarada Ladies Union, Sarada Home, Model Elementary School, Sarada Vidyalaya etc. to train and help widows, adult women, adult unmarried girls, students and slum children. She campaigned for the abolition of child marriage. Appreciating her service to the girls and widows of the Presidency she was awarded *Kaiser-i-Hind* medal. To her credit she had left behind pupils to carry on her work.

S. Muthulakshmi Reddy (1886 - 1968) was a remarkable champion of women's rights. She became a Doctor in 1912. She was the first woman to sit in the Madras Legislative Council, and the first woman deputy president of the council (1926). She saw it her duty as an educated woman to speak on behalf of women. In her first speech in the council she expressed her desire to ameliorate the condition of women and sought the help of her colleagues in the council in this regard. She thought that no country or nation would prosper without the active support and cooperation of its women. She not only campaigned to obtain legal rights for women, promote girls education and eradication of social evils but also worked to improve the health condition of women and children. Regarding the system of education her opinion was "We have to formulate a system in which our religion, our past culture and tradition should have a large share and at the same time suitable to modern conditions of life". She was associated with many social organisations and associations for women and worked for the well being of women through these organisations. She called meetings, attended many meetings, wrote articles in *Stri-Dharma* and other magazines for the uplift of women. She established "Auvai Home" in 1930 for the orphans and destitute women. Her services for the uplift of women and the society should be remembered for ever.

Apart from them, a powerful movement for social reform

and political freedom was carried on by men of letters. Early part of the twentieth century witnessed a renaissance in Tamil literature. There were several writers and poets in Tamilnadu who were forceful proponents of women's emancipation. The foremost among them was Subramania Bharati (1882-1921). He advocated modernity and reform, while asserting a cultural identity against imperialism. He championed the cause of India's independence and denounced the subordination of women. He insisted on female education and the rights of women and criticised the Tamil conservative society for keeping women in subordination.[44] He glorified Tamil women with his verses and poetic potential. He dreamt of a 'New India' with modern women devoid of shyness, fear, ignorance, walking with unbent head and sobriety. He argued for modernity and progress as fit behaviour for women. In his famous poem *'penn viduthalai'* (Women's Freedom) he sang to the glory of modern women who were equal to men. He often used the image of 'Mother India' and linked the subjection of India with the subjection of women.[45] He wanted to burn all the factors which were responsible for keeping the women suppressed. As a mighty exponent of Indian nationalism, he wrote series of articles requesting women to come forward to fight for the freedom of the country. He thought that the root cause of all these evils lay not in customs, but in political subjugation and economic system. For women's liberation, he advocated a *dharmayutha* (war of Justice). He placed female education as the first and foremost requirement of women's liberation.[46]

Emphasising women's liberation he wrote a lot of poems and articles. His poems titled, 'Women too have the right to be free', 'Women's liberation', 'Modern Women' 'Feminity' etc. were aimed at women's liberation. He felt that inorder to have their voices heard the participation of women in the civic and public life of the country was necessary. For the attainment of that object women should receive sufficient education. Unlike the ancient writers he placed chastity common to both the sexes. "Chastity? Yes - for both the sexes in the same measure" he said.

Bharati wanted to break the tradition which treated women as slaves of their husbands. The moment a girl accepted a man as her husband even in thought, she would virtually become his wife and so from that moment she had to worship him as God. She was a subordinate ally to him in life, obedient and devoted house wife. The lesson that a girl would learn from her mother was that she should always remember that she had no God except her husband. But Bharati wrote that women were not slaves to their husbands, rather the best companions and best partners in their life. He was against forced marriages and wanted women to marry any one whom they liked. He was anxious that responsible persons throughout the country should seriously consider the question of woman's status and do something immediately to make Indian womanhood free, enlightened and really human that was to say 'divine'.[47]

Bharatidasan, an ardent advocate of women's rights and a staunch disciple of Bharati strongly attacked the traditional customs and practices which made women inferior and advocated female education through which these social evils could best be eliminated. He equated the uneducated women to barren land.[48] The female characters in his novels were mainly educated women. He wrote in his famous Tamil novel *`kudumba vizhakku'* that if all women would come to politics and rule the country, there would not be any war and bloodshed. Although he thought that women could play an useful role in public life, and that their noble nature would purify it, he did not consider that this should be at the expense of their domestic roles. The novel portrayed that he welcomed the birth of female children contrary to the existing customs.[49] He wanted to abolish child marriage and polygamy and advocated widow marriage and freedom of speech.[50] He called upon women to shed their inferiority complex.

Thiru V. Kalyana Sundaranar (Thiru Vi. Ka), a labour leader and a freedom fighter believed that denial of rights to women was the main cause for the backwardness of India. He compared the status of women with the proletariats. Just like the capitalists exploited the proletariats, women were exploited by men. Like other writers he also wanted female education to improve their status. To produce leaders, philanthropists and statemen, it was necessary that sufficient education and training should be given to mothers. It would strengthen the national cause and help to bring up the new generation in the right spirit. Therefore the purpose of education was to develop their character and make them serve the community and the country. Education was an all round training and as such it should be given to both the sexes. He was of the opinion that there were fixed spheres for men and women and that education for women should therefore have a different emphasis. He emphasised that to bring up children properly and to help men in all public affairs women should have knowledge in medicine, maths, politics and above all religion.[51] Without sufficient education they could not fulfil their duties as mothers and responsible citizens. He defined womanhood as incorporating humility, patience, sacrifice, care for others, pity, co-operation and service. A woman according to him "is born, brought up, educated, married and lives for services".[52] Contrary to him, Subramania Bharati wanted women to give up all these traditional qualities.

According to Thiru.Vi. Ka rights and duties were different. Rights were common to both men and women where as duties were different because of the biological nature. Since the rights were denied to women they were in the subordinate status which affected the children born to them also. Hence women should be given all rights equal to men. At the same time he did not want women to fight with men to get the rights as the westerners. Women should help and co-operate with men in all walks of life. Love and affection should bind them together thereby they should live happily.[53] He believed in the unique contribution of women, through their special qualities to the harmonious continuance of human society. His vision in this respect was essentially traditional and sentimental. He was against the ban on widow marriage and inter-caste marriage, at the same time he accepted voluntary widowhood. He wrote series of articles in *Desabhaktan* attacking the institution of *devadasis*. He visualised a charitable raising of the status of the *devadasis* to that of good wives. Since non-marital status was responsible for their immoral life, he requested men with social reform attitude to marry the *devadasis*.[54]

His writings displayed the need for sexual decorum and restraint and the need to pay careful attention to rear children to be proper citizens. Also important was the idea that a woman should be a companion to her husband, a person he might turn to, when he needed to unburden himself, one who would share his troubles and joys. At the same time he wanted women to be treated as individuals in their own rights with full potentialities for self-development and not merely as sex symbols.

Periyar E.V. Ramasamy (1879-1973) was of the opinion that religion and lack of property rights were the main causes for women's subordination. He asked 'despite there being a Goddess of learning and a Goddess of wealth in Hindu religion why do they not grant women their education and right to property?' Economic bondage was also responsible for the troubles of the Indian women. He clearly perceived that superficial reform would not serve the cause of their emancipation. "If a woman cannot have the right to property and the liberty to love whom so ever she chooses what is she but a rubber-doll for the selfish use of man?".[55]

Right from the beginning, he insisted on equality of women with men in all matters including education, right to property and securing government jobs. He encouraged widow marriages and discouraged child marriage, *devadasi* system and prostitution in any form. Right to divorce and the need for increasing women's marriageable age were also advocated by him.[56] Attacking social evils pertaining to women he wrote articles on love, chastity, prostitution, women's education, birth control, etc., in *Kudi Arasu.* He also wrote a pamphlet "why women are enslaved?" in Tamil. He told that men should adopt the contraceptive methods if they were really kind to their wives. Since child bearing was one of the major handicaps in women's life he exhorted women also to follow birth control. His birth control policy was against bringing forth an unlimited number of children.[57]

He criticised all the sacred laws which imposed chastity only for women. Since the wife's chastity was the pillar of Tamil marriage, he advocated a thorough revision of the marriage system. There were many obstacles to the advancement and independence of women. He wanted many changes to take place in the economic and social spheres. He wondered how could a woman without money, without independence and without equal rights with man in social affairs become free and experience progress?[58] The self respect movement launched by him passed resolutions for women's education, implementation of Sarda Act, inclusion of women in police and army, fifty per cent reservation in government services and the right to divorce.[59]

M. Kodhainayaki, W/o V.M. Parthasarathi Iyangar, started the Tamil Magazine *Jaganmohini* in 1925. She had a prolific output of 115 novels. Her novels focussed on women's education, abolition of child marriage, removal of caste distinctions, social and economic uplift of Harijan's and raising the quality of life of the poor, infirm and handicapped. She became an ardent propagator of Gandhian principles through the medium of her novels.[60]

These reformers and writers focussed attention on social evils. Their writings created an awareness of realities in the minds of the people. They rejected the prevailing religious and social practices. The most striking feature of the movement was that every one wanted to promote female education and placed chastity for both the sexes. Their writings were concerned primarily with modifying relationships in the families and sought only "limited and controlled emancipation of their womenfolk". These writers often challenged the traditional subordination of women. The concept of the `perfect wife' was being redefined. They enumerated the various disabilities under which the Indian women were labouring in regard to the inheritance of property, child marriage, prostitution and *devadasi* system and wanted to change them. They felt that without sufficient education women could not fulfil their duties as mothers and responsible citizens. Their activities acted as a stimulus and encouragement to reform minded individuals in other areas and gradually reform organisations with an all India identity began to emerge.

Organisations

Starting from the later part of the nineteenth century organisations were formed to work for the uplift of women in the Madras Presidency. The Madras Hindu Widow Marriage Association was founded in 1874 by P. Chentsal Rao, Rama Iyengar, Muthusamy Iyer and Ranganatha Sastri to promote widow marriages. In 1882 Raghunatha Rao from Tanjore reorganised it and had given the name Hindu Women's Remarriage Association. Raghunatha Rao believed that women were deprived of their civil rights mentioned in the sastras and were forced into child marriage and enforced widowhood. He thought that the success of the movement depended on preaching to the people that these evils were opposed to the sastras. He held that reforms should be effected on the basis of the sastras. The association submitted a petition to the Government of India requesting it to invalidate section II of the Widow Remarriage Act of 1856 which disallowed the right of a widow to get her husband's property if she was remarried.

The first conference of the association was held in 1884. In that three resolutions were passed to the effect that every graduates should actively work for women's education, they should discourage child marriage and should work for widow marriages. The first widow marriage under the auspices of the association was celebrated at Mylapore on 7th June 1883. Discussions on the Age of Consent Bill gave rise to differences of opinion in Madras. Raghunatha Rao and Chentsal Rao were traditionalists and felt that reforms should be effected on the lines of the sastras and so the government should not interfere in it. G. Subramania Iyer and K. Subbarao were radicals and were opposed to the sastras. Hence the latters formed the Madras Hindu Social Reform Association in 1892. Its objectives were to promote female education, marriage reforms, domestic reforms and the general amalgamation of castes.[61]

Another organisation called the Madras Tamil Mission was founded by G. Joseph Israel, an European in the year 1884 with the object of educating the Pariah children of Madras. Within a short time it showed tremendous progress and by 1897 it had a Day Night Industrial School, the orphan home, women's section to work among Paraiah women, village Evangelistic work, distribution of tracts, clothing, free dinners and social work among christian poor. The Mission had fifteen schools, 876 pupils with forty seven workers in the year 1896-97.[62]

The first women's association in Madras, the Sree Sathya Samajam (The Hindu Women's Association) was established in 1896 with T.A. Thayarammah as Secretary. Its objectives were establishing schools for Hindu girls, carrying on zenana education through Hindu women teachers, teaching of needle works and other useful occupations to poor women with a view to enable them as teachers to earn an honorable livelihood, the teaching of Hindu religion and morality, giving help according to their respective position to Hindu women of families which though respectable and well-to-do had then been reduced to bad circumstances. This association had established a school for Hindu girls at Madras run by Hindu women.[63]

In 1903, a group of enthusiastic persons started the Madras Hindu Association. Besides other objects, it aimed at raising of the age of marriage, discouraging dowry, advocating single marriage and educating widows.[64] In 1908 a Women's Congress was held at Madras attended by women from all over South India, where nineteen women presented their papers in Tamil, Telugu, Malayalam, Marathi and English.[65] All these associations were short lived. But the most important women's association formed in Madras was the Women's India Association. It was established in 1917 by Annie Besant, Margaret E. Cousins and Dorothy Jinarajadasa, wife of Jinarajadasa, a theosophist from Ceylon. The moment was ripe, for the foundation of such an organisation was evident from the fact that within the first year itself thirty three branches were formed in important towns.[66]

The objectives of the association were:

1. To present to women their responsibilities as daughters of India.
2. To secure for every girl and boy the right of education through schemes of compulsory primary education including the teaching of religion.
3. To secure the abolition of child marriage and other evils.
4. To secure for women the vote for municipalities and legislative councils on the same terms as it may be granted to men.
5. To secure adequate representation of women in municipalities, taluk and local boards, legislative councils and assemblies.
6. To secure for women the right to vote and to be elected for the council of state.
7. To establish equality of rights and opportunities between men and women.

8. To help women to realise that the future of India lies largely in their hands, for as wives and mothers, they have the task of training, guiding and forming the character of the future rulers of India.
9. To band women into groups for the purpose of self-development and education and for the definite service of others.

The political policy of the association was to work for reforms through legislative councils[67]. The aims, ideals and works of the association were on a religious but non sectarian basis. The association started in 1917 had grown and increased steadily ever since. It had by 1935 seventy two branches, twenty four centres and over 4000 members representing women of all castes, cultures and religions. The Association began its work by approaching the subjects, committees of the provincial conferences and the National Congress. In response to their request for women's suffrage the Muslim League, the Congress and the Home Rule League also pronounced their support. Its branches kept themselves active in serving the sick in times of epidemics, needy in distress and arranged fund raising campaigns for such worthy causes. While concluding the five year period, 1917-22, the report stated "Only men and women cooperating as equals can make the wonderful era we dream of and bring into actuality our ideals. To bring this about it is the work of the Women's India Association".[68]

References

1. Padmini Sengupata, *The Story of the Women of India,* pp. 27-42.
2. Tripat Sharma, *Women in Ancient India*, pp. 8-12.
3. *Thirukkural*, poem-400.
4. C. Balasubramanian, *Status of Women in Tamilnadu during the Sangam age*, p. 8.
5. *Purananuru*, poem, 279; Susie Tharu (ed.), *Women Writing in India*, p. 77.
6. *Purananuru*, poem, 312; K.K. Pillay, *A Social History of the Tamils*, vol. I, p. 327.

7. *Purananuru*, poem-278; K.K. Pillay, *A Social History*, p. 327.
8. Kanakasabhai, *The Tamils Eighteen Hundred Years Ago*, p. 53.
9. *Nanmanikkadikai*, poems, 22, 101.
10. *Ibid.*, poem-20.
11. K.K. Pillay, *A Social History...*, p. 384.
12. Nilakanta Sastri, *The Colas*, p. 552.
13. Raju Kalidas, *History and Culture of the Tamils*, p. 196.
14. *Kalithokai*, poems, 63, 64.
15. N. Subramanian, *History of Tamilnadu (to A.D. 1565)*, pp. 343-44.
16. S. Sundararajan, *Ancient Tamil Society: Its Social and Economic Structure*, p. 148.
17. *Nanmanikkadikai*, poem -15.
18. T.V. Mahalingam, *South Indian Polity*, pp. 283-284.
19. K.A. Nilakanta Sastri, *The Colas*, pp. 91-92; 152
20. *Thirukkural*, poem-54.
21. *Ibid.*, poem-55.
22. *Namanikkadikai*, poem-91.
23. S. Sundararajan, *Ancient Tamil Society...*, p. 82.
24. *Thirukkural*, poems, 141-150.
25. S. Sundararajan, *Ancient Tamil Society...*, p. 155.
26. C. Balasubramanian, *Status of Women...*, p. 20.
27. Abbe J.A. Dubois, *Hindu Manners Customs and Ceremonies*, pp. 357-60.
28. Papers relating to East India Affairs viz Hindu Widows and Voluntary Immolations, 1821, p. 269; Edward Thompson, *Suttee : A Historical and Philosophical Enquiry into the Hindu Rite of Widow burning*, p. 125.
29. S.Jayalakshmi, "Women Poets and Musicians of Tamilnadu", pp. 123-25.
30. Thiru Vi. Kalyanasundaranar, *pennin perumai allathu vazhkaithunai* (Tamil), p. 48.
31. F.R. Hemingway, *Madras District Gazetteers, Trichinopoly*, p. 60.
32. Rajukalidos, *History and Culture of the Tamils*, p. 228.
33. *Ibid.*, 229.
34. A.Ramaswami, *Gazetteer of India, Tamil Nadu State, Ramanathapuram District*, pp. 100-101.
35. R.Annasammy Ayer (compiler), *The Sivaganga Zemindary; Its origin and its litigation*, vol.I, 1730-1890, p. III.
36. N.Subramanian, *History of Tamilnadu AD 1565-1984*, P. 71
37. A.Ramaswami, *Gazetteer of India, Tamilnadu State, Ramanathapuram District*, pp. 100, 103.
38. Kuzhathur Vedannayagam Pillai, *pennkalvi, penn manam, penn mathimalai, (Tamil)*, pp. 27-28.

39. Sarala Raja Gopalan, *puratchi kavignarum pennmaiyum (Tamil)*, p. 186.
40. Yajnesvara Chintamani, (ed.) *Indian Social Reform*, Vol. II, pp. 356-57.
41. D.Sadasivan, *Growth of Public opinion in the Madras Presidency*, p. 115.
42. Muthulakshmi Reddy, "Dr. Annie Besant: An appreciation" in *Stri-Dharma*, Nov.1931, p. 15; Geraldine Forbes, *The New Cambridge History of India, IV - 2, Women in Modern India.*, pp. 43-44.
43. Seetha Neelakantan, "Margaret E Cousins", in Butchi Arumugam, et al. *Some Illustrious Women...*, pp. 43-45.
44. Kumari Jayawarduna, *Feminism and Nationalism in the Third World*, p. 86.
45. P. S. Sundaram, (Trans) *Poems of Subramania Bharati*, p. 67.
46. Pa.Chu.Mani, *bhartiyum samoogha seerthiruthamum (Tamil)*, p. 114.
47. C.Subramania Bharati, *AGNI and other Essays, Poems and Translations and Essays and other Prose Fragments*, p. 85
48. Chu. Sivakami Sundari, "pavendar parvaiyil pennmai" in *pavender bharatidasan noorandu vizha malar (Tamil)*, pp. 86-88.
49. *Kudumba Vizhakku*, p. 148 ; Sarala Raja Gopalan, *puratchi kavignarum pennmaiyum (Tamil)*, p. 18.
50. Chu. Sivakami Sundari, "pavendar parvaiyil...", p. 187.
51. Thiru. Vi. Kalyana Sundaranar, *pennin perumai...*, pp. 37-76.
52. C.S. Lakshmi, *The Face behind the Mask*, pp. 46-76.
53. Thiru. Vi.Kalyana Sundaranar, *thiru vi. ka valgai kurippukal (Tamil)*, p. 600.
54. *Ibid.*
55. K. Veeramani, *Periyar on Women's Rights*, p. 76.
56. B.S. Chandrababu, *Social Protest in Tamilnadu*, p. 107.
57. *Kudi Arasu*, 10 September 1933.
58. K.Veeramani, *Periyar on Women's Rights*, pp. 20, 92.
59. B.S. Chandrababu, *Social Protest...*, p. 110.
60. *The Hindu*, 4 February 2001.
61. C. Paramarthalingam, *Social Reform Movement in Tamilnadu in the 19th Century with Special Reference to St.Ramalinga*, pp. 115-35.
62. *Asylum Press Almanac*, vol.II, 1897, p. 1094.
63. *Ibid.*, p. 1107.
64. G.O. No. 860, Pub., 3 June 1915.
65. Radha Kumar, *The History of Doing*, p. 54.
66. *Women's India Association Golden Jubilee Celebration, 1917 to 1967*, p. 1.
67. *Stri-Dharma*, March - April 1935, p. 1.
68. Women's India Association Golden Jubilee Celebration 1917-1967, p. 2.

Two

The Suffrage Movement 1917-1947

The rise and rapid growth of political agitation for Self Government in the country from the early years of the twentieth century made the women of India also conscious of their exclusion by British law from any share in the government of their land. Apart from the fact that women form half of the community, the fact that this country was passing through a phase of women's emancipation from ancient social and economic bondages had made women conscious of their political rights. The Home Rule Movement of Annie Besant was also instrumental in creating a general political consciousness among the educated women of India. The result was the formation of the Women's India Association in 1917 at Madras. The first challenge the Women's India Association faced in the political sphere was the question of women's right to vote.

Voting is the basic activity by which the citizen get assimilated into the political process. 'Politics' was a word that scared a large number of women. To attend a political meeting, to enter into political work seemed to them to be an adventure only to be undertaken by men for a woman to be interested in politics was to be unwomanly.[1] It had traditionally been viewed as a male domain. So Women's India Association thought it necessary to impart political training to women. It was conscious that the mistake made by the western countries of leaving women out of the democratic and representative system should not be repeated in India.[2] As an association it wanted to do political work of a nonparty but national in character on constitutional lines. It enabled the association to attract women of all shades of opinion who all wanted women to gain political rights.[3]

Annie Besant and Margaret E. Cousins linked it with the suffragette movement in the west.[4] Margaret E. Cousins was one of the pioneers of the women's suffrage movement both in Ireland and in England and suffered imprisonment twice for that cause in both the countries. She identified herself with the cause of India's political struggle and with the cause of women in particular. Both wanted the Indian women also to gain the same rights as the women in the west. Though the women's problems in England and its solution were bound to have an effect in India, the situation in India was different. Since India was under the control of the British Government, even if Indians were ready to grant political rights to women, they could do so only in the Home Rule Government.[5] Hence the nationalists wanted India to attain Home Rule first and sidelined women's issues, where as leading women of India wanted nationalist movement and women's movement to go simultaneously.

The First Phase

The campaign for political representation in India was not always uniform. It had two phases. Since women had no political rights and the basic political right was voting, in the first phase (1917-1926) the issues were enfranchisement of women and eligibility for the legislatures. In the second phase (1927-1947) the movement was for adult franchise and increasing women representation in the legislatures.

The first part deals with the various steps taken by the women to attain voting rights and the eligibility for the legislatures. Getting voting rights in the Indian context was not an easy task. Various arguments were advanced by the opponents of women's suffrage such as "women are naturally unfit for the proper exercise of the franchise", "it is unfeminine", "it is contrary to nature".[6]

The British Government was also against granting voting rights to women, because it thought, it would have a great effect on the people of India who did not happen to know anything about that question. Lord Curzon openly opposed it by saying that Britain would loose India if Indian women were given voting rights.[7]

First Women Deputation

It was the situation when the chief members of the Women's India Association presented an address to E.S.Montague.[8] On Ist December 1917, when he was in Madras, the memorable All India Women's Deputation consisting of fourteen women headed by Sarojini Naidu asked him women's franchise in India on the basis of sex equality.[9] Leading Indian women gave for the first time public expression of their feeling. It follows :

> "... the precedent for including women in modern. Indian political life has been a marked feature of the Indian National Congress, in which since its inception women have voted and been delegates and speakers and which this year finds its climax in the election of a woman as its president. Thus the voice of India approves of its women being considered responsible and acknowledged citizens and we urgently claim that in drawing up of all provisions regarding representation, our sex shall not be made a disqualification for the exercise of the franchise for service in public life".[10]

The cruz of the demand of the deputation was that when franchise conditions for India were being drawn up women should be recognised as people.[11]

It really marked the beginning of a conscious women's movement in India. Since then Women's India Association identified itself with the cause of women's suffrage and the removal of sex disqualification for election to all the governing bodies. Women also sent representations to the Indian National

Congress to consider a resolution infavour of the enfranchisement of Indian women. It had its repercussions in the Congress also. The Indian National Congress in its Calcutta session in 1917 stated that "women should not be disqualified on account of sex that the same tests be applied to women as are applied to men with regard to franchise and eligibility to all elective bodies". Subsequent annual sessions of the Indian National Congress as well as many Congress committees also passed resolutions recommending the removal of sex disqualification in voting.[12] The purport of all the resolutions was

> "that the word `people' or `persons' should be taken to refer to both men and women instead of men alone and that women should not be put on par with children, foreigners and lunatics in any scheme of reforms to be given to the country".

Further it added

> "that women possessing the same qualifications as are laid down for men in any part of the scheme shall not be disqualified on account of sex".[13]

Thus the Congress endorsed the resolution for women's equality with men in matter of franchise. Soon the whole country was aware of the issue. The Muslim League also passed a resolution in 1918 saying that women should be given the power to vote.[14]

When the Southborough Committee came to India in 1918 to examine the question of franchise, women leaders carried on propaganda and constant agitation to acquaint the committee with their demands. Resolutions passed by the forty five branches of the Women's India Association expressing their demand for vote was sent to the committee by them.[15] But their efforts proved fruitless. The committee reported in April 1919 that the social conditions of India made it premature to extend the franchise to Indian women at that juncture.[16] They said that until the custom of seclusion of women followed by many classes and communities was relaxed, female suffrage would hardly be a reality. Immediately protest meetings were held in all parts of India by the combined women's associations and resolutions were passed, cable grams and telegrams were sent to England asking the Secretary of State for India to give a certain measure of franchise to Indian women in the reform scheme which was under consideration.[17]

After the introduction of the Government of India bill in the Parliament in 1919, on behalf of the Women's India Association, a committee consisting of Sarojini Naidu, Annie Besant and Mrs and Miss Herabai Tata gave evidence in London before the Joint Select Committee for the extension of the franchise to them.[18] On behalf of all the branches of the Women's India Association the following cablegram was sent by its General Secretary Dorothy Jinarajadasa to the Joint Select Committee, London asking votes for the women of India. "forty five branches of Women's India Association controverts Southborough's evidence, they claim votes, protest against sex disqualification".[19] Members of the Women's India Association were also conscious of their dependence on the British Government for a change in the electoral laws. Hence they conducted campaigns to educate British public opinion on the needs of such reforms. Public meetings were held in many parts of Great Britain and many women's associations in England showed sympathy and took interest in the cause of Indian women.

As a result, the Parliament granted the right to decide the voting rights of women to each provincial council by a council resolution.[20] Since the power was then shifted to the provincial legislatures, Women's India Association put pressure on the members of the Madras Legislative Council to sponsor resolutions for the same purpose.[21] As a result Madras took the lead and Dewan Bahadur M.Krishnan Nayar brought the following resolution for the enfranchisement of women,

"This council recommends to the government that the sex disqualification prescribed in sub-clause (b) of clause (1) in rule 7 of the Madras Electoral Rules for registration of the electoral roll be removed in respect of women and that the qualifications which entitle men to vote be made applicable to women".[22]

After it became known that this resolution was to be moved in the Madras Legislative Council women held meetings all over the presidency and sent deputations to meet the Law Member, and the Minister for Development to get the resolution passed.[23] As a result many voted for the resolution and was declared carried.[24] Madras was the first legislature in British India to pass the women's suffrage resolution in 1921 by a considerable majority. It granted women voting rights on the same terms as men. Bombay followed close on Madras.[25] Thus the first effort of the Women's India Association was successful in Madras after four years of struggle. The resolution received mixed response from the press. Both *Desabhaktan and Swadesamitran* appreciated it though it was passed by a legislative council which was not a really representative body. But *Navasakti* opposed it on the ground that it was a right granted by the bureaucratic council which only restricted such rights. According to it the liberty of women was only in the teachings of Mahatma Gandhi and in the spinning wheel and to follow him without getting deceived.[26]

This however was only half the battle. Though the resolution had given the right of electing members to the legislative council, it did not enfranchise women to stand as candidates for the legislatures. This right was reserved to the British Parliament. An agitation was soon set afoot for the removal of this disqualification. The women asserted their right to enter the legislatures at many largely attended public meetings, and also through deputations and representations which met the government. So after 1921, women diverted their attention for getting admission to the legislatures either by election or by nomination.

The women were more particular in getting the right to enter into the legislatures. Margaret E. Cousins moved heaven and earth to secure the entry of women into the legislatures. She wrote, when she was campaigning for women's suffrage in Ireland and England she suffered much cruelty and injustice from the men politicians, the male dominated press and the men in the street. But in contrast during her work in India for the same cause, the Indian men showed great statemenship, understanding of democratic values, sympathy and support for the women's cause.[27] A number of meetings were convened by the leading women of Madras. A deputation of women under Mangalambigai W/o Sadasiva Iyer met the Governor of Madras, asked him to amend the rules to make women eligible for entry to the provincial and imperial legislatures.[28] As a result, the report of the Reforms Enquiry Committee called the Muddiman Committee on Franchise Reforms recommended to empower the legislative assembly and the provincial councils to legislate in this regard.[29] This recommendation bore fruit in the Madras Presidency. Once again Dewan Bahadur M. Krishnan Nayar moved a resolution in 1926 in the Madras Legislative Council in favour of admitting women into the Legislative Council by nomination and by election and was passed unanimously[30] The Government of India accepted it.[31] Thus the Madras Presidency threw open the legislature to women. In 1925 Assam Legislative Council as a first one permited women to seek election.[32] Other legislative councils in India followed it. Between 1921 and 1926 the major Indian states and all the provinces of India consecutively voted that suffrage should be granted to women of India along with the right of election to the central and provincial legislatures on exactly the same terms as men.

The Association maintained international links with other international women's organisations. It representatives attended the International Conferences. In May 1923 Dorothy Jinarajadasa, Ms.M.Patwardhan, Herabai Tata and Mithan Tata attended the Congress of International Women Suffrage Alliance in Rome. S.Muthulakshmi Reddy, Ammu Swaminathan, Rukmini Lakshmipathi, Ms. Bosnic and

Dr. Menon attended the same at Paris in May 1926 and created a great impression. Dorothy Jinarajadasa, Kamaladevi Chattopadyaya, Ms. B. Rama Rao and Ms. Mathai attended the Berlin Conference in 1930.[33]

It was only about the middle of 1926 that women were granted the right to be elected or to be nominated. Therefore there was not much time before the election for women candidates to do any canvassing among the electorates.

Since it was difficult to secure the election of any women to the new councils as the time was short, the Women's India Association requested each political party to put up and to support some women of their party for some seats of which they were reasonably sure.[34] The Congress which promised to support women's issues neither choose any woman candidate for contest, nor supported the woman candidate put up by the Women's India Association. Both Kamaladevi Chattopadhyaya and Hannen Angelo jumped into the arena of election in Madras.[35] Kamaladevi Chattopadhyaya from Mangalore[36], by then was a reputed leader of younger women and who had thrown herself whole heartedly into the political struggle. She had participated in the Non-Cooperation movement. She stood as an independent candidate in her home constituency South Canara which was a part of Madras Presidency at that time. In the election Kamaladevi Chattopadhyaya secured 4,461 votes only fifty one votes less than the successful Congress candidate by a few days work. She was the first Hindu woman to stand forth as candidate for election to the legislative council.[37] Hannen Angelo, Secretary of the Nurses Association, Madras contested the seat reserved for the Anglo-Indian community. She also lost her seat.[38] Though no woman won the election, there had been an appreciable increase in the use of vote by the women electors for the various legislatures.

The following table indicates the total number of voters, votes polled, total number of women voters and votes polled in the Madras Presidency in different elections.

Year	*Total No. of Voters in contested constituencies*	*Votes polled*	*Percentage*
1	2	3	4
	Madras Legislative Council		
1920	12,14,581	3,03,558	24.9
1923	11,74,808	4,25,983	36.26
1926	12,37,039	5,98,360	48.6
	Women Voters		
1923	82,367	9,361	11.36
1926	1,06,274	20,418	19.2
	Legislative Assembly		
1920	2,19,442	60,167	27.6
1923	2,52,545	1,03,386	40.9
1926	1,95,495	94,700	48.0
	Women Voters		
1923	13,091	1,363	10.41
1926	13,179	2,910	22.00
	Council of State*		
1923	2,290	1,694	73.9
1926	2,691	2,357	87.5

*: Women not eligible

Source: *Memoranda of the Madras Presidency on the working of the Reformed Government : Submitted to the Statutory Commission*, pp. 315-16, 335; IFC, vol. IV, p. 56.

The women having failed to get their candidates elected, then sought to make good through nomination. This demand persuaded forcefully by the Women's Indian Association led to the nomination of Dr. S. Muthulakshmi Reddy, (1886-1968) the Vice President of the Women's Indian Association, a devoted social worker and the medical woman graduate of Madras University to the Madras Legislative Council.[39] She was the first woman to sit in the Madras Legislative Council.[40] She accepted the nomination at the request of several women's associations in Madras.[41] She was then chosen unanimously as the Deputy President of the Madras Legislative Council, the first woman to hold that office.[42] Even before that the Princely State of Travancore made Dr. Poonam Lukose as the Health Minister in Travancore in 1925. She was the first woman member of the Legislative Council in India. Mrs. Madhaviammal of Trichur was nominated as a member of Cochin Legislative Council. Both were the active members of the Women's Indian Association.[43] By 1927 there were seven women legislatures in India including those in the Indian States.[44]

The Madras Legislative Council had given the lead to the other legislative councils in British India in the matter of giving privileges to women. It was this council that first passed the resolution giving the voting right to women, and to be nominated as member of the council. It was also a first instance in which a woman had been elected to preside over the deliberations of the legislative council. Travancore was the first Indian State to grant vote to its women in 1920. Assam was the first state to permit its women to contest the election in 1925. Inspite of all these positive steps it must be remembered that the total number of women enfranchised throughout India was not more than roughly one million.

The proportions of men and women enfranchised in the several provinces are shown in the following table.

Province	*Women*		*Men*
Madras	1	-	10
Bombay	1	-	19
Bengal	1	-	26
United Province	1	-	29
Punjab	1	-	29
Bihar and Orissa	1	-	62
Central Provinces	1	-	25
Assam	1	-	114

Source: *Indian Franchise Committee*, Vol. I, p. 78.

The reasons for this disproportionate voting strength of women as compared to that of men were the high property and education qualifications. The majority of women did not hold property in their own rights and very few of them were graduates. These limitations were quite sufficient to prevent a large number of women from being placed on the electoral rolls. In consequence under the then franchise the proportion of women as voters was still extremely low. The place that women should occupy in the reformed constitution soon became problem that exercised the minds both of the framers of the new constitution and of the politically conscious women of India. Hence the Women's Indian Association started demanding adult franchise. With that the second phase of the suffrage movement began.

The Second Phase

In the second phase, political situation was more complex. The relationship between the British authorities and the Congress deteriorated sharply. The Indian political elite was divided within itself on many issues of importance. In the women's movement also two factions emerged. One argued for increased representation and special qualifications for women that was supported by the British Government and the other was for adult suffrage and no special privileges. They adopted an equal right perspective and was supported by the Congress. In the British Government, fear of instability and administrative problems loomed large and thus the government rejected adult suffrage.[45] At the same time it compromised with the first faction.

This period witnessed series of enquiry commissions, which culminated in the Government of India Act, 1935. The Statutory Commission, the first in that series which came to India in 1928 to draw up a scheme of reform recommended the addition of two special qualifications for women voters namely, (1) Being the wife over twenty five years of age whose husband had the property qualification to vote, (2) Being a widow over that age whose husband at the time of his death was so qualified. In addition under the commission's scheme women over twenty one years of age who possessed the suggested educational qualification would also be enfranchised in their own right.[46] The scheme of reform laid special stress on the need for enfranchising a much larger proportion of women for the future legislatures.

Wifehood and widowhood qualifications were criticised by all women's organisations. Hence it was suggested that the question of enfranchisement of women should be further investigated by the Franchise Committee.[47] The women were more particular in getting adult suffrage. The Congress too wanted adult suffrage and moved a token cut in favour of it in the Madras Legislative Council. It desired that the suffrage should be extended to all sane persons over twenty one years of age.[48] Before nothing was finalised the fourth election to the Madras Legislative Council approached. Women had to compete with men on equal terms. At that time the political condition of the country was so disturbed and unsatisfactory and the Congress decided to boycott the election, under such condition, women also did not stand for election. But they conducted election campaigns.

Political campaigning had been a difficult experience for most women but it had not disillusioned them. They did lot of propaganda. Several women's associations framed a questionnaire which consisted of reforms to be carried out, to men candidates who stood for council election.[49] Since the Women's Indian Association was not affiliated to any political party it encouraged the women to vote for the candidates who positively answer the questionnaire irrespective of the party.[50] Special provisions were made by the government for the recording of women's votes. For the convenience of women voters, separate entrances and exists were arranged at every polling station and that as far as possible for identifying purposes in each polling station, a woman health staff of the corporation was posted.[51] As a result considerable number of women voted. In the urban constituency it was found 73 per cent exercised their franchise. In the south central land lord constituency, there were forty three men and five women and all the five voted. For the southern landlords constituency there were eighty two men and nine women and eight women voted.[52] But in the rural constituencies women votes polled was less. Women voters in the contested constituencies in the Madras Presidency were 98,680, but women votes polled was only 17,836.[53] It was mainly because of the boycott of the elections by the Congress. This time also through nomination, a woman candidate Alamelu Mangathayarammal became the member of the Madras Legislative Council.[54] Inspite of the low per centage of polling, the efforts of Women's Indian Association for the uplift of women did not go in vain. Because of its efforts, Indian Women had become members of the legislatures, town councillors, honorary magistrates, university senators, barristers and lawyers. Margaret E Cousins became an Honorary Magistrate in 1923. She was the first woman in India to hold that post. In the next year four women Honorary Magistrates were appointed in the Bombay Presidency. Mangalambigai Sadasiva Iyer, Ms Panduranga Rao and Ms Hume Stanford were appointed to that post in 1925.[55] The highest honour was the election of women as presidents of the Indian National Congress twice. One woman was elected unanimously as the deputy president of the Madras Legislative Council and in the Indian State of Travancore, an Indian woman Dr. Poonam Lucose was the Minister of Health for three years. Women also participated in the national movement.

After the election, women conducted vigorous propaganda for adult suffrage. Taking advantage of the Gandhi-Irwin settlement which brought temporary peace in the country, women representatives of the various associations, political views and interests met at Madras and drafted a memorandum on the status of Indian women. It proposed adult suffrage.[56] Similar representative gathering of Indian women met in Bombay under Sarojini Naidu also drafted a similar memorandum and was adopted by the Women's India Association and All India Women's Conference. This joint memorandum demanded among other things no reservation of seats for women or special nomination. It wanted women to fight elections on equal terms with men in mixed general elections as in every other country.[57] This memorandum was presented to His Excellency, the Viceroy of India in May 1931 and to the members of the Second Round Table Conference in August 1931.

Indian National Congress also allied with these women in demanding adult franchise and abolishing sex discrimination. The fundamental rights, drafted in its Karachi session included adult suffrage and no sex discrimination in regard to public employment.[58] Mahatma Gandhi also promised to a deputation of the South Indian women who presented the Madras Memorandum to him that he would secure adult franchise for women.[59] The women's organisations also wanted their representatives in all the committees meant for the framing of the constitution for India. Whenever due representation of women were not granted, women staged protest. Women's India Association protested against the non-inclusion of any Indian and of any women in the Simon Commission though each of the draft constitutions for Indian Home Rule contained a clause stating that sex should not be a disqualification for any of the rights and responsibilities of citizens.[60]

The Association sent protest to the South African Government against their continued exclusion of women from the rights of citizens. It also wrote to the League of Nations to include women on their committees. It supported Japanese women's just demands for attending political meetings and of forming political associations.[61]

As soon as the idea of the Round Table Conference had taken shape, women's organisations put forward their claim to be represented it by women of their own choice and they submitted a panel of names including Sarojini Naidu to represent them.[62] Ignoring the names suggested by them, Radhabai Subbarayan and Begum Shah Nawaz were selected by the British Government to represent women. Though both were long standing members of women's organisations, they were not accepted by the women's organisations.[63] Sarojini Naidu was selected by the British Government only to represent the Round Table Conference on general issues. Hence women's organisations at once cabled to the authorities concerned that Sarojini Naidu would be their spokes person in all matters pertaining to their status in the new constitution.[64] It was rejected by the British government. Contrary to the joint memorandum, Radhabai Subbarayan in the Round Table Conference demanded that there should be a special franchise for women and a fixed proportion of women to the legislatures through reservation during the first formative years.[65]

Both Begum Shah Nawaz and Radhabai Subbarayan supported those of the Simon Commission's proposals. They also wanted the age of voting to be lowered to twenty one to make it consistent with the voting age for men.[66] But women's organisations stick on to the joint memorandum.[67] By then it was obvious that there were two opinion regarding women's suffrage. One group supported the British Government's idea of slowly increasing the franchise and special representation and the other along with the Congress wanted adult suffrage and equal rights.

Inspite of the repeated request of the women's organisations with the backing of the Congress, the Franchise Sub-committee of the Round Table Conference which met in London felt that special qualifications should be prescribed for women to reduce the disparity between the voting strength of the two sexes.[68] It pointed out that some qualification other than the then one was needed and it was very difficult to suggest the most satisfactory method. Hence it supported the recommendations of the Simon Commission.[69]

But majority of the women stood by the opinion expressed in the joint memorandum asking for adult suffrage. They considered wifehood qualification as objectionable on the ground that it placed a premium on marriage and perpetuates the idea of women's dependence on men and did not recognise their independent right of suffrage. Apart from that, the controversy also raged around what was called the application condition. Women voters who claimed special qualification would be enrolled only on making an application to the authorities concerned. It was felt that this condition would defeat the very object for which special qualifications were devised and would reduce the number of specially qualified women as few would be in a position to fulfill the latter condition. Inspite of the repeated protests from all major women's organisations, the application condition was not removed.

Then another Franchise committee known as Lothian Committee was appointed to suggest ways and means for increasing the franchise rights. It came to India twice first in the winter of 1931 and then in the spring of 1932. It circulated a questionnaire to various organisations. In response, the representatives of All India Women's Conference and the Women's Indian Association met and prepared a memorandum and answers to the questionnaire and circulated it to various branches for approval. They also elected some women to give evidence before the committee in various provinces on the lines of policy enunciated in the memorandum. In addition, a declaration was issued to the press and was sent to the Government of India and England reiterating their firm belief in the principles given in the joint memorandum.[70]

There were difference of opinion among women regarding special representation. In Madras on behalf of the Women

Graduates Union, Lakshmi Ammal and Mrs.L.Devasahayam advocated reservation of seats for women in the legislature.[71] Radhabai Subbarayan, the only woman in the committee and also the Government of Madras had the same opinion. Alamelu Mangathayarammal, a member of the Madras Legislative Council in her individual capacity and Lakshmi Menon on behalf of the All India Women's Conference were the important persons who opposed the reservation of seats for women.[72] Disapproving the government's stand S.Muthulakshmi Reddy refused to give evidence before the committee and charged that the committee was not a true representative of all the people of India.

In every province, women including some in strict purdah came forward as witnesses either representing organisations or individually asking for an extension of the franchise, while there had been no expression of opinion to the contrary written or oral from the women themselves.[73] Regarding reservation of seats in the legislatures, leading women's organisations were opposed to the granting of any special facilities and wished women to be returned by "open door of competition". On the other hand a large number of witnesses both women and men who gave evidence individually or as representatives of associations, felt strongly that although women should be free to contest the elections on the same terms as men, some minimum representation should be secured for the first ten years.[74] The Government of Madras suggested that eight seats should be reserved for women in the provincial legislative council as a special interest group, but no special representation for women in the upper chamber.[75] The Madras Provisional Franchise Committee was of the opinion that since Madras was far ahead of other provinces in the ratio of men to women voters, there was no need for increasing the number of women voters by enfranchising women merely because they were wives or widows. Majority of them were in favour of a low educational qualification for women aged twenty one and over in addition to and independent of the ordinary property qualification.[76] The Prime Minister also in his instructions to the Franchise Committee said that special importance should be given to the question of securing a more adequate enfranchisement of women than the existing system.[77]

After analysing the questionnaire, the Franchise Committee realised that it was necessary to expand women's franchise to compel candidates to consider their interests and opinions, to awaken political interest among women and to make their vote an effective lever particularly in providing reforms of special concern to women and children. The proportion the committee aimed at was 1:4. It also wanted that from two to five per cent of the seats in the provincial council should be reserved for women for the first ten years. The committee considered it essential that during the formative period of the constitution, there should be in the legislatures quite a number of women sufficient to express their views and make their influence felt.[78] Taking into consideration all these points, apart from the wife or widowhood qualification the committee proposed mere literacy as a qualification for vote. Unlike education, literacy means mere ability to read and write a letter in any language, and so any woman who had the will, could acquire it. Again it would increase the number of women voters year by year as opportunities for education improve. Regarding enfranchisement through husband's qualification, the commission argued that it was not necessary that a woman should be under the influence of her husband, because her name was on the electoral roll for one reason rather than for another. Moreover this qualification was approved of in a memorandum signed by a large number of women of Bengal and by other organisations and individual witnesses.[79]

The ratio of men to women who would be qualified in each province as a result of independent property qualification, literacy and husband's property qualifications were as follows.

Province	*Independent Property Qualification*	*Literacy*	*Husbands Property Qualification*	*Total Women Electorate*	*Ratio of Men to Women*
Madras	7,18,000	3,45,000	7,00,000	15,00,000	4:1
Bombay	50,000	1,63,000	5,92,000	7,50,000	4:1
Bengal	5,00,000	3,77,000	8,00,000	15,00,000	4:1
United Provinces	4,14,000	1,28,000	11,00,000	15,00,000	4:1
Punjab	1,01,000	85,000	3,76,000	4,50,000	5:1
Bihar and Orissa	46,000	77,000	2,80,000	3,50,000	9:1
Central Provinces	70,000	40,000	2,66,000	3,50,000	5:1
Assam	30,000	40,000	1,92,000	2,20,000	4:1

Source: *IFC*, vol.II, p. 85.

This franchise proposal increased the men's electorate four and a half times and the women's no less than twenty one times.[80] Even then the voting strength of women as compared to that of men would be 1:4 in most provinces and there was in Bihar and Orissa even 1:9. Though the women's organisations were very firm on adult franchise, the British Government did not want to treat women on equal terms with men. They wanted to perpetuate the dependency status.

In 1933 the Joint Parliament Committee's report known as White Paper incorporating the recommendations of the Lothian Commission was published. Until then only property owners could exercise the vote, now that right was extended to their spouses.[81] No effort was made by those responsible for white paper to abolish sex disqualification. All efforts made by the women's organisations till then went unheeded.

One of the reasons given for enfranchising the wives and widows of husbands who possessed the prescribed property qualification was "the enfranchisement of married women is the recognition of the family unit as the basis of national life and of the equal partnership of men and women in that unit". This statement was criticised by the *Stri-Dharma* which submitted that there could never be an equal partnership where women were not only economically dependent upon their male relations but also made to depend upon them for their citizens rights.[82] Women through their several organisations totally rejected it as unworthy of their inherent fundamental rights as the citizens of the country. It should be borne in mind that all the women's organisations of some standing and status had repeatedly urged uniform adult suffrage to eliminate all inequalities and discriminations.

The Alternative Proposal by Women: Memorandum-II

Since the demands of the women were totally rejected, in March 1933 representatives of three woman's organisations met once again at Bombay and prepared an alternative proposal for an intervening stage. It would enfranchise a large number of women on equal terms and offer them opportunities for service in the legislatures without communal basis or through separate electorates. The result of these deliberations known as memorandum II was issued in June 1933.[83] Three representatives namely Raj Kumari Amrit Kaur, S. Muthulakshmi Reddy and Ms.Hamid Ali were elected on behalf of the three leading women's organisations to give evidence before the Joint Select Committee in London which was once again considering the new constitution in 1933.[84] During the examination they made it clear that their organisations had throughout stood for adult franchise, which was the only logical and desirable method of fairly enfranchising the whole population. Until then the alternative proposal described as the 'second best' should be considered.[85] Apart from the mere literacy tests and the same property qualifications as men, the alternative proposal suggested adult franchise in urban areas, joint electorates, direct election, and no reservation of seats on communal basis.[86] They urged that there should be a clear pronouncement to the effect that there should be "equal rights and obligations of all citizens without any bar on account of sex"[87]. The British press made the following comment, "representatives of Indian women's organisations have stated their case in commendable manner and we have been struck with their courage and vigour as well as the lucidity with which they have criticised and condemned the British proposals and focussed on their own". "The Indian women are firm and resolute and they speak soberly and distinctly" S. Muthulakshmi Reddy said to the press categorically "we have come to tell you what we want and not hear from the committee or even friendly English people what they want".[88] They made it clear that they were against the communal and separate electorates as also against the reservation of seats. S. Muthulakshmi Reddy asserted that when women saught political rights it was not to weild power in competition with men, but to be able to discharge the normal civil duties and have an equal right in determining the course of national life.

Joint Select Committee Report had also retained the wives and widows votes and nomination which were so definitely opposed by all the leading women's organisationas all over India.[89] Though women were disappointed over the report, they were undeterred. On the one hand they were working for adult franchise on the other hand they were working hard either to send women to legislatures or any person who would support their cause irrespective of the politcal party. When the by-election to the Madras city was announced, S. Muthulakshmi Reddy convened the meeting of the Women's India Association and requested the women voters to give a mandate to any candidate irrespective of politcal party who would promise to work for the improvement of women.[90] Since Rukmini Lakshmipathi, the Congress candidate pledged to support the Women's India Association's manifesto, the association requested its members to cast their votes infavour of her.[91] *The Hindu* too supported her and wrote, "Rukmini Lakshmipathi has a record of service and sacrifice to her credit which entitled her to the unstinted support of all who place national interests before communal and sectional ends".[92] In the election she won the seat by securing 8,758 votes and returned to the council by a thumpig majority.[93] She was the first elected woman member in the Madras Legislative Council.[94] After examining all the committees' reports, the Government of India Act 1935 was passed. It was the product of long discussion and ultimately of compromise between ideologies. The Simon Commission report of 1930, Round Table Conferences held in London between 1930-32, White Paper proposals for Indian Constitutional reforms 1933, and the Joint Select Committee report 1934 served as the basis for determining the new constitution.

The Act of 1935 enfranchised a large number of women. Women of twenty one years of age and over were eligible to vote provided they had any one of the following qualifications: hold the same property or taxation qualifications as men;were able to read and write in any Indian language or dialect in common use; wives or widows of the eligible voters.[95] Except in the case of women who held the necessary property or taxation qualifications in their own rights, it was imposed on them that they should apply to be enrolled as voters.

Even the alternative proposal put forward by the women's organisations had been wantonly rejected on the ground of administrative difficulties, inability on the part of Indian men to come to an agreement over the communal question and the fact that in the opinion of the government 'social conditions make too quick an advance dangerous'. Thus the sex bar had not been removed. The wifehood qualification had been imposed on women thereby denying them their inherent right of citizenship.

Both in the federal and provincial legislatures women were given reservation of seats on the communal basis.[96] On the whole fifteen seats were reserved for women in the central legislature. Out of that, six seats were for the Federal Council of State (Upper House), one each for Madras, Bombay, Bengal, United Provinces,

Punjab and Bihar. Seats for Bombay and United Provinces were to be filled for three years, Bengal and Bihar for six years, and Madras and Punjab for nine years. Rest of the nine seats were reserved in the Federal Assembly (Lower House)[97].

Forty one seats were reserved for women in the provincial assemblies as follows.

Province	*General*	*Muslim*	*Indian Christian*	*Anglo Indian*	*Sikh*	*Total*
Madras	6	1	1	-	-	8
Bombay	5	1	-	-	-	6
UP	4	2	-	-	-	6
Bengal	2	2	-	1	-	5
Punjab	1	2	-	-	1	4
Bihar	3	1	-	-	-	4
Central Provinces & Berar	3	-	-	-	-	3
Sind	1	-	1	-	-	2
Assam	1	-	-	-	-	1
Orissa	2	-	-	-	-	2
Total	28	9	2	1	1	41

Source: Radhakrishna Sharma, *Nationalism, Social Reform...*, p. 94.

Regarding the eight seats reserved for women in the Madras Legislature, three were general urban seats assigned to Madras city, Ellore and Tellicherry cum Calicut, three general rural seats to Cuddalore, Bellary and Dindugul taluks, one Muhammadan seat to Madras city, one Indian Christian seat to the municipalities of Tirunelveli, Palayamkottai and Tuticorin.[98] As far as the selection procedure was concerned, women to fill the seats in the upper house would be chosen by the persons whether men or women who held seats in the chamber or as the case might be the chambers of the legislature of that province. Men would be elected to the lower house by the provincial legislatures, but for women, nine special electorates of women composed of all the women members in the provincial legislatures would be created.

Madras, Bombay, Bengal, United Province, Bihar and Assam were given the upper house (PLC). In these no seats had been reserved for women. But during the course of the debate on the Indian Act in Parliament, the government informed, that the Governors would be recommended to fill some of the seats allotted to them for nomination by women.[99] It was left to the Indian Delimitation Committee to decide the qualification for women candidates and the nature of the constituencies that would return forty one women representatives to the provincial legislatures. It recommended that enrolment as a voter in any constituency in that province would be a sufficient qualification for women candidates. It also recommended that special constituencies would be created for electing women members. The argument infavour of these special constituencies were

> ... to ensure that the constituencies in which the women's seats are filled, are small and select and so framed as to minimise the difficulties of canvassing the hardships of communication in rural areas in their constituencies and the obstacles likely to be met by a member in maintaining contact with her constituents".[100]

These special constituencies would consist of men and women voters except in the Muhammadan constituencies. As the need for women representatives of rural areas had been emphasised by several local governments, the Delimitation Committee had recommended that rural seats be reserved wherever possible.[101]

The principle of reserving seats for women was one which had never been acceptable to any of the representative women's organisation. Inspite of that the system of reserved seats on communal lines had been introduced in the future framework of the Indian constitution. The creation of the special constituencies again stressed the tendency to segregate women into a separate compartment and it was indeed unfortunate that the committee could not accept the other alternative of reserving seats for women in the fuller territorial multi-member constituencies. But women were not debarred from contesting elections from the general constituencies. Application condition was also not removed.

The application condition also did not find favour with the women's organisations. The Government of Madras required the voters to present their application in person to the registration officer.[102] As a result registering of women voters presented the greatest difficulty, especially for women in purdah or for women who were sick or out of town of register. To further complicate the situation, the last date of application was the month of June, the holiday season when many qualified voters would be away. The government yielded to the request of the Women's India Association and extended the last date to the month of July and liberalised the rules of registering women in purdah by allowing them to register through their husbands or other male relations.[103] S.Muthulakshmi Reddy again requested the government to extend the similar concessions to other women.[104] The electoral roll for women's constituencies were the same as that for the general, Muslim or Indian Christian constituencies. All persons, men or women whose names were included in the electoral roll for that area were entitled to vote in the women's constituencies as well as in the general, Muslims or Indian Christian constituencies for which they were electors.[105]

When the election approached, women's organisations became very active in enrolling women voters as well as contacting various political parties to nominate atleast some women for the general constituencies. Suitable names of women candidates were also given to various political parties by S.Muthulakshmi Reddy.[106] But no woman had been nominated even by the congress to stand for any of the four urban general constituencies in Madras. The Women's India Association also called upon all men and women to cast their votes without fear or favour in support of those candidates who would work for national freedom and also for removing the disabilities under which women and children suffer.[107] A manifesto was drawn by the All India Women's Conference and sent to all political parties asking for the support of their candidates in regard to the various measures of reform for which All India Women's Conference stood.[108]

In the 1937 election, eight women were elected from general constituencies and forty one from reserved constituencies. On the whole eighty women entered the legislatures of the various provinces and states. Women came to hold the posts of ministers, deputy speakers and parliamentary secretaries. Rukmini Lakshmipathi and Jothy Venkatachalam had joined the Madras Cabinet.[109]

The number of women voters in the 1937 elections to both reserved and unreserved seats of the various provincial legislatures are shown in the following table:

PLA	*No. enrolled*	*No. enrolled in contested constituencies*	*No. who voted*	*Percentage*
1	2	3	4	4 on 3
		PROVINCIAL LEGISLATIVE ASSEMBLIES		
Madras	15,84,784	15,23,248	4,79,278	31.50
Bombay	3,35,890	3,05,750	1,29,535	42.50
Bengal	9,70,033	8,96,588	46,758	5.20
U.Provinces	5,20,380	4,94752	95,553	19.30
Punjab	1,89,105	1,73,459	58,216	33.56
Bihar	2,29,044	2,15,490	17,037	7.90
C.P. & Behar	2,63,331	2,59,750	63,744	24.50
Assam	45,336	29,680	8,678	29.23
N.W.F.P.	4,895	4,895	3,498	71.40
Orissa	79,208	70,526	4,670	6.62
Sind	32,668	27,940	9,705	34.70
Total	42,54,674	40,02,078	9,16,672	23.30

1	*2*	*3*	*4*	*4 on 3*
		PROVINCIAL LEGISLATIVE COUNCILS (PLC)		
Madras	2,796	2,578	1,420	55.10
Bombay	1,755	1,636	932	56.20
Bengal	3,673	2,136	437	20.50
U.P.	2,262	1,684	598	35.50
Bihar	1,060	882	594	67.34
Assam	1,127	559	512	91.57

Source: Shai Ved Prakash Gupta, *Franchise in India*, p. 53.

The government's estimate to franchise nearly six million women voters fell far below the expectations in the elections of 1937.

Things remained as they were till independence regarding franchise question. But the political scenario witnessed radical changes. The ministry formed in 1937 resigned in 1939 as a mark of protest against the British decision on the war question.

In the meantime Radhabai Subbarayan was nominated from the Madurai Ramnad cum Tirunelveli non Muhammadan rural constituency in the by-election in 1938.[110] From 1939 to 1945 mostly all the works were stumbled on account of the II world war. Ammu Swaminathan was elected to the Central Assembly from the Madras city constituency in November 1945.[111] The second general election took place in 1946 and 20.57 per cent of enrolled women in Madras used their franchise. Total number of women elected was twelve. In addition to the seats reserved for women three were elected from general rural constituencies and one from the general urban constituency, Madras.[112] All elected women were from the Congress Party only. The Congress Party swept the poll again and formed the ministry under T.Prakasam. His cabinet consisted of eleven ministers including one woman Minister Rukmini Lakshmipathi. She was incharge of the Public Health and Medical Department. Ms.C.Ammanna Raja was elected as the Deputy Speaker.[113] The Congress Party had given its full support to the issue of women's suffrage partly because of the women's movement and campaigns around the issue, partly because of their gratitude at the women's part in the national movement and above all to portray themselves as more progressive than the British.

Though political campaigning had been a difficult experience for most women, their political ambition was stimulated as was evident by their enthusiasm to be elected as representatives to the Constituent Assembly in 1946. It was the result of Indian women's continued fight along with men, that representatives of the various women's organisations scattered throughout India were asked to participate in framing the Indian constitution. The idea behind this was to enable them to get a place of equality and honour similar to that of men. The Constituent Assembly of India formed in 1946 had fourteen women members and from Madras Presidency Ammu Swaminathan M.L.A from Central Madras[114] and Durgabai Amma were selected. Sardar Vallabhbhai Patel had been struck by Durgabai's knowledge of law and her plain speaking. A man of action himself, he recognised her mettle and she was elected to the Steering Committee and nominated to the panel of chairperson, an honour accorded to no other woman.[115]

At independence, the Congress Party instituted universal adult suffrage and a constitutional guarantee of sex, caste and religious equality and thereby fulfilled the commitment made during the national movement. It was adopted by the India Constituent Assembly in 1949. Article 325 of the constitution says,

> "no person to be ineligible for inclusion in or to claim to be included in a special electoral roll on grounds of religion, race, caste or sex".

Article 326 says,

> "election to the House of the People and the Legislative Assembly is to be on the basis of adult suffrage".

Every person who is a citizen of India and is above twenty one years of age and is not otherwise disqualified shall be entitled to be registered as a voter. The disqualification can only be on the ground of non-residence, unsoundness of mind, crime or corrupt practices. Thus sex and possession or non-possession of any property are no longer any considerations for the grant of the franchise or the right to vote.[116] Women got thus equal rights with men and a beggar will be a voter side by side with a multi millionaire.

Local Bodies

The local self government in India was a representative organisation responsible to a body of electors enjoying wide powers of administration and taxation and functioning both as a school for training in responsibility and a vital link in the chain of organisms that make up the government of the country. Municipalities and District boards formed the basic units on which rested the super structure of the large administration of the country. If women were to participate in the discharge of civil duties and to realise their civic and political responsibilities they should acquaint themselves increasingly with the working of these bodies and exercise their right of franchise as well as enter them in large numbers. Apart from serving as a training ground for wider responsibilities, the works in these departments of administration were of vital importance to the day to day existence of a nation.

Realising its importance, for the first time in the annals of India, section 48 of the Madras Act IV of 1919 conferred on the women of the city of Madras the privilege of exercising the right of franchise in the Corporation of Madras. Later on that privilege was extended to mufassal municipalities and local boards.[117] This act was amended in 1923 to enable women to stand for election. As a result, a large number of women were appointed as municipal councillors and local board members most of them belonged to the Women's India Association.

For the first time women voted in the election of the Corporation of Calcutta in 1924. In Bombay four women stood for election and all were successful.[118]

Hannen Angelo, an Anglo-Indian who was well known for the good work as a nurse was elected as a member of the Madras Municipal Corporation. This was the first time that a woman had entered the corporation by election.[119] Though Anglo-Indian community was provided with a special electorate, she had contested in an open constituency and won the election.

Already Ms. Devadass was nominated by the government to the corporation. Ms.Thomas, Secretary of the Women's India Association, Tirunelveli branch was nominated as a member of the municipal council.[120] In the municipal elections held in 1925, quite a number of women exercised their vote.

Women called on the provincial governments, municipal councils and local boards to reserve a proportionate number of nominated seats for women representatives until the Municipalities Act and Local Boards Act were suitably amended.[121] In the municipal elections in the cities of Madras and Bombay held in 1928, some women had been returned. One of them Amma Kutty Ammal, Headmistress of the Kanchipuram Girls School had been nominated to the Kanchipuram Municipal Council.[122] In Madras out of the total of 2,18,751 voters both men and women in the seventy four municipalities 1,54,446 recorded their votes. Among the women it was 63 per cent.[123] The Madras Legislative Council accepted the principle of women's representation on the public bodies and had legislated that in every local boards, taluk boards and district municipalities seats should be reserved for women side by side with other minority communities.

As a result in 1931 Mahalakshmi was elected as a councillor of the Salem municipality. Ms.Davamoni Manuel, Secretary of the Tuticorin Ladies Association was elected as a councillor of the Tuticorin Municipality and Ms. K. Rama

Subbama Kodi Reddi was elected as a councillor of the Cuddappah Municipality.[124] In Madras Hannan Angelo returned unopposed to the Corporation of Madras thrice. She had faced an open municipal election and had been elected by a joint electorate consisting of all castes and creeds.[125] The Madras city Municipal Act No. X of 1936 divided the city into four divisions, raised the number of councillors from fifty to sixty and provided for election of five Aldermen of whom one should be a woman. The Act of 1947, which amended the 1919 Act, increased the strength of the Madras Council to eighty five, reserved seats for women, certain communities and trade and industry.

The introduction of adult suffrage together with the removal of all discrimination on ground of sex provided under the new constitution had been a great step towards the complete emancipation of Indian women. The granting of adult franchise implied the recognition of the right of women to participate in the decisive sphere of the national life, the sphere of politics where all important decisions affecting the economic, social and cultural life of the people would be taken. The political consciousness, their claim and interest to have a say in the laws made for them and the social and general reforms undertaken by various social institutions towards their betterment led to more pressing demands of women. Their organisations compelled the introduction of radical change in the exercise of vote.

The three organisations had developed branches all over India, annual and bi-annual meetings, journals and memberships which ran into thousands. Through their branches they had established contact with the majority of India's educated women. These organisations claimed the authority to speak for the women of India followed up this claim with a steady stream of resolutions, reports and deputations, which finally resulted in the adult suffrage.

References

1. *Indian Ladies Magazine*, Vol. VIII, September - October 1935, p. 171.
2. *Stri-Dharma*, April 1928, p. 1.
3. *Ibid.*, July-August 1930, p. 385.
4. Rama Mehta, *Socio-Legal Status of Women in India*, p. 43.
5. *New India*, 21 January 1918.
6. Annie Besant, *The Political Status of Women*, p. 4.
7. Annie Besant, *Women and Politics : The way out of the present difficulty*, Pamphlet, p. 16.
8. E.S. Montague, the Secretary of State for India came to India to investigate and study Indian conditions prior to the framing of the new constitution for India.
9. *Stri-Dharma*, April 1928, p. 6; *Women's India Association Golden Jubilee Celebration, 1917-1967*, p. 1; *Status of Women in India : A Synopsis of the Report of the National Committee on the Status of Women, 1917-1974*, p. 103.
10. Aruna Asaf Ali, "Women's Suffrage in India" in Shyam Kumari Nehru(ed) *Our Cause : A Symposium of Indian Women*, p. 352.
11. Kamaladevi Chattopadhyaya, *Indian Women's Battle for Freedom*, p. 94.
12. *Ibid.*, p. 96 ; Herabai A. Tata, *A Short Sketch of Indian Women's Franchise Work*, p. 22; PMLC, April 1921, p. 1016.
13. Herabai A.Tata, *A Short Sketch* ... p. 3.
14. PMLC, April 1921, p. 1016.
15. Herabai A. Tata, *A Short Sketch* ..., p. 4.
16. *Report of the Indian Statutory Commission*, Vol. I, Survey, p. 49; G.O. No.172, Pub., 31 March 1919 ; G.O. No. 568, Pub., 5 October 1919.
17. Herabai Tata, *A Short Sketch* ...., p. 6.
18. *Women's India Association Golden Jubilee...*, p. 4; JSC consisting of members of the Parliament was appointed to take the evidence of the representative Indians on the suggested reforms and to place them on a workable basis. (Aruna Asaf Ali, "Women's Suffrage in India" in Shyam Kumari Nehru (ed), *Our Cause...*, p. 353).
19. Herabai Tata, A Short Sketch ..., p. 8.
20. *Report of the Indian Statutory Commission*, Vol. I, *Survey*, p. 49; *Government of India's Despatch on Proposal for Constitutional Reform*, p. 25.
21. *Women's India Association Golden Jubilee...*, p. 2.
22. *PMLC*, April 1921, p. 1015.
23. *Ibid.*, p. 1016.
24. *Ibid.*, p. 1030.

25. Aruna Asaf Ali, "Women's Suffrage...," p. 356.
26. *Desabaktan* and *Swadesamitran*, 2 April 1921, p. 466. (MNR).
27. Seetha Neelakandan, "Margaret E. Cousins" in Butchi Arumugam, et.al, *Some Illustrious Women...*, p. 45.
28. Radha Krishna Sharma, *Nationalism, Social Reform...*, pp. 86-87.
29. *Stri-Dharma*, October 1925.
30. *Ibid.*, August 1926, p. 145.
31. *RAMP*, 1925 - 26, p. xvii; FR, 17 July 1926.
32. *Women's India Association Golden Jubilee...*, p. 4.
33. *Ibid.*, p. 3-5.
34. *Stri-Dharma*, August 1926, p. 145.
35. Kamaladevi Chattopadhyaya, *Indian Women's Battle...*, p. 97.
36. Bornin 1903, Kamaladevi Chattopadhyaya was a child widow and then married Harindranath Chattopadhyaya, brother of Sarojini Naidu.
37. *Stri-Dharma*, October 1926, p. 179; December 1926, p. 17; Kamaladevi Chattopadhyaya, *Indian Women's Battle...*, p. 97.
38. *Stri-Dharma*, December 1926, p. 17.
39. Kamaladevi Chattopadhyaya, *Indian Women's Battle...*, p. 98.
40. RAMP, 1925 - 26, p. ix.
41. *Indian Ladies Magazine*, August-September 1927, p. 14.
42. *Ibid.*; *Women's India Association Golden Jubilee...*, p. 14.
43. *Women's India Association Golden Jubilee...*, p. 4.
44. *Stri-Dharma*, May 1928, p. 68.
45. Rama Mehta, *Socio-Legal Status...*, p. 44 ; Everest Jana Matson, *Women and Social Change...*, p. 101.
46. *Government of India's Despatch on proposals of Constitutional Reform*, p. 24; *Indian Franchise Committee*, Vol. II, p. 3.
47. *Government of India's Despatch...*, p. 24.
48. *Memoranda...*, pp. 318-19.
49. *Stri-Dharma*, May 1929, p. 301 (See Appendix-I).
50. *Ibid.*, July - August 1930, p. 385.
51. *Memoranda...*, p. 336; Selections from Memoranda and oral evidence, etc. 1932, in IFC, Vol. IV, p. 57.
52. Leg-Election Department, Government of Madras, Circular No. 9 in IFC, p. 61.
53. General Election 1930 Statistics in G.O. Nos. 570-571, Law (Leg.), December 1930.
54. PLMC, Vol. LIV, November 1930, p. 12.
55. *Women's India Association Golden Jubilee*, p. 5; Stri-Dharma, 1932, p. 367.
56. *Ibid.*

57. All India Women's Conference was established in 1926 mainly to promote female education. Indian National Council for Women was started in 1925 by the Bombay Women's organisation to uplift the women (*Stri-Dharma*, May 1931, p. 286).
58. *The Indian Annual Register*, Vol. I, January-June 1931, p. 277.
59. *Stri-Dharma*, May 1931, p. 286.
60. *Ibid.*, May 1928, p. 65.
61. *Women's India Association Golden Jubilee...*, pp. 3-5.
62. *Ibid.*, July 1931, p. 387.
63. Geraldine H. Forbes, "Votes for Women : The demand for Women's Franchise in India 1917-1937" in Vina Mazumdar (ed.,) *Symbols of Power : Studies on the Political Status of Women in India*, p. 11.
64. Amrit Kaur, "Women Under the New Constitution", p. 366.
65. B.G. Paul and Co., *Gandhiji in England : And the proceedings of the second Round Table Conference*, pp. 47-61 ; Shai Ved Prakash Gupta, *Franchise in India*, p. 24.
66. Radhabai Subbarayan, *The Political Status of Women under the New Constitution*, pp. 2-3.
67. *Annual Report of the Women's Indian Association, 1930-31*, pp. 6-7.
68. *IFC*, Vol. I, p. 78.
69. *Ibid.*, p. 80.
70. Armit Kaur, "Women under the New Sonstitution", p. 368.
71. "Madras Provincial Franchise Committee to the Indian Franchise Committee Questionnaire", in IFC, Vol. II, pp. 13-14.
72. *Stri-Dharma*, 1932, pp. 301-4.
73. *IFC*, Vol. I, p. 80.
74. *Ibid.*, p. 86.
75. *IFC*, Vol. II, pp. 19-21.
76. Views of the Madras Provincial Franchise Committee on the Questionnaire, *IFC*, Vol. II, p. 27; IFC, Vol. I, p. 78.
77. *IFC*, Vol. I, p. 78.
78. *IFC*, Vol. II, p. 82.
79. *Ibid.*, p. 84.
80. *Ibid.*, p. 85.
81. Kamaladevi Chattopadhyaya, *Indian Women's Battle ...*, p. 99; *Stri-Dharma*, June 1933, p. 403.
82. *Stri-Dharma*, June 1933, p. 403.
83. Amrit Kaur, "Women Under the New Constitution", p. 371.
84. Stri-Dharma, June 1933, p. 424; *Women's India Association Golden Jubilee..*, p. 8.
85. "Minutes of Evidence given before the Joint Committee on Indian Constitutional Reform", *Joint Committee of Indian Constitutional Reform*, Vol. II, p. 1618.

86. Amrit Kaur, "Women under the New Constitution", p. 371.
87. *Joint Committee...*, p. 1619.
88. Kamala Devi Chattopadhyaya, "Blazing a Trail" in Aparna Basu (ed) *Dr. Muthulakshmi Reddi: The Path Finder*, p. 20.
89. *Stri-Dharma*, December 1934, p. 78.
90. *Ibid;* November - December 1934, p. 22.
91. *Ibid*, March 1935, p. 221; Rukmini Lakshmipathi was an old member of the Women's India Association, one of the pioneer women workers, and the first Secretary of the All India Women's Conference.
92. *The Hindu*, 8 April 1935.
93. G.O. No.103, Pub., (Conf.) January 1935.
94. *Stri-Dharma*, April 1935, p. 252.
95. Amrit Kaur, "Women Under the New Constitution", p. 374.
96. *Ibid.*, p. 375.
97. Radha Krishnan Sharma, *Nationalism, Social Reform...*, p. 94.
98. Amrit Kaur, "Women Under the New Constitution", p. 379.
99. *Ibid.*, p. 375.
100. Aruna Asaf Ali, "Women's Suffrage in India", pp. 360-61.
101. *Ibid*, p. 362.
102. *Stri-Dharma*, May 1936, p. 101.
103. *Ibid.*, p. 102; *Annual Report of the Women's India Association, 1935-36*, p. 3.
104. *Stri-Dharma*, May 1936, p. 101.
105. Press Communique, in G.O. No. 325, Pub. (Elections), 15 February 1937.
106. Proceedings of the All India Women's Conference, Ahmedabad, 23-27 December 1936 ; G.O. No. 3499, Home, 3 September 1937.
107. *Report of the Women's India Association 1936-37* and *1937-38*, p. 3.
108. G.O. No. 3499, Home, 3 September 1937.
109. Radha Krishna Sharma, *Nationalism, Social Reforms...*, p. 96; *RAMP 1937-38*, p. 2.
110. G.O. No. 984, Pub. (Elections), 13 June 1938.
111. Sushila Krishna"Ammu Swaminathan" in Butchi Arumugam et.al, *Some Illustrious Women...*, p. 4.
112. V.Rajalakshmi, *The Political Behaviour of Women in Tamilnadu*, pp. 79-84.
113. *Madras in 1946*, p. 1.
114. Vijay Agenew, *Elite Women in Indian Politics*, p. 129; Kiran Devendra, *Status and Position of Women in India*, p. 40.
115. Tara Ali Baig, "Durgabai As I see Her" in *Social Welfare*, August-September, 1978, p. 13.

116. S. Krishnaswamy, *The Role of Madras Legislature in the Freedom Struggle*, 1861 - 1947, p. 334.
117. *PMLC*, April 1921, p. 1028.
118. *Women's India Association Golden Jubilee...*, p. 3.
119. *Stri-Dharma*, September 1925.
120. *Ibid.*, October 1927, p. 178.
121. *Ibid.*, January 1928, p. 38; *Indian Ladies Magazine*, October 1929, p. 144.
122. *Stri-Dharma*, May 1928, p. 65.
123. *IFC*, Vol. II, 1932, p. 56.
124. *Stri-Dharma*, December 1931.
125. *Ibid.*, June 1933, p. 598.

Three

Women in the National Movement

It is without doubt that the national movement had been the most important cause of women's emergence in the socio-political life of the country. There emerged a common purpose that was the freedom of the country. For that the collaboration between men and women was no option, it became a matter of survival. All reformers including Mahatma Gandhi welcomed women's participation both as an opportunity for their own growth as individuals and as a force for the national movement.

Though there were one or two scattered incidents to prove the heroism of women in Tamilnadu, it was the national movement of the late nineteenth and early twentieth centuries which attracted a lot of women. Velu Nachiar, the ruler of Siva Ganga was the first woman of India to resist the British imperialism as early as 1770s. Then under the leadership of Mahatma Gandhi, Thillaiyadi Valliammai of Tamil Nadu joined the South African Movement and lost her life. But women of Tamil Nadu played an active role in the national movement only from the Home Rule movement.

Women had been taking increasing interest in socio-political affairs, fillip to this was given by the partition of Bengal, the ill-treatment of Indians in South Africa, the first world war, the Home Rule Movement and the Women's India Association.

Annie Besant

The Home Rule Leagues founded by Annie Besant and Bala Gangadhar Tilak, dominated the political scene of India from their formation in 1916 to the emergence of Mahatma Gandhi in 1919. Annie Besant, an Irish born theosophist was very active in the Madras politics since 1914. The outbreak of the first world war in Europe gave a new dimension to the Congress demand for Self Government or Swaraj. Having the Irish nationalist background, she jumped into the fray to achieve Swaraj by adopting some new methods. By starting two news papers The *Common Weal*, a weekly and *New India*, a daily, she popularised the demand for Self Government.[1] Knowing that without unity Self Government was impossible she advocated the need for unity through her papers and platforms.

As a delegate to the Madras Congress session held in 1914, she pleaded for Self Government not as a reward but as a right.[2] On 24th September 1915, Annie Besant made a formal announcement of forming the Home Rule League to work both in India and in England. Its main objectives were educating the masses, inculcating in them the idea of liberty and the formulation of a detailed scheme of Home Rule on the lines of colonial Self Government.[3] She wanted to start it as an auxiliary body to the Indian National Congress and moved a resolution to that effect in the Bombay Congress session held in December 1915.[4] Fearing that the Congress would be weakened, the Moderates in the Congress did not approve of the idea of any organisation within the Congress and asked to postpone its formation until the Congress and the Muslim League submitted their reports.[5] Annie Besant accepted that suggestion and the formation of the League was thereby postponed.[6] But Bala Gangadhar Tilak established the Home Rule League on 28th April 1916 in Pune and defined its objectives as 'attaining Self Government within the British Empire by all constitutional means and to educate and organise public opinion in the country towards the attainment of the same.

Annie Besant however founded the Home Rule League

for India in England on 7th June 1916, to educate the British public in relation to India and to place before them the demand of the Congress for Self-Government.[7] Before starting the same in India she toured throughout India and spread the ideal of Home Rule every where. However, to the great dismay of many, the Congress and the Muslim League failed to submit the report within the stipulated time. It made Annie Besant to inaugurate the Home Rule League in Madras on 3rd September 1916 with herself as its President, C.P. Ramaswami Iyer, B.P. Wadia and G.S. Arundale as its General Secretary, Treasurer and Organising Secretary respectively.[8]

As said earlier, it emerged as an auxiliary forum to the Indian National Congress. Its objectives were; to secure Self-Government for India through law-abiding and constitutional activities; to maintain the connection with Great Britain by becoming a free nation within the British Empire under the Imperial Crown and his successors; to support and strengthen the Indian National Congress which had laboured for more than thirty years to lay the foundation of Indian Self-Government and to carry on a continuous educative propaganda on the necessity of Home Rule for India.[9] Annie Besant wrote in the *New India,* that India should have some sort of Self-Government within the British Empire and the Indians wanted to have all the rights and privileges of the citizens of the British Empire. Hence, Home Rule within the British Empire was the only panacea suitable to India.[10] With this aim, she suggested that the Congress should formulate the plan of Self-Government and the Home Rule League should popularise it by all possible means. In order to get the approval of their plan in the Congress, Annie Besant and Bala Ganghadhar Tilak worked to send those delegates who pledged to vote for Home Rule to the Lucknow Congress session to be held in December 1916.[11]

The result of their propaganda was the dominance of the Nationalists in the Lucknow Congress session. In that session, a resolution on Self-Government jointly prepared by the Congress and Muslim League was passed. It exhorted the British Emperor to issue a proclamation conferring Self-Government to India at an early date.[12] By Self-Government, the leaders meant representative government controlled by the people. However, the British Government felt that the Indians were unfit for Self-Government. In order to retaliate this stricture, the Congress carried on an effective propaganda through the organs of the Home Rule Leagues.

Home Rule League and Justice Party

Fearing that the dominance of Brahmins in the Congress and the Home Rule League would result in the assumption of political power by the Brahmins, some of the non-Brahmin leaders like P. Thyagaraja Chetti, a Telugu Devanga businessman, T.M. Nair, a Malayalee Physician and C. Natesa Mudaliar, a Tamil Vellala Physician formed the South Indian Liberal Federation, later called the Justice Party on 20th November 1916.[13] Its chief aim was to launch non-Brahmin movement to oppose the Brahmin domination not only in public services but also in the Congress and the Home Rule League.

The South Indian Liberal Federation issued a manifesto with the signature of P. Thyagaraya Chetti criticising the Home Rule movement in Madras. The manifesto stated that though the non-Brahmins formed 400 lakhs out of 450 lakhs of the population and comprised the bulk of tax prayers, land-holders, zamindars and agriculturists, they remained practically without any political power. Public bodies and public services were practically monopolised by the Brahmins who had been using official powers and political influence for their own advantage.[14] It demanded equal justice for the non-Brahmins in all walks of life. The tone of the manifesto was little militant and it aimed at giving resistance to the Home Rule movement. However, the manifesto had come under severe criticism in the hands of the pro-Congress organs. Reacting to the manifesto, *The Hindu* commented that it gave a distorted and unfair representation of many of the matters it had referred to and that it could serve no good, instead it could create ill-feeling between the same Indian community.[15] Criticising it, the *New India* wrote that it showed distrust in the ultimate objective of independence. It opined that in the case of India gaining Home Rule, it mattered little whether Brahmins or non-Brahmins, Hindus or Muslims were most powerful, for all were the children of the same mother *'the Bharatmata'*.[16] Denouncing the non-Brahmin movement as an enemy of the nation, it further said that it was an instrument to oppose the works of the Indian National Congress and the Home Rule Leagues. Besides, it condemned the movement as unpatriotic, shortsighted and narrow-minded.[17]

On the other hand, the non-Brahmin movement enjoyed the support of three journals namely *Dravidian* in Tamil, *Justice* in English and *Andhra Prakasika* in Telugu.[18] In their attempt to attract the non-Brahmins from the Congress, they attacked the programmes and the proceedings of the Congress through these papers almost daily. But a considerable number of non-Brahmins in the Congress did not like the non-Brahmin movement. They wanted not only to contradict the claims of the Justice Party to represent the entire non-Brahmin community, but also to check the defection of non-Brahmins from the Congress to the Justice Party.[19] At the same time they were not satisfied with the Congress-Leauge Scheme, because it provided for the minimum constitutional demands of the Muslim League and the Congress but said nothing about the non-Brahmins. Hence they began to think in terms of an organisation that would seek communal representation to safeguard their own interests in the elections.[20] However, they did not want to break away from the Indian National Congress, of which they had long been members. Encouragement to that was so great that in a meeting held in Madras, the non-Brahmin members of the Madras Provincial Congress Committee such as E.V. Ramaswami Naicker, Thiru V. Kalyana Sundara Mudaliar, George Joseph, P.Varadarajulu Naidu and some others formed the Madras Presidency Association.[21] The chief aim of this association was to place before the Secretary of State for India, a scheme of reforms designed to give the non-Brahmins full communal representation.[22] The Madras Presidency Association insisted that communal representation for non-Brahmins should be embodied as an integral part of the Congress-League Scheme.[23] This was in a way to counteract the claims of the Justice Party as the sole spokesman of Non-Brahmins. Except communal representation, the members of the Madras Presidency Association supported the Congress ideals and goals. Surprisingly many of them happened to be members of Annie Besant's Home Rule League, which worked for the Home Rule for India.

Home Rule Movement

In the Lucknow Congress session in 1916, a resolution was passed recognising the Home Rule Leagues of Bala Gangadhar Tilak and Annie Besant as a body affiliated to the Indian National Congress and permitting them to carry on a vigorous propaganda in favour of the Congress-League Scheme.[24]

As decided in the session, Bala Gangadhar Tilak and Annie Besant visited many parts of India and addressed several meetings. In support of their intensive campaigns, many Moderates came forward to join the Home Rule movement. Among them G.A. Natesan, V. Krishnaswami Iyer, V.S. Srinivasa Sastri, S. Subramania Iyer and C.P. Ramaswami Iyer were the important Moderates of Tamil Nadu.[25] Important among the Nationalists who attacked the Home Rule League at first and later joined it were C. Rajagopalachari, S. Satyamurti, A. Rangaswami Iyengar and T.S.S. Rajan.[26] For a moment, the Home Rule League united all the disgruntled political factions of Madras under Annie Besant. Using Tamil, the language of the people she attracted the attention of the people to her Home Rule movement. Two of her staunch non-Brahmin supporters of the Madras Presidency Association were Thiru V. Kalyana Sundara Mudaliar and P.Varadarajulu Naidu who spread her message among the people.[27] At once the movement became very popular. In February 1917, the Home Rule League had 110 branches and over 5,000 members in the Madras Presidency alone.[28] The Congress also adopted the Home Rule movement and continued the work by committees connected with it.[29] Her attacks on the castles of political power had electric effect on the people. Agitation for Home Rule became widespread throughout India and the government resorted to repressive measures. At first she was expelled from Bombay and subsequently from Central Province and Bihar.[30] Determined to achieve Home Rule, she continued her attacks on government policies. To draw the students to the agitation, she convened a protest meeting of students in Madras against the failure of 2,800 students at the Secondary School Leaving Certificate and the Intermediate Examinations. Denouncing the government and the university authorities for their reactionary measures she wrote that the authorities in order to keep India down, wanted to strangle higher education. As a result, many students joined the Home Rule movement. On one occasion the students of Madanapalle college which was then under her direct control, wrote on the black board 'We do not ask for Home Rule, we demand it'.[31]

The entry of a large number of students into the agitation alarmed Lord Pentland, the Governor of Madras who decided to curb the political activities of the students. At first he warned and directed them not to take part either in political meetings or join any political association or take part in any movement. The educational authorities also informed the heads of colleges and schools, both under political management and otherwise to strictly enforce these directions.[32] Annie Besant in her *New*

India strongly condemned the action of the government.[33] Lord Pentland reacted quickly by prohibiting Annie Besant from writing or speaking or publishing anything political in *New India*.[34] Again on 7th June 1917, he passed another order restricting the movements and activities of Annie Besant and her co-workers, B.P. Wadia and G.S. Arundale. According to the order, on or before the expiry of a period of fourteen days from the date of service of that order, Annie Besant and her colleagues should take up their residence in any one of the following six places; Nilgiris district, Coimbatore district, Bellary, Palni hills, Shevaroy hills and the municipal town of Vizagapatinam.[35] Another government order issued on 14th June 1917 reduced the period fixed for Annie Besant and her colleagues from fourteen days to seven days to leave Madras and Chengleput district for their place of confinement.[36] Obeying the order she and her colleagues selected Ottacamund in the Nilgiris district.[37] There they hoisted the flag of the Home Rule League. Immediately, the District Magistrate issued an order under section 144 Cr.P.C prohibiting them from hoisting the flag. Despite such restrictions, Ottacamund at once became a centre of political activities and a place a pilgrimage for the Home Rulers.[38]

Their internments earned more popularity and support for the Home Rule movement. Motilal Nehru, Tej Bahadur Sapru, Munshi Narayan Prasad Asthana, C.Y. Chintamani and several others joined it as a protest against the arbitrary action of the Government of Madras.[39] Almost all the papers criticised the internments. For example, *The Hindu* in its editorial described it as a violent and unconstitutional act of aggression upon Indian constitutional agitation. It, thus, induced a campaign against the government action.[40] Though Mahatma Gandhi, who was then rising up, did not like her political propaganda during the world war, he wrote to the Private Secretary to the Viceroy, Lord Chelmsford stating that the internments were a big blunder.[41] Moreover the appeal of the

Home Rule League did not confine itself within the frontiers of India. S. Subramania Iyer, a senior Congressman and a leader of the Home Rule movement appealed to President Woodrow Wilson of the United States of America to apply his war message of democracy and self-determination of nations to India.[42] A printed copy of the letter was placed on the desk of the Senators and the Congressmen. It created great sensation in America and the American Labour Party at once wanted Home Rule for India as in Canada and Australia. An Indian Home Rule League was established in New York.[43] Though the spark of the agitation spread throughout the world and there was a persistent demand for her release, the government was not moved to cancel the internment punishment.

This induced many women to join the movement. Their active participation in the movement calls for specific reference. It was this movement which brought the women of Tamil Nadu to the forefront. Women theosophists like Ms. Arundale, daughter of Mr. G.S. Arundale, Dorothy Jinarajadasa and Sivakamu Ammal were notable women Home Rule members.[44] Sivakamu Ammal was a medical student studying at Bombay left the college and became a Home Rule worker as a protest against the order forbidding students to take part in politics.[45] She felt that she could serve the country more by joining the Home Rule movement than by becoming a doctor. To welcome her, a meeting was convened at Madras by the Madras Home Rule League on 9th August 1917.[46] Abadi Bano Begum, mother of Ali Brothers sent a letter appreciating Home Rule movement and Annie Besant. The patriotism, courage and the firmness shown by her were praiseworthy.[47] It was auspicious for the Home Rulers that even conservative Muhammadan women gave up their ancient traditions adopted themselves to the times with courage and firmness and rallied round the Home Rule banners. The letter was a source of courage to Indian women. Though she was poor, she rendered considerable help to the Home Rule cause.[48]

In order to get Annie Besant released, a special meeting was held at Triplicane on 14th September by some women including Dorothy Jinarajadasa and another English woman from Adayar settlement. The meeting was addressed among others by Sivakamu Ammal and was followed by a procession to an adjacent temple, bearing a portrait of Annie Besant and flying a large Home Rule flag. On the temple they offered prayers. In other parts of the country also prayers were offered up in many temples and sacred places of pilgrimage. Thus Home Rule movement became so intertwined with religion. The procession was undertaken in order to test whether the police would interfere having regard to the orders previously issued prohibiting general processions.[49]

A large number of Home Rule placards and invitations to undertake the 'Swadeshi Vow' were pasted on the walls. Pictures and postcards bearing the portraits of the internees were sold on large scales. A booklet entitled the 'Swadeshi Vow, Why Indians should take it'? was sold.[50] Pattabi Sitaramaya, a member of the Home Rule League took an active part in the protest meetings. Moreover, he, in the Indian Legislative Council moved a resolution asking its members to stay away from the proceedings of the council until the internment order was cancelled.[51] Even then they were not released. So, on 31st July 1917, the All India Congress Committee and the Muslim-league together held a meeting to work out a plan to secure the release of Annie Besant and her followers. A resolution was also passed to launch passive resistance.[52] On this issue opinion was gathered from provincial congress committees. When the opinion was in favour of that, the Home Rulers held a meeting in Madras on 9th August 1917 to formulate a policy of passive resistance and to gather support for that. They welcomed all those who were desirous of joining the Home Rule League, even though they were not prepared to become passive resisters. The *New India* and The *Common Weal* exposed the various aspects of passive resistance.

The underlying idea was that everyone should personally refuse obedience to any law or executive order which in his/her private judgement would be morally wrong to be obeyed. The Indian Press Act (1910) and the Defence of India Rules (1915) were cited as specific instances of law coming under that category. Meanwhile the leaders of the Home Rule League popularised the idea of passive resistance among the mofussil people by distributing vernacular leaflets, illustrated post cards, public meetings and processions. This had its immediate effect on the people. For instance, Sivakamu Ammal, a student of the Bombay Medical College left that institution to join the passive resistance movement. On its side, the Government of Madras directed the District Magistrates to discourage protest meetings, especially street processions.[53]

Before passive resistance was approved of and Annie Besant was still in internment, the question of election of the president for the next Congress session came up before various Provincial Congress Committees. In recognition of her sacrifices and in appreciation of her contribution to the cause of Indian nationalism, all the provinces suggested that Annie Besant should be elected.[54] The Madras Provincial Congress Committee also on 12th August 1917 in its special meeting nominated Annie Besant as the President of the Indian National Congress by fifty to twelve votes.[55] On finding her release very urgent, the Madras Provincial Congress Committee on 14th August 1917 approved of passive resistance.[56] Fearing that, the launching of such passive resistance would wreck the government at a time of the world war, the authorities immediately changed their attitude towards India. The result was the historic Declaration of Responsible Government by Montague, the then Secretary of State for India, on 20th August 1917 in the House of Commons, as the goal of the British policy in India.[57] It was the first time the word 'Responsible Government' appeared in any of the British reform schemes. However, it did not incorporate the Congress-League Scheme.

Any how for the time being, the Declaration pacified the passion for passive resistance.

But the declaration evoked mixed feelings. The Moderates welcomed it as the Magna Carta of India. The Nationalists held that it fell far short of the legitimate expectations of the Indians and characterised it as a concession to intensive agitation.[58] It also did not escape the press criticism. According to *The Hindu* it was an uninspiring and disappointing declaration which would cause great dissatisfaction throughout the country.[59]

On finding, the country was not in favour of the declaration, and at any time passive resistance might be launched which would affect his mission to India, Montague asked the Government of India to release the political prisoners. Still the Government of Madras did not consider the release of Annie Besant advisable and informed Montague accordingly.[60] Therefore, to get her released, a manifesto was published in the *New India* approving the policy of passive resistance.[61] The meeting of the Madras Provincial Congress Committee convened on 25th August 1917 approved it in theory, but strongly opposed to resorting to it at the critical time of Montague's mission to India. But the party in favour of passive resistance gained upper hand and the resolution in favour of it was passed by a large majority.[62] Fearing worst consequences, the Government of Madras requested the Government of India to remove the restrictions imposed on Annie Besant and her colleagues.[63] On 15th September 1917, the Government of India announced its decision to release them.[64] Finally Annie Besant and others were released owing to the personal intervention of Queen Mary. On their release, the move for passive resistance was also given up.[65] When Annie Besant came to Madras a large assemblage of women tendered her congratulations.[66]

After her release, a series of meetings were held in honour of her which culminated in a special celebration at the head quarters of the Theosophical Society, Adayar on Ist October by Mr. and Mrs. Dorothy Jinarajadasa and other residents.

Sivakamu Ammal played so prominent a part in the Home Rule movement. She attended almost all the meetings held at Madras in connection with it.[67] Members of the Women's India Association also took part in the meetings and processions connected with the internment of Annie Besant and after her release.[68] The Home Rule idea spread like wild fire and many women joined the movement. Annie Besant in her presidential address in the Indian National Congress in 1917 told, "the strength of the Home Rule Movement was rendered ten fold greater by the participation of a large number of women".[69] It is significant to note that the movement was led by a woman and also it attracted a lot of women. Owing to the Home Rule agitation between 1916 and 1917 women began to wake up and realised their exclusion from political movement.

Thereafter Annie Besant toured Madras, Calcutta, Benares, Allahabad and Bombay to gather the opinion of every class in order to present an united front for Home Rule to Montague who was scheduled to visit India in November 1917. On 26th November 1917, Bala Gangadhar Tilak and Annie Besant, on behalf of the Home Rule Leagues and the Congress presented a memorandum to Montague demanding Home Rule. In the memorandum, they stated in clear terms that nothing less than the Congress-League Scheme would satisfy the Indians.[70] The Justice party, while welcoming the Declaration, stressed the need for granting representation to the Non-Brahmins.[71] Montague also discussed the reform proposals with the then Viceroy, Lord Chelmsford.

The Calcutta Congress session met in December 1917 under the presidentship of Annie Besant passed a resolution expressing its satisfaction over the Montague Declaration. At the same time it emphasised the necessity for the immediate enactment of a parliamentary statute providing for the establishment of Responsible Government in India within a fixed time. Further, it stated that the Congress-League Scheme should be immediately implemented as the first step in the process.[72]

Describing that Congress session Margaret E. Cousins remarked "I remember vividly being impressed by the three women who occupied the place of power and honour on the platform at that Calcutta Congress - Mrs. Besant in the President's Chair, on her right Mrs. Sarojini Devi Naidu, representative of the great Hindu race, on the left Begum Ammam Bibi, (Abadi Bano Begum) mother of the brothers Muhammad and Shaukat Ali, and the veiled daughters of the strong Muslim people. The three women were deeply significant in the new era in Indian social and political history. Womanhood had come out of its seclusion to share with manhood the struggle for gaining freedom for Bharat Mata - the Motherland".[73]

On 11th March 1918, the Madras Provincial Congress Committee, while disapproving of Montague's Declaration, passed a resolution stating that no reform could be inaugurated or worked out which did not confirm to the principles of Congress-League Scheme. It called upon the Congress propaganda committee, the Home Rule League and all other affiliated associations to carry on a vigorous and active campaign for securing the Congress-League Scheme of reforms. Public meetings were held in various places to emphasise it as the minimum demand.[74] The Madras Presidency Muslim League also declared that the attainment of Self-Government within the British Empire was their goal.[75] The Justice Party demanded separate communal electorate as the only panacea for them.[76] As an alternative to separate communal electorate, the Madras Presidency Association suggested reservation of seats for non-Brahmins in plural member constituencies.[77] It was only after much effort, the Madras Presidency Association convinced the Madras Provincial Congress Committee to accept the demand for communal representation.[78]

Dissatisfied with the attitude of the Nationalists, the Madras Moderates and few other staunch Home Rulers, published a manifesto in May 1918, stating that the path of wisdom lay not in the rejection of the scheme, but in effecting considerable modifications in it.[79] This however did not lead to their permanent separation from the Congress. But the Nationalists' rejection of the Mont-Ford Reform Scheme forced them to depart the Congress.

The Montague mission to India resulted in the announcement of Mont-Ford Reform Scheme on 8th July 1918. Public opinion was sharply divided on that scheme. The Congress had three lines of thinking. The Moderates stood for the total acceptance of the scheme.[80] The Nationalists urged total rejection of it, and the Home Rulers favoured a middle path of responsive cooperation. In Tamil Nadu many Nationalists changed their previous stand and proposed for some modifications in the scheme. On 3-4th August 1918 the Madras Provincial Congress Committee held a meeting to discuss it. It elected C.Vijayaraghavachari as President, Annie Besant as Chairperson of the Reception Committee and S.Kasturi Ranga Iyengar, as one of the Chairperson of the meeting. In that meeting, the great debator, S.Satyamurti advocated total rejection of the scheme, but was voted down by 187 to 154 votes. The *New India*, The *Common Weal* and *The Hindu* which at first advocated total rejection, then changed their stand.[81] After the Delhi Congress session in December 1918, Annie Besant and her associates openly accepted the scheme. Many Nationalists considered this change as betrayal and attacked Annie Besant severely.[82] Annie Besant and her associates were criticised for being too moderate in their demands and too conciliatory to the British Government. Under such situation, on 18th March 1919, Annie Besant resigned from the Provincial Congress Committee taking with her several prominent moderates and Home Rulers.[83]

Non-Cooperation Movement

Having total faith in the declared aim of Britain and her allies that they were fighting to make the world safe for democracy, during the first world war India responded to the call of the British Empire. After the war, Mont-Ford Reform Act of 1919 was passed, which was unsatisfactory to the Indians. Further, it was followed by Rowlatt Act[84] which was enacted on 21st March 1919 amidst the united opposition of all the Indian members of the Legislative Council, the Congress, press and the public.[85] Rowlatt Bills evoked much opposition and condemnation. Even before it was passed the Madras Provincial Congress Committee held a meeting and constituted an Anti-Rowlatt Committee with S.Kasturi Ranga Iyengar, and others to oppose the Rowlatt Bills. In its meeting held at beach on 17th March, Sarojini Naidu moved the following resolution.

> "That this public meeting of the citizens of Madras once again earnestly urges on His Excellency, the Viceroy and the Govt. of India, that they should drop the Rowlatt Bills, atleast at this stage in as much as they are unjust, subversive of the principle of liberty and justice and destructive of the elementary rights of individuals on which the safety of the community as a whole and the state itself is based".[86]

She added that the contemplated legislation was an insult of insults and tyrany of tyrannies.

At the request of the committee Mahatma Gandhi visited Madras on 18th March and they had discussion with him and decided to oppose the Rowlatt Bills through Satyagraha.[87] While welcoming Mahatma Gandhi, Sarojini Naidu said that the secret of success either in war or in politics lay in the followers' obeying their leaders implicitly and blindly. She fervently exhorted all to rally round the flag of Mahatma Gandhi.[88] Then satyagraha sabhas were formed to enlist volunteers and force the government to withdraw the Rowlatt Bills. A satyagraha pledge was drawn up by Mahatma Gandhi and all the Indians were asked to sign it.[89] He fixed 6th April 1919 for an all India satyagraha and as a day of national humiliation by fasting, prayer and penance.[90] In the meantime

Rowlatt Act was passed. Throughout Tamil Nadu, satyagraha was observed by observing twenty four hours fasting, processions and meetings. Shops were closed. It is remarkable to note that in Madras Muhammadans and women were present in large numbers than in any other political meetings. In short, Tamil Nadu presented quite a remarkable appearance. To bring down the raising tempo of the *satyagraha*, the government issued explanatory leaflets in Tamil justifying the Rowlatt Act.[91] The culmination of this movement, atlast ended with the tyrannical display of force and massacre of participants at Jallianwallabagh in Punjab, on 13th April 1919. The satyagrahis were brutally shot dead by General Dyer.[92] The news of the Jallianwallabagh massacre shook the whole of India. Immediately, C. Rajagopalachari, Secretary of the Madras Satyagraha Sabha, suspended the satyagraha in Tamil Nadu on the advice of Mahatma Gandhi. Following this, martial law was declared in Punjab. In spite of the official secrecy, the reports of the martial law atrocities leaked out. Throughout India, people became angry. But the Congress did not take any action expecting that the Hunter Committee appointed by the British Government to enquire into the matter would do justice. The Amritsar Congress session held in December 1919, though condemned all these atrocities, permitted the Congressmen to contest elections to the Legislative Council, according to the Mont-Ford Act.[93]

The Congress also appointed a sub committee of non-officials to collect evidence relating to the outbreak of the Punjab disturbances and the methods employed for their suppression. The subcommittee termed the firing at Jallianwallabagh, a calculated piece of inhumanity unparalleled for its ferocity in the history of modern British administration. The report concluded with a demand for the recall of the Viceroy and the dismissal of the various officials who were involved in the atrocity. The Hunter Committee did not examine the evidence produced by the sub-committee of the

Indian National Congress.[94] Added to that, the report published by the Hunter Committee justified the action of General Dyer and believed that a state of rebellion existed necessitating or justifying the adoption of martial law.[95] It came with an added shock to the public opinion, both in India and in Great Britain.

Meanwhile, the Khilafat agitation continued with renewed force. A number of Khilafat meetings were held in Madras and the vows of non-cooperation, boycott and swadeshi were advocated.[96] S. Satyamurti and S.Kasturi Rangai Iyengar delivered a number of lecturers on Khilafat problem in Madras, in which they emphasised the necessity of the Hindus cooperating with the Muslims, in the Khilafat agitation.[97] The draft terms of peace reached between the Allied powers and Axis powers in April 1920 was unsatisfactory to the Muslims and it served to stimulate the agitation. The meeting of the All India Khilafat Committee held in Bombay on 12th May 1920 sought the support of Mahatma Gandhi. He advised them to resort to non-cooperation programme, drawn up by the Congress Sub-Committee.[98] Mahatma Gandhi also requested the Hindus to join the movement. Thus, he had taken the unprecedented step of identifying himself with a Muslim religious movement. The meeting of the All India Congress Committee held in Benaras, on 30th May 1920 decided to convene a special Congress session in Calcutta in September to consider the question of non-cooperation.[99] From then on, until September 1920, the scheme of non-cooperation was published in the columns of Mahatma Gandhi's *Young India*. Having pursued for months an elaborate campaign through the press and the platforms, Mahatma Gandhi prepared to launch the non-cooperation movement in August 1920. When the leadership of the Congress movement passed over to Mahatma Gandhi, he chartered out the national programme in such a way as to give opportunities to all class of people. In order to include women Mahatma Gandhi introduced khadi as an important Congress programme. It was he who gave a new direction strength and inspiration to the freedom movement and drew into it women in large numbers.

Constructive Programme

For Mahatma Gandhi, the national movement was not merely a political struggle but a means of regenerating and rejuvenating society. He encouraged women to participate in the constructive programme and the non-violent satyagraha initiated by him. Mahatma Gandhi believed that women's nature was particularly suited to non-violent satyagraha for it required not physical strength but moral courage and spiritual determination. The three essential qualities required of a satyagrahi were a capacity for love, non-violence and self sacrifice.[100] They were naturally found in women.

From Tamil Nadu, there were some women who participated actively in the Congress programmes of boycott of foreign clothes, promotion of khadi, the picketing of liquor shops and conducting meetings. Press also played a leading role in mobilising women. A correspondent to the *Desabhimani* recommended the Non-Cooperation movement to the acceptance of women. It requested the women to play their part in making the movement a success and concluded with the exhortation, "... Ascend the steps of Swaraj, secure freedom to India, fame to yourselves, happiness to your sons and disgrace to our rulers".[101] It also requested women to help men in carrying out swadeshi and boycott movement.[102]

Picketing of liquor shops was a notable item in the Non-Cooperation movement. From the beginning the Indian National Congress viewed with much concern the growing consumption of intoxicants. The Allahabad Congress session held in 1888 passed a resolution urging the Government of India to adopt some such improved system as would discourage drinking.[103] In the subsequent Congress annual sessions as well as in the provincial and district conferences, the same matter was discussed and passed resolutions against the use of it. Thus, towards the end of the nineteenth century and the beginning of the twentieth century there began a prohibition movement. The Congress and its conferences passed a number of resolutions demanding the government to eradicate the evil of drinking that bore no fruit. Instead, year after year more shops were opened for the sale of intoxicants. In the Madras Presidency in 1920, the number of coconut and palmyra trees tapped for toddy was 12,47,841 and the number of toddy shops was 10,729.[104]

The details of income and expenditure incurred by the Government of Madras through the sale of intoxicants are indicated hereunder:

Year	*Income Rs.*	*Excise*	*Total Duty Rs. (2)+(3)*	*Expense Income*	*Excess (4)–(5)*
(1)	*(2)*	*(3)*	*(4)*	*(5)*	*(6)*
1880-81	31352260	3798360	35150620	954040	34196580
1885-86	41521320	4198100	45719420	1243720	44475700
1890-91	49477800	6009000	55486800	1749810	53706990
1895-96	57224170	6625860	63850030	2079570	61770460
1900-01	59088030	6938205	66026235	2417640	63608595
1905-06	85317300	9740000	95057300	3871740	91185560
1910-11	110545475	12053394	122598869	6089904	116508965
1915-16	129483132	11790000	141273132	7061095	134212037
1917-18	154425590	10996886	165422476	7300000	158122476
1918-19	173552770	11065351	184618121	8200000	176418121

Source: *Navasakti*, 18 March 1921.

It is apparent from the table that the income derived from the sale of intoxicants also increased year after year. The total revenue from country spirits in excise tracts of the Madras Presidency for the year 1919-20 amount to Rs. 22,06,905 while it was Rs. 18,89,630 in 1918-19. The increase occurred under both excise duty and rentals. The proportion of head duty to total revenue was 72.21 per cent. Trees marked for toddy also increased year after year.[105]

It was the non-cooperation movement which gave a momentum to prohibition and the movement was launched throughout Tamil Nadu. But the original non-cooperation resolution did not contain any provision for prohibition campaign. It was not planned or anticipated by Mahatma Gandhi or the Congress. It was purely a spontaneous move by the masses, but the Congress encouraged it once it had read the pulse of the masses and included it in the non-cooperation programme.[106] From then onwards, prohibition was made a major item in the Congress programme. Most of the resources of the Congress had been utilised in carrying out this message to the people.

As early as 1920, the Madras Provincial Congress Committee in its election manifesto included prohibition as one of its legislative programmes. Under dyarchy, the transfer of the excise portfolio to an Indian Minister brought prohibition within the realm of practical politics. Even the Justice Party claimed that prohibition was one of its aims.[107] The Congress took it as an easy way to provoke the government to arrest and imprison them thereby earn mass support and sympathy for the Congress cause.

Prohibition movement had spread in almost all the districts of the Madras Presidency before the end of February 1921. The sales of arrack and toddy shops had been boycotted in many places.[108] The campaign reached its zenith at the time of the auction sales of toddy shops in August 1921 and lasted till the end of that year. C. Rajagopalachar, E.V. Ramaswami Naicker and N.S. Rangaswami Iyer organised volunteers corp known as *thondarpadai* to picket liquor shops throughout Tamil Nadu. Picketing took place in innumerous parts of Tamil Nadu.[109] The volunteers induced the workmen employed in the liquor shops to leave their masters. They prevented the cartmen from carrying liquor to the depots and shops. The volunteers burnt down few arrack shops. They persuaded the owners of the coconut trees not to give the trees to the renters for tapping or where such persuasion failed, they instigated the breaking up of pots on the trees and cutting of the spathes. All these naturally affected toddy sales so much, that in several places resale of shops was ordered.[110]

The Government of Madras placed substantial reliance on its income from excise duties and the prohibition campaign put it under serious pressure. At first the government disguised the impact of the agitation by attributing the sharp fall in income from toddy shop auctions to factors other than picketing. But in October 1921 the Government of Madras was compelled to intervene directly because it lost nearly a quarter of its revenue came from duties on liquor.[111] Prosecutions were started on a large scale. E.V. Ramaswami Naicker, C. Rajagopalachar, M.V. Subramanya Sastri and others were imprisoned thinking that the movement would die in the absence of leaders. After their arrest, E.V. Ramaswamy Naicker's wife Nagammal and his sister Kannammal along with many other women were drawn into the moment. They pursued passive resistance to make it a success at Erode.[112] On seeing this, a number of women from Erode also participated in this agitation. Fearing that the law and order situation would get out of control if all the women were arrested, the government lifted the 144 ban order.[113] When the Congress asked Mahatma Gandhi to stop the movement, he replied that it was not in his hands and it was only in the hands of two women from Erode.[114] Such was the involvement, Nagammal and Kannammal had in the movement.

Another aspect of the movement was the boycott of foreign clothes. Inorder to make this movement a success and also to make the people economically self reliant it was necessary to increase khadi production. Khadi industry had multi-dimensional advantages to the country. Economically it would increase the production of cloth in the country without much additional investment and the foreign exchange consumed in importing foreign clothes could be diverted to more urgent necesssities of capital goods. It would also make the people economically self dependent and save them from starvation. Socially it would serve as a bond between classes and masses.[115] If hand spinning, and hand weaving were carried on by all, the gulf between the rich and the poor, the educated and the uneducated would be bridged and in its place a bond of unity would be established. Psychologically khadi alone could teach the village population to depend on their own efforts to improve their lot and thus to learn the first lesson in real independence. Politically organisation of manufacture and distribution of khadi on a nation-wide scale would prepare the country for the non-violent disciplined organisation of political struggle for freedom. Further the curtailment of revenue from importing foreign clothes would force the alien government to leave India. Hence Mahatma Gandhi saw in it, the revival of the entire economic, social and political life of the villages. *Charka* thus become a symbol of non-violence and of economic and national struggle against foreign domination.

Hand spinning and hand weaving functioned as an integral part of Indian economy from ancient times. On account of British domination, hand spinning and hand weaving had been ruined and Indian market was flooded with foreign clothes. Out of the total imports, nearly one-third consisted of foreign clothes. It was one of the reasons for India's poverty. Even the early nationalists wrote and spoke about India's growing poverty and linked it with the British exploitation of the economy of India. They criticised the official economic policies for bringing about the ruin of India's traditional handicraft industries. However, the first world war induced them to take immediate action for its revival. While the country was passing through the period of series of economic crisis on account of the first world war and the increasing competition of the mill industries, a competition largely made possible by the tariff policy followed by the Indian Government, the Congress realised the urgent need of economic revival. Hence, it decided to revive village industries, the most important one being hand spinning and hand weaving.

The work of popularising khadi was undertaken by the Congress since 1919 as a part of its national programme.[116] Subsequent Congress sessions also reiterated its resolution on khadi. Along with the non-cooperation resolution the Congress advised the stimulation of further manufacture of khadi on a large scale.[117] The Ahmedabad Congress session held in 1921 advised the Congress organisations to boycott foreign clothes and to open depots for the supply of khadi, spinning wheels, charka, hand looms and other accessories required for spinning and weaving. It also requested the Congress volunteers to collect foreign clothes from consumers for destruction or use outside India in their option.[118] For the successful boycott of foreign clothes, it would be necessary to increase the output of khadi clothes. In order to encourage khadi, charka was put in the center of the national flag made in khadi cloth in 1921. Mahatma Gandhi held the view that in cent percent swadeshi lies Swaraj and khadi was the symbol of true swadeshi.[119]

In order to promote khadi, with the help of the Tilak Swaraj Fund, *charkas* were distributed every where.[120] In Tamil Nadu E.V. Ramaswami Naicker was in the forefront to popularise it. From ancient times, in Tamil Nadu centres like Kanchipuram, Madurai and Tanjore produced and exported very superior quality of cotton textiles to foreign countries. There are references for that in the Sangam Classic like *Silappadikaram* and *Manimekalai*.[121] Spinning and weaving stood next to agriculture. Not only the weaving communities, but also agriculturists in their leisure time did that. Like other parts of India, the weavers of Tamil Nadu also suffered due to foreign rule. Since 1871, the output of hand spun yarn had diminished by 22.5 per cent.[122] It was then that machine and science sought to replace men. Manchester, Lanchashire and Glasgow mills (Britain) began to export to Madras and other places in India cheaper yarn and cheaper cotton piece goods. In 1900 Indian mills began to compete with English mills in producing yarn and cotton piece goods.[123] The hand spun yarn was rapidly superseded by yarn made in the Indian mills. As every factory hand would displace thirty weavers and spinners it was obvious that the deterioration of these classes were even more rapid than in the past.[124] These mills were mostly owned and controlled by British firms. In 1931 for example, British controlled mills accounted for 73.1 per cent of spindles, 66.1 per cent of looms and 71.9 per cent of employment in the cotton mills of the Madras Presidency.[125] The result was exports of handloom cloth dwindled, import of mill made clothes increased. Hand spun yarn gave place to English and Indian mill made yarn. Chemical dyes drove out indigenous dyes. It was for these reasons spinning was completely given up. Weaving was done by a few people, but they were exploited by the middlemen. The hand weavers of Tamil Nadu were either indebted to master weavers or other persons who made the investment in the yarn. Thus, the main benefits of the labour of weavers was generally taken off by merchant communities such as the Komati Chetti, Tamil Muslims, Balija Naidus, Reddis or Thondaimandala Vellalas. Generally these master weavers or brokers brought the thread and sold it to *coolies* (wage labourers) for the actual weaving.[126] In Tirunelveli district weaving was done in the Ambasamudram taluk and particularly in the towns of Ambasamudram and Tirunelveli. In Ambasamudram, Brahmin brokers advanced money to the Senguntha weavers who lived in the Brahmin settlement of agraharam village of Kalladaikurichi and took the finished products. The output supplies were strictly controlled by Brahmin brokers.[127] When charka and yarn were distributed with the help of Tilak Swaraj

Funds, weavers were relieved from the exploitation of middlemen.

In the Tanjore district, weaving was carried on mainly in Tanjore, Kumbakonam, Mannargudi and Ayyampettai. Once the clothes woven there with a silk warp and a cotton wool were very popular. But the English cambrics had lessened the demand for that clothes. As a result, this handicraft was ruined and many weavers were drifted to other employments.[128] In Madurai, in the olden days handloom industries flourished in many places and contributed to supplement the income of even the agriculturists in the off-season. The Saurashtras who lived mostly in Madurai town, have through centuries acquired a great skill in weaving superior cotton as well as silk fabrics. Nest to them, came the Devangas who wove silk and art silk and who were found chiefly in the Dindugal and Nilakottai taluks.[129] But from the late nineteenth century, due to the increasing importation of foreign cotton yarn they suffered severely. Such was the condition when the Congress took up the khadi programme.

E.V. Ramaswami Naicker thought that by urging the people to use khadi he could, not merely give a fillip to cottage industries in the country, but also enforce sanctions against British economic interest by boycotting their textiles.[130] To give an impetus to the khadi movement, volunteers were asked to picket the shops of foreign cloth dealers if within a fixed time they did not dispose of their stocks of foreign clothes.[131] On 31st July 1921 Mahatma Gandhi made a bonfire of old foreign clothes in Bombay and the example was soon followed in other parts of the country. In Tuticorin bonfire of old foreign clothes was witnessed as a result of the non-cooperation propaganda.[132] With the suspension of the non-cooperation movement, foreign clothes boycott movement lost its vigour.

Then the Congress Working Committee adopted the constructive programme in which production of khadi was assigned an important place.[133] As a logical step to promote khadi, the Tamil Nadu Congress Committee opened the Tamil Nadu Congress Khadi Board in March 1923. E.V. Ramaswami Naicker, P. Varadarajulu Naidu and T. Prakasam were the members of it.[134] The Coconada Congress session held in December 1923 was also much impressed by the progress of khadi movement and it passed a resolution to form an All India Khadi Board to oganise and carry on khadi works all over India under the general supervision of the All India Congress Committee.[135] Accordingly, the All India Khadi Board was formed in 1924. In order to organise its provincial branches, the members undertook a tour to select places. In Tamil Nadu, they found Tirupur in Coimbatore district to be the biggest centre of khadi production.[136] In about 1,500 villages around Tirupur, there were about two lakhs *charkas*, some of them were said to be older than 100 years, but they were idle. After the starting of the khadi movement, a few merchants took up khadi manufacture as a business and about 5,000 *charkas* started plying again. After the tour, the All India Khadi Board met in Bombay and directed the Tamil Nadu Congress Committee to start a provincial board at Tirupur.[137] On their advice, Tamil Nadu Congress Committee met on 21st January 1924 and established the Tamil Nadu Khadi Board at Tirupur with K. Santhanam as its Secretary, and E.V. Ramaswami Naicker as its President. The other important members of the Tamil Nadu Khadi Board were T.S.S. Rajan, C. Rajagopalachari, C.N. Muthuranga Mudaliar, K.S. Ramaswami Gounder and N.V. Krishna Chetti.[138] District and taluk boards were also formed. It had also opened a training centre near Tirupur and was placed under the charge of Sabarmati khadi worker who trained the spinners how to improve the locally used *charka* and the carding. They were of low working power and would get the yarn spun finer and make cheaper the clothes thereby.[139]

Instructions in spinning were given in several schools that were under the control of the local bodies captured by the

Congress.[140] In order to stimulate the movement, C. Rajagopalachari announced the year 1924 should be a khadi year and the programme of work for that year centred around khadi only. The Congress also emphasised its members to have atleast a live *charka* under them.[141] Mahatma Gandhi requested that every man, woman and child who understood the necessity of the *charka* for the national well being should religiously spin for sometime everyday.[142] But the most important attempt made by the Congress to promote khadi was the introduction of spinning franchise by abolishing four anna franchise. The Belgaum Congress session held in December 1924 adopted spinning franchise.[143] Since it was considered to be too much to pay, opposition arose from all sides. Hence the All India Congress Committee meeting on 22nd September 1925 reduced it from 2,000 yards per month to 2,000 yards per year. It also made compulsory to its members to wear khadi on all occasions. Even the Swaraj Party made it obligatory on every member of that Party to accept spinning franchise.[144]

The Tamil Nadu Congress Committee not only accepted that, but also in its meeting at Erode on 17th January 1925, decided to give a prize worth of Rs. 250 in the form of silver *rattinum* (spinning wheel) to a taluk that would enroll more members to the Congress through spinning franchise.[145] On the whole 2,239 members joined the Congress in Tamil Nadu until August 1925. Madurai received the silver *rattinam* for enrolling more members.[146] The Saurashtras of Madurai who found this system as a means to preserve their traditional occupation, came forward to support the Congress. Due to the effort of the Congress, in Tamil Nadu itself Rs. 4,72,364 worth of khadi was produced in 1923.[147] Tamil Nadu stood first in the production of khadi as well as enrolment of members through spinning franchise. Due to the effort of the Congress from being an importer of khadi in 1921, Tamil Nadu was self sufficient by 1924.

Khadi movement was successfully carried out by Padmasini Ammal from Madurai. When her husband Srinivasa Varadhan was arrested and imprisoned in connection with the picketing of liquor shops, she successfully managed the Bharat Ashram[148] sold khadi, and encouraged a lot of women to join the Congress movement. Until her husband's release, she gave up all her ornaments, only one time food, that too though she was rich enough, she ate from the income of the sale of khadi. Everyday evening she used to spin khadi, after that she would sell them by door to door visits. Though spinning and selling of khadi were prohibited by the government, violating that order she forced all people including government servants to buy atleast one metre of khadi. She compelled women atleast to buy one blouse piece. She was a good orator. Sometimes in her speech she emotionally quote about the valourous activities of the sepoy mutiny soldiers. At the end of the meetings there would be a bonfire of foreign clothes. She spread the swadeshi message through speeches, discussions, songs, lectures and door to door visits. As a result many women refused to use foreign goods including foreign dresses. By her efforts more than 500 women joined the Congress. Such was the impact of her speech. Later in her plot of land at Thoppur, nine miles away from Madurai, she established a Swarajya Ashram and made it a centre for constructive programme of the Congress. Its name was later changed into Bharathi Ashram.[149] Even after the non co-operation movement was suspended, she continued to weave khadi. In order to promote khadi, in 1924 with the support of the Congress she along with Thayammal, Mrs. Joseph, Mrs. Sundaram Iyengar, Subbulakshmi Ammal and Mrs.Soundaram Ramachandran started the 'Association of Sisters' at Madurai. Along with them Thayarammal, Seethaiammal, Muniammal, Dr. Pichaimuthu Ammal also worked. There every Friday nearly thirty women wove khadi for two hours. Cotton and *charka* needed for them were supplied from the national school. They were not only given training in *charka* but also in general education.[150] This association helped a lot of women to join the national movement. It is notable that this association played a significant role in the boycott of foreign cloth shops.

Not only Indian women, but also European women belonging to the Theosophical Society, Madras learnt the art of spinning and weaving and promoted khadi production. Madame de Manziarly was the first woman to do it within the compound of the Theosophical Society. She introduced hand spinning in the school opened in the Theosophical compound for the benefit of the neighbouring villages in October 1924. Later other women learnt to spin and by December 1924 in their new vocational division belonging to Miss. Barrie's Montessori School, Mrs. Peramma gave lessons to eleven village women besides several women and children of the compound. The *charkas* were made by the carpenter belonging to the vocational division. As a result by the end of the year 1924 atleast a dozen women from there did spinning regularly. Yarn was made by women into cloth in the craft division and out of the cloth little jackets of the South Indian fashion were made and were introduced as uniform of their school. They spin from the seeds directly without any intermediate process.[151]

At the request of Annie Besant, Devadas Gandhi came to Theosophical Society, Madras in December 1924 to help the women there to learn the art of spinning. He at first taught it to Annie Besant and later to other European women residing in Theosophical Society who were in charge of important branches of educational works under Annie Besant. A number of them decided on the spot to avail themselves of the earliest chance of learning spinning. Madame de Manziarly, Margaret E Cousins and Miss.Barrie took no time to master all the little secrets of spinning. Madame de Manziarly was very much interested in handspun and handwoven khadi and when C. Rajagopalachari asked her if she thought khadi was beautiful enough she said "I would not be wearing khadi if I did not think it immensely beautiful". Devadas Gandhi was surprised to see Kamalamma Garu Ramarao, an Andhra woman settled at Madras was able to spin 380 counts. Mrs. Kamalamma accompanied Devadas Gandhi to Women's Home of Service run by Margaret E. Cousins to give a demonstration of spinning and other auxiliary processes. There she taught the audience how to spin. At the close of the function, Kamalamma was besieged from all sides with women eager to shower their blessings and gratitude upon her. Devadas Gandhi remarked "no mill can spin so fine a count as this gifted woman".[152] To encourage khadi, exhibitions on khadi were held. Kasturiba Gandhi presided over one such exhibition at Salem.[153]

The khadi propaganda gained momentum and the Congress found it necessary to entrust the work to an autonomous organisation free from political influence. Hence, the All India Congress Committee in its meeting at Patna on 22nd September 1925 authorised the starting of the All India Spinners Association as an integral part of the Congress but with an independent existence and powers. Membership in the association was opened to any person above eighteen years old who should be a habitual wearer of khadi and pay an annual subscription of 2,000 yards of self spun yarn well twisted and uniform. Any yarn paid to the association for membership of the Congress was considered a part of the subscription to the association.[154] Mahatma Gandhi was its first President.[155] It took over all the funds and assets belonging to the All India Khadi Board and all provincial khadi boards with full powers to administer these and other funds.[156] The All India Spinner's Association also provided funds to its regional branches. Its Tamil Nadu branch at Tirupur in Coimbatore district controlled sixty nine branches which were either producing or selling khadi. Of these thirty nine were run directly by the association. Among them fourteen were for production and twenty five for sale. The rest were managed by the organisations in private sector. The capital made available for work in Tamil Nadu during the year 1927-28 by the All India Spinners Association was Rs. 5,07,118. The worth of total khadi produced in Tamil Nadu during the same year was Rs. 9,97,465 and the year's sales amounted to Rs. 10,01,840.[157]

Khadi movement derived a lot of support from C. Rajagopalachari. His ashram at Thiruchengode had a school where spinning and weaving were taught.[158] It served more than twenty villages and supplied cotton for nearly 750 women.[159] The members of the ashram spun yarn by hand organised schemes. They also collected hand spun yarn from outlying rural areas and made arrangements for marketing.[160] The Tamil Nadu Khadi Board had invested about Rs. 44,000 in the ashram.[161] In addition, Kallakurichi in South Arcot district, Vadaseri in Tiruchirapalli district and Tissaiyanvillai in Tirunelveli district also produced some quantity of khadi. On the whole, the activities of the khadi production centres in Tamil Nadu extended over 925 villages and supported 18, 225 spinners and 1,474 weavers.[162]

Mahatma Gandhi's khadi tour to Tamil Nadu in September 1927 stimulated some of the prominent persons in Tamil Nadu to join the movement. Important among them were A.Vaidyanatha Iyer and A.Vedarama Iyer who gave up their practices as lawyers and became active members of the spinners association. Mahatma Gandhi also collected a large sum of money for khadi funds. All people irrespective of castes and creeds contributed to it especially the Saurashtras of Madurai.[163] Every year since 1920, 7th April in the national week was devoted mainly to propaganda in favour of khadi and the boycott of British goods.[164] On that day processions were taken out and competitions in *charka* and *takli* spinning were held.[165] All these efforts automatically promoted khadi and reduced the foreign cloth trade. Hence the government decided to contain it. At first the government prohibited wearing of khadi by government servants while on duty.[166] Then it issued orders under rule 23(1)

Government Servants Conduct Rules prohibiting government servants from subscribing to the khadi fund in aid of the All India Spinner's Association.[167] The reason on which the instructions were based was that the fund was political, because All India Spinner's Association was affiliated to All India Congress Committee, a political body. The Justice Party too went against khadi movement. For instance, a resolution was moved in the Madras Legislative Council by the Swarajists to introduce khadi clothing in the government departments including police. It was declared lost due to the opposition of the Justice Party.[168] A resolution moved in the Madras Corporation to introduce khadi uniforms to its employees was also defeated. The Swarajists also asked for introducing hand spinning in jails. That too was defeated.[169] Added to this, A.P. Patro, the Justice Party Minister issued an order prohibiting the imparting of instructions to children below fourth standard in spinning in the absence of provision for weaving.[170] A Madras Inspectress of Education had pronounced sentence against the spinning wheel for Brahmin girls. This judgement of hers had given rise to criticism against her. If the *charka* was good enough for non-Brahmin girls why not, it was argued for brahmin girls.[171] Whatever the rules were the Congress was undismayed.

Another programme of the Non-Cooperation movement was the boycott of the Duke of Connaught. In this programme Congress leaders tried to include women. One suggestion made by them was that as a sign of mourning, men should appear without upper garments and women without jewels, that labourers should prostrate themselves infront of the Duke's carriage and that all shops should be closed as a sign of hartal.[172] Sarojini Naidu was a great soul behind the Non-Cooperation movement. She often visited Madras.[173] Her visits and speeches encouraged other women also to join the movement. She was elected as the President of the Indian National Congress Calcutta annual session in 1925 and was the first Indian woman to occupy that chair.

Though the Non-Cooperation movement failed to achieve its objective namely redressal of the khilafat wrongs and the attainment of swaraj, it was an important step in the development of Indian nationalism. No doubt it led to a general awakening of the masses to their political rights. Though the Non-cooperation movement was suspended, the constructive programme initiated at that time continued.

Neill Statue Satyagraha

The idea of the Neill statue satyagraha came when the people read the book, "The First War of Independence". Even before that the sword satyagraha was started at Madurai. In February 1927 General Avari, the Chairman of the Nagpur Municipality inaugurated the sword satyagraha at Nagpur against the Arms Act. This aroused the enthusiasm of young people in Madurai. They called for a meeting at Ramnad which was attended among others by Padmasini Ammal and decided to start the satyagraha at Madurai. Accordingly on 16th June 1927 the "Deshabandu day" the movement was launched by N. Somayajulu of Madurai, K.V. Ganapathy of Madras and Muhammed Sali of Ramnad at Madurai.[174]

Another achievement to stand to the credit of Madurai was the translation into Tamil and publication of the book "The First War of Independence" written by Vinayak Savarkar. It was proscribed by the government. The translation of the book was very ably done by Mrs. Soundaram Ramachandran who sat day and night and finished the work. The translation had so fully kept up the spirit of the original that no one would consider it a translation. About Rs.1000/- were collected for the publication of the book and two workers Pichu Sivam and V. Ramachandran went to Karaikal where work on the printing of the book began at a local press. R. Chidambara Bharathi had also gone there for the purpose and when forms were ready he took over thirty forms of 240 pages each of 2000 unbound copies to the Madras Congress in 1927. At the Madurai delegate camp in the Congress about six people sat one night and assembled the forms to make the books. Then they were taken to the city and brought back after being bound. That very night copies of the book were distributed free to all those who had helped the venture with their financial support. Only after reading about the atrocities committed by General Neill, the idea of demolition of the Neill statue originated.[175] At any cost they decided to remove the statue. Mahatma Gandhi had apparently approved of the Satyagraha on the ground that the "the statue is an elaquent proof of the British Government's stand for terrorism and falsehood". He added "Great Britian reminds us of the people's helplessness and subjection at the hands of the foreigners everyday and every hour and need not add it by the bronze piece of statue in the Mount Road".

R. Chidambara Bharathi, R. Srinivasa Varadan and Padmasini Ammal planned the strategies for the satyagraha and contacted Subbarayalu Naidu of Tirunelveli and Mohammed Salia of Ramnad to start the agitation at Madras. Their expenses to go to Madras were met by Padmasini Ammal by pledging her anklets. On 11th August 1927, Subbarayalu Naidu and Mohammed Salia, dressed in khadi started from the Tamil Nadu office armed with axes and hammers began hacking away at the statue. They succeeded in breaking a portion of the sheath of the sword in the hands of Neill and hoisted the national flag on it, and garlanded the flag. Two satyagrahis made speeches about the atrocities committed by Neill on Indian people during the sepoy mutiny. Immediately policemen came and arrested the satyagrahis under section 427 IPC and sentenced them to six months rigorous imprisonment. Others continued the agitation. On 29th August K.V. Ganapathi Iyer went to break the statue, inspite of the police protest. He was arrested and given fifteen days imprisonment.[176] He observed fast for 84 hours in the jail until the Congress promised that it would continue the satyagraha. Women also participated in the movement.

On Ist September disobeying police orders, Salem Angachi Ammal along with Cintathripettai Mrs. Lokaiya Naidu went to deface the statue beating with hammer. Immediately they were arrested and Angachi Ammal was charged with Rs. 7/- as fine and kept under court custody that day. Mrs. Lokaiya Naidu was given fifteen days imprisonment and Rs. 50/- as fine. Another woman was Anchalai Ammal from Cuddalour in South Arcot District. She made her twelve years daughter Amma Kannu Ammal[177] also to participate in the movement. They were arrested on 6th September and Anchalai Ammal was convicted by the city police Magistrate under section 75 of the City Police Act and sentenced to imprisonment till the rising of the court and a fine of Rs. 25/- or indefault one week rigorous imprisonment. She was a good orator and was considered as Velu Nachiar of South Arcot District. She was instigated by none her own courage made her to join the freedom struggle. In this connection she travelled throughout India.[178] Her daughter Amma Kannu Ammal being a girl of twelve years was ordered to be detained in Children's Home for four years. Including Amma Kannu Ammal four women and eighteen men were arrested until mid September.[179] Mrs.Lakshmi Ammal was arrested and imprisoned for seventeen days in connection with this satyagraha.[180] People from other part of the country also joined the movement. A party came from Rajahmundry was led by an old woman of seventy.[181] By October-November 1927 the number of people arrested increased to thirty four.[182] In the meantime inorder to continue the satyagraha Tamil Nadu Congress Committee formed an executive committee consisting of Hiralal Shat, Thirumalacharia, Srinivasa Vardhan and Padmasini Ammal. It also passed a resolution asking the government to remove the statue immediately.[183] But the government didn't pay heed to the Congress demand. Hence, the satyagraha was continued. *Swaraja, Swadesamitran, Tamil Nadu* and *The Hindu* contributed a lot for the promotion of the satyagraha. With all difficulties they continued the agitation until it was suspended due to the expected arrival of Simon Commission and the holding of the Indian National Congress session at Madras. When the Congress formed ministry in the Madras Presidency in 1937, it ordered for the removal of the Neill statue from Mount Road and its preservation in the Government Museum, Madras. Accordingly it was removed and tranferred to the Museum on 22nd November, 1937.[184]

Simon Commission Boycott

The announcement regarding the Statutory Commission headed by John Simon made in November 1927 was a blessing in disguise to the Congress. The Congress took it as an opportunity to oppose the government. Swarajists,[185] Congress No-changers and Independents after a long time joined together to boycott the commission.

The commission was scheduled to visit India in February 1928 to examine whether the people of India were entitled to a further measure of Self-Government. The Congressmen had repudiated the right of the British Parliament to constitute a commission for examining the right of the Indian people for Self-Government and self-determination. The other political parties in India had taken it as an insult because no Indian was included in the commission.[186] The Madras Congress session held in December 1927 passed a resolution advocating the boycott of the commission.[187] The Khilafat conference held in Madras in December 1927 also endorsed that decision. It appeared for a time that the appointment of the commission might bring the Congress and the Muslim League together again on a common platform. However, the Justice Party decided to cooperate with the commission.[188]

Annie Besant and Hansa Mehta played a leading role in opposing the commission. In order to plan the boycott, Annie Besant convened a meeting of important leaders of Madras at New India building on 9th November 1927.[189] Early in

December 1927, local women formed a committee to organise and regulate the boycott movement. All the merchants in Madras also joined and organised a meeting at Pudupet on 25th January 1928 with Rukmini Lakshmipathi in the chair. She spoke urging the audience to boycott the commission.[190] On 28th January Sami Venkatachalam Chetti presided over a meeting held at Madras. It was attended by a good number of students and was addressed by Yamini Poorna Thilagamma and others. Masilamaniammal, the editor of the *Tamil Makkal* appealed to the women to join the boycott.[191]

Again on Ist February 1928, at a women's meeting held at Madras Yamini Poorna Thilagamma, Masilamaniammal, Rukmini Lakshmipathi and others spoke in support of the boycott.[192] Padmasini Ammal also supported the decision.[193] Women's India Association opposed the commission for two reasons, exclusion of Indians and exclusion of women from the commission. In the Madras Legislative Council, Sami Venkatachalam Chetti moved a resolution on 24th January 1928, recommending the government to the effect that the council had no confidence in the Statutory Commission as it was consisted of only Britishers and therefore they had nothing to do with the commission.[194] After a debate it was accepted by the council. This decision was greeted with much satisfaction in the Swarajist circle. But while making the final decision, the Chief Minister was absent and the other two Ministers remained neutral without voting.[195] This was critised by the Congress and they decided to deal with the commission independently. They formed Simon Boycott Propaganda Committee with S. Satyamurti as its President. Its object was to carry on intensive propaganda in the press, platform and by posters and leaflets. They decided to organise hartal on 3rd February, 1928,the day of the arrival of the commission in Bombay.[196] There were some violence by local Congressmen in Madras on 3rd February 1928. A car was burnt and a shop was bombed. The police opened fire on the crowd, killing three persons.[197] Orders under section 144 Cr.PC were issued by Chief Presidency Magistrate prohibiting meetings, processions, demonstrations and propagandas inconnection with any future hartal on the occasion of the commission's visit to Madras. The commission visited Madras on 18th February 1928 and was welcomed by the Chief Minister and the members of the Justice party.[198] The commission, however could not escape the fury of the people. They conducted processions carrying black flags and banners paraded from George Town to Triplicane beach where the meeting was held in the evening. P.Varadarajulu Naidu exhorted the people to keep up the boycott campaign. Almost all shops were closed on that day.[199] D. Kolandai, a Congress member organised processions and shouted slogans like "down with Subbarayan and his Ministerialists who cooperated with the commission". Before the meeting began effigies of P. Subbarayan and others who cooperated with the commission were burnt.[200] The commission came to Madras for the second time on 18 February, 1929 received and replied several addresses from the representative bodies. This time also the Congress boycotted the commission. Many shops were closed.[201] In the beach meeting, Rukmini Lakshmipathi spoke against the Simon Commission. The students of Presidency College who attended the meeting shouted slogans against the commission.[202] Because of the incessant effort of the Women's India Association, in the Simon Commission report there were five pages devoted to women.[203]

The Congress-1927

It was a proof for the patriotism of women when the annual session of the Indian National Congress was held at Madras in 1927, there were sixty women volunteers wearing orange red khadi sarees on constant duty at the Indian National Congress. They were under the captaincy of Rukmini Lakshmipathi and Kamaladevi Chattopadhyaya and did splendid service both for the thousands of women visitors and as part of the musical corps.[204] Rukmini Lakshmipathi was appointed as the Secretary of the women's section of the Congress and was assigned the task of looking after the guests who came for the Congress. She welcomed Jawaharlal Nehru and others who came to Madras.[205]

Civil Disobedience Movement

The declaration of 'Purna Swaraj' or Complete Independence by the Congress as its goal was a significant turning point in the struggle for freedom. Mahatma Gandhi himself sponsored in the Lahore Congress session in 1929, a resolution proclaiming 'Purna Swaraj' as the immediate goal of the country and authorised the launching of civil disobedience movement to achieve it.

The civil disobedience movement of 1930-34 was both a continuation as well as improvement over the non-cooperation movement of 1920-22. But what distinguished the civil disobedience movement from the non-cooperation movement was the stress Mahatma Gandhi laid in 1930 on the economic grievances of the masses and the meaning of political freedom for them. He endeavoured to give a new orientation to the national demand that insisted on 'familiarizing the nation with the contents of independence'.[206] He emphasised the economic, political, cultural and spiritual ruin of the country under British rule and pleaded for immediate relief to the masses from what he described as 'the killing weight' of an expensive top heavy administration. Whereas the non-cooperation movement was launched to secure the redressal of Punjab and Khilafat wrongs.[207]

As a preliminary step towards organising a campaign for independence and in order to make the Congress policy as consistent as possible with the change of creed, the Congress called upon all Congress persons not only to boycott the elections but also to resign their seats in the legislatures.[208]

As a protest against Mahatma Gandhi's arrest

S.Muthulakshmi Reddy resigned her seat in the Madras Legislative Council and also her office there in as Deputy President of the council.[209] In her letter to His Excellency, the Governor of Madras she stated, "I am obliged to take this step as a mark of respect for that great soul, Mahatma Gandhi who has been arrested and imprisoned by the government. I feel it my bounden duty to express to Your Excellency on this occasion that his life has been a source of inspiration to me in all my activities".[210] Kamalabai Lakshman Rao of Tirunelveli resigned the post of Honorary Magistrate.[211]

The voice of the Women's India Association had been strong in support of political freedom for India. It had also protested against terrorism and cruelty on the part of the police, yet as an association it kept unity between its members who were of four classes, those members who were ready for any sacrifice of an unconditional, but non-violent nature, those who were under the control of government either through their employment by the government or by their connection with government servants, and those opposed to Congress propaganda. The association consequently served the national march forward in every path of constructive, constitutional, philanthropic effort open to it.[212] The association had also continuously supported the claim of India to the right of Self Government and pressed in many ways for the grant of Swaraj. It also sent representatives to the conferences which formulated the constitution for India called "The Common Wealth of India Bill". In that bill there was a clause, "the rights, privileges and duties of citizens shall be without distinction of sex".[213]

When the Viceroy announced the Round Table Conference in November the association immediately asked that women should be chosen amongst its personnel including at least one woman from their Association. It also passed a resolution requesting the government to give an undertaking that the framing of a self governing constitution was the duty of the Round Table Conference, that being the first essential step for restoring peace and good will in India.[214] Since the Viceroy and the government refused to give that undertaking, Women's India Association did not support the Round Table Conference.[215] Thus Women's India Association did constitutional agitation continuously.

Though Women's India Association did not involve directly in the national movement, many of its women participated in it. Women's India Association, London committee did most splendid work in educating the British public on the real Indian situation. It had also successfully enlisted the sympathy and co-operation of some of the British women leaders for the cause of India's freedom.

Salt Satyagraha

In March 1930, Mahatma Gandhi opened the new phase of satyagraha by announcing that he would break the salt law. The avowed object of it was to break the salt laws openly and defy the authority.[216] When Mahatma Gandhi planned this non-violent battle for independence, it became an open invitation to women, for this technique suited them. But at first Mahatma Gandhi was reluctant to permit women to join the salt raid and asked them to confine their activities to picketing of liquor and foreign cloth shops.[217] But women felt it their duty to shoulder responsibilities connected with national struggle on an equal footing with men. The editorial note in *Stri-Dharma* written apparently before Mahatma Gandhi approved of women taking part in the campaign testified to the eagerness of Indian women to serve the motherland.

> "Whatever be the opinions of individual readers on the details whereby self government shall become the possession of India, every woman not only in India but throughout the world must watch anxiously the result and the reaction following Mahatma Gandhi's appeal to a new method of war, soul force, self sacrifice without blood shed or violence".[218] It was the only alternative to

> ordinary war, women welcomed this alternative way of achieving the desired end. Not withstanding that, Mahatma Gandhi had refused to allow women to participate in that heroic march because he explained that it would complicate things. Women in different parts of India were not satisfied with this explanation and had protested against their arbitrary exclusion when they were just as full of health and patriotic as their marching brothers. Women wanted them to be included not only in the conferences, congresses or commissions, but also in the marches, imprisonments and demonstrations organised for the welfare of India.[219]

When Mahatma Gandhi had given the green signal, many women joined the movement. A lot of women from Tamilnadu joined the salt satyagraha.[220] The nationalist movement picked up momentum after that. For conducting salt satyagraha Vedaranyam in Tanjore district was selected. Because Vedaranyam was favourably situated for the salt campaign, as it was near the Agastyampalli Salt Factory, a government concern and a big swamp, that would be covered with salt from the month of May. Also it was a home of Sardar. A Vedaratnam Pillai, an active Congress worker and the owner of salt pans at Vedaranyam who had promised all help.[221] Another reason for staging the march in Tanjore district was that C. Rajagopalachari wanted to include people from rural society who had grievances against the government. He knew that there were much discontent among the land holders and others in the Tanjore district. Despite the government claims that the tax reassessment in the district was done rationally the facts were otherwise.[222]

Using Mahatma Gandhi's march as an example, C. Rajagopalachari appealed to the people of Tamil Nadu to participate in the manufacture of salt against salt tax. He along with his adherents went around Tamil Nadu, collected funds and enlisted volunteers who were prepared to march to Vedaranyam in order to break the salt laws. Important leaders in Tamil Nadu like T.S.S. Rajan, S. Srinivasa Iyengar, Thiru V. Kalyana Sundra Mudaliar[223] and K.Santhanam held a number of meetings to earn mass support as well as for money collections.[224] In addition to the Rs. 30,000 collected by them, the other districts also collected and sent considerable sums.[225]

Owing to the propaganda, about 1,000 applications were received for recruitment as volunteers. After a scrutiny of the applications, C. Rajapalachari selected 100 volunteers including a woman volunteer Rukmini Lakshmipathi and formed the first batch to be led by himself to Vedaranyam and arranged for regular despatch of volunteers to break the salt laws. They were housed and trained in T.S.S. Rajan's clinic at Tiruchirapalli. First, an advance guard of outsiders was sent along the route to be taken by C. Rajagopalachari and his volunteers. They worked hard for arranging accommodation and supplies at each halting place and also to gain sympathy for the satyagraha march.[226]

While preparations for the satyagraha march were going on, J.N. Thorne, the then District Magistrate of Tanjore, decided to take necessary action to keep the movement in check. But the Government of Madras directed him that so long as the movement was non-violent and legal, action should not be taken. The government was of the opinion that the object of the demonstrators was to force the government to arrest them and produce them in court for prosecution thereby attract general sympathy. But the object of the government was to disappoint them as far as possible without any arrest.[227] In spite of that, J.N. Throne issued a circular to terrorise the people by declaring that the salt satyagraha party headed by C. Rajagopalachari was an unlawful assembly under section 141 IPC.[228] He further ordered that those who would receive the marchers or give them food should be punished with imprisonment for a term of six months, in addition to fine.[229] Police officers were ordered to arrest any person found manufacturing salt.[230]

Inspite of severe warnings, many people from other districts also came to join the movement. The march was started from the house of T.S.S. Rajan at Tiruchirapalli on 13th April 1930 at 5 p.m. with 100 volunteers headed by C. Rajagopalachari.[231] All along the route they were accorded with tremendous and spontaneous receptions. Women supplied food for the volunteers. They reached Vedaranyam on 28th April. The next day was observed as a day of fast and prayer. On 30th morning C. Rajagopalachari with sixteen volunteers proceeded to the salt swamp and violated the salt law.[232] Immediately the officers came to the scene and the District Superintendent of Police arrested C. Rajagopalachari.[233] The volunteers were not arrested but were asked to surrender the salt they had picked up. They refused to do so and returned to the camp with the salt they had collected. C. Rajagopalachari did not participate in the court proceedings except pleading that everything necessary had been said by Mahatma Gandhi. He was convicted for the offence under section 74 of the Madras Salt Act and was punished with a fine of Rs. 200 or in default to undergo six months simple imprisonment.[234] The latter C. Rajagopalachari preferred.

C. Rajagopalachari nominated K. Santhanam of the Thiruchengode ashram to be incharge of the satyagraha camp at Vedaranyam.[235] For a month the volunteers of Tamil Nadu waged a strenuous battle at Vedaranyam. Every day batches of volunteers entered the swamp and collected large quantities of salt and were distributed in the villages around. Soon orders under section 144 Cr.PC were served on all principal workers and on the people of Vedaranyam and even on some of the surrounding villages.[236] The police surrounded the camp and asked the volunteers to surrender the salt. They refused to do so and K. Santhanam, their leader answered that it was their duty to defend it. Then the volunteers formed a close and compact cordon around the salt they collected. On the order of the District Superintendent of Police, the police attacked them and the scuffle lasted for an hour. On 4th May, K. Santhanam, Sardar A. Vedaratnam Pillai and some other volunteers were arrested and were sentenced to six months simple imprisonment and a fine of Rs. 200 in default of which six more weeks imprisonment.[237]

When leaders were arrested one by one for collecting salt S. Rukmini Lakshmipathi, the only woman volunteer became the leader.[238] She visited Agastyampalli camp and the quarters of the police and distributed pamphlets designed to undermine the loyalty of the constables and peons.[239] On 14th May she was arrested at the camp and sentenced to simple imprisonment for one year. Before leaving the camp, she asked with a bright smile, "Are you not all envious of me now? Victory to the Satyagrahis. Be Brave and carry on the fight".[240]

She was the only woman among 200 men. She lived in the camp with men and then became their leader. She was prominent both in speeches and activities. Her moral repute also did not suffer from her association with the satyagrahis. She was the first woman to be arrested in India during the Civil Disobedience movement.[241] Her arrest caused excitement among the members of Youth League. Mahatma Gandhi congratulated her as she was the first woman to be so honoured[242] With the arrest of the volunteers the movement in Tanjore came to an end.[243]

Women continued to be conspicuous throughout the Salt Satyagraha. At Madras the movement began on 13th April led by T. Prakasam, Nageswara Rao and Durgabai Amma.[244] They boiled sea water first on the beach and then in Prakasam's house and sold them in the evening beach meetings.[245] On 15th April, at 6.30 a.m. T. Prakasam, Nageswara Rao and others along with five women volunteers, Durgabai Amma, Angachi Ammal, Venkatarammal, Kamatshi Ammal and Saraswati Ammal started a procession carrying national flag and signing national songs from the Swarajya Office and reached the beach at 8.30 a.m. There they prepared salt with nearly 10,000 people witnessing. They were convicted for being members of an unlawful assembly and were fined Rs. 500 each.[246]

On 20th April 1930, twenty women with Mrs.Hanumayamma and Durgabai Amma in the lead started the procession from the Swarajya Office to the High Court beach where more women joined and they boiled the sea water in six pots. On hearing this, Assistant Commissioner went to Nageswara Rao's house and arrested him. As a protest, a hartal was announced for the next day. Durgabai Amma, Angachi Ammal and Prakasam were given a great welcome when they came there. Police arrested Prakasam. His arrest did not check the agitation which had acquired a momentum of its own.[247]

When the leaders were arrested, Durgabai Amma took charge of the city campaign. She requested all women to join the movement. She acted as 'Madras City Dictator'. She also formed a Council of Action to offer Salt Satyagraha.. She set up a camp at Udayavaram in Mylapore.[248] Accompanied by her about 100 volunteers left the Swarajya Office on 25th April in procession to prepare salt in the High Court beach. But their advancement was resisted by the police. When they refused to disperse, a lathi charge was made. For two or three minutes, there were merciless beating till some fell to the ground. Durgabai Amma and Varahalamma had given them first aid and the satyagrahis scattered. Their pots, ovens and firewood were seized.[249] On 30th April seven women started the procession, others joined on the way. There were about thirty women present when six pots of sea water was boiled.[250] They were dispersed with lathi, thereby the progress of the movement was curtailed. On 5th May Durgabai Amma and Krishnamma accompanied by other women defied the salt law and the order under section 144. The police broke the salt pots, causing boiling water to fall upon the hands of leading women and they were scalded.[251] She conducted the campaign for over a month and ran the Udayavaram camp sending out eighty to ninety volunteers every day.[252] Though she was not arrested at that time an order was served on her prohibiting her political activities. She was jailed several times after that and given rigorous imprisonment including solitary confinement. There she kept herself engaged in educating other women prisoners in the jail and made their lives more pleasant, happy and cheerful with music, dance and crafts.

Besides, a sizeable block of women participated in the Salt Satyagraha movement in Tamilnadu. Asher Padmavathi, Taiyalnayagi Ammal, Tayammal, Saraswathi Pandurangam, Rajamani Ammal, Venkatasammal, Gomathi Ammal were a few among them. Mrs. Sakuntala Iyer discontinued her medical studies to join the movement. The salt campaign brought out a lot of women from their seclusion and showed to the country that they could also serve the country on equal terms with men. Salt Satyagraha was conducted in coastal areas only. Contemporaneous with that, in other areas defiance of orders under section 144 Cr. P.C., reading and distribution of proscribed literature, picketing of foreign cloth and liquor shops, hartals, meetings, processions, etc. were conducted.

From the middle of May the second stage of the movement began. Almost all the districts had joined the movement. When the political speeches became more violent, orders under section 144 Cr.P.C. were passed forbidding meetings, processions and demonstrations for a month. Violating the order already served on her, Durgabai Amma came to North Arcot district on 21st May and spoke at Gudiyattam, Vellore and Arni. After that she went to Madras.[253] She again returned to the district on 25th and began a series of speeches. This time she was arrested and sentenced to nine months imprisonment.[254] As a result there was a considerable excitement at Arcot and Vellore. At Arcot the mob attacked some of the busmen in the bus who had carried political prisoners to Vellore. They also attacked with stones the Deputy

Superintendent of Police who was going from Vellore to Arcot with a party of the reserve. Then they went to the police station and threw stones at the police.[255]

In the Chengleput district during the course of these events twenty three persons were sent to prison including one woman.[256] On 2nd May 1930, Durgabai Amma, Rukmini Lakshmipathi and Bakthavatsalam visited Chengleput district and spoke in many meetings. On 28th July, Varahalu Ammal spoke about the satyagraha. There she was arrested and sentenced to six months simple imprisonment and was put in the 'B' class jail.[257]

Khadi and the Boycott of Foreign Clothes

Spread of khadi and the boycott of foreign clothes was a vital item in the Civil Disobedience movement. When the women of Ashram insisted on being taken along with men, something within Mahatma Gandhi told him, that they were destined to do greater work in the movement than merely breaking the salt laws. He found that work, it was picketing of liquor shops and foreign cloth shops. The picketing of liquor shops and foreign clothshops by men though it succeeded beyond expectations upto a point for a time in 1921, failed because violence crept in. If a real impression was to be created picketing should be resumed.

Drinks and drugs sap the moral well being of those who were given to the habit. Foreign clothes undermined the economic foundations of the nation and threw millions out of employment. The distress in each case was felt in the home and therefore by the women. Only those women who had drunkards as their husbands knew what havoc the drink devil works in homes that once were orderly and peace giving. Millions of women knew what unemployment meant. The Charka Sangh covered over one lakh women against less than ten thousand men. Mahatma Gandhi said,

"Let the women of India take up these two activities

> specialize in them; they would contribute more than men to national freedom. Their appeal to the merchants and buyers of foreign cloth and to the liquor dealers and addicts to the habit cannot but melt their hearts.... the charm will be in the agitation being initiated and controlled exclusively by women, they may take and should get as much assistance as they need from men, but the men should be in strict subordination to them."

In this agitation thousands of women, literate and illiterate could take part.[258] Therefore, Mahatma Gandhi appealed to women,

> "Boycott is impossible unless you will surrender the whole of your foreign clothing ---- you can ensure the fruitfulness of your blessings by giving up your foreign cloth and during your spare hours by ceaselessly spinning for the nation".[259]

Tamil dailies played a remarkable role in spreading the movement among women. *Bharati* had an article,

> "It is the primary duty of every woman born in India to carry on a struggle for the liberation of the country. Everyone of us should wear khaddi dress and make even the unwilling men in our homes do so. Women should without wasting their time in idle talk and playing at draughts spin yarn on the *charka*".[260]

Women's India Association also helped the khadi and swadeshi movement.[261] It was very particular in waging struggle against the economic exploitation of the Indian market which could otherwise be self contained.[262] Spinning classes sprang up every where. Every branch of the Women's India Association organised making and the sale of home made articles especially Indian made clothes.[263]

A Swadesi League was established in Madras to carry on swadeshi propaganda in the different divisions of the city particularly in the collection of swadeshi pledges in the following form.

> "I hereby undertake to purchase from today only khadi or swadeshi cloth and never under any circumstances British cloth".[264]

It also made considerable propaganda for the sale of khadi and swadeshi goods and opened swadeshi exhibition in Madras in that a variety of khadi dresses were exhibited.[265]

Many women gave up foreign clothes and started wearing khadi. One such woman was V.M. Kodhainayaki. Once when Mahatma Gandhi came to the South she came face to face with him. She, in her youthful exuberance, thought it was proper to meet the great man in all her finery of silk sari, gold waist band, gold bangles, diamond ear studs, nose ring etc. Mahatma Gandhi took one look at her and with his charming smile said, "when our Bharata Mata is shakled with heavy iron fetters, is such ostentation necessary? Kodhai felt a deep sense of guilt and shame and from that day, she shuned silk sarees and ornament and wore hand spun khadi.[266]

Women like Krishnabai and Kameshwari also started a separate national association for women known as 'Women's Swadeshi League'. Manjubhashini, Ambujammal and her aunt Gnanammal also joined it. Apart from spreading khadi it conducted Hindi classes. They toured all over the state and organises exhibitions and shows of khadi and swadeshi goods. Its work expanded and 'Swayam Sevika' a band of women volunteers was formed to help organising meetings in an orderly manner to sell swadeshi goods and also to promote khadi.[267] Every member of it wore khadi though it was rough. They went from door to door and propagated the use of swadeshi articles and boycotting foreign clothes. They collected signatures from the people who agreed to them. In support of them, *The Hindu* donated a van, a car and a hand push cart. With the help of them they were able to do door to door sale.[268] Apart from that, prohibition, removal of caste feeling and untouchability were adopted as equally important goals. To achieve these, exhibitions, processions and picketing were being conducted regularly.

The Congress also formed foreign cloth boycott propaganda committees.[269] They organised meetings throughout Tamilnadu in which they delivered lectures advocating picketing of foreign cloth shops along with other demands.[270] They also requested the foreign cloth dealers to stop their trade in foreign clothes. In many places foreign garments were consigned to flames.[271] Thus vigorous picketing of foreign cloth shops was launched.

The marked feature in the picketing of foreign cloth shops was the participation of women. Bagyalakshmi Ammal and Lakshmi Ammal of Kallidaikuruchi, Mrs. T.Madhava Rao, Mrs. Lakshmana Rao and Kamalabai Amma were arrested and imprisoned for six months for picketing. Later on the movement was carried on by women under the leadership of Mrs. K. Bashyam, L. Krishnabai and Kameswari Ammal of Swadeshi League. Ambujammal, Gnanammal, and a number of other women played an active role in the movement and courted imprisonment.[272] It was Ambujammal who set the pace for the conservative women folk in the south to throw off the shackles and boldly leap into the fray for the liberation of the motherland from foreign rule.

K.P. Manjammal was arrested and sentenced to six months rigorous imprisonment for picketing the foreign cloth shop in Rajapalayam in 1930. Again in 1932 when she sang the *Vande mataram* song with the national flag in her hand she was arrested under Section 17(2) of Cr.Law Amendment Act and was sentenced to three months imprisonment and lodged in the Vellore Jail.[273] These women marched to the foreign cloth shops, requested them to abandon their trade which was improvising the country. But most of the dealers ignored the women's request. Hence the women posted themselves at the shop entrances, pleaded the customers not to buy foreign clothes.[274]

Their presence intimidated the merchants and the patrons. A few merchants were persuaded by the picketers to give an undertaking promising not to trade in foreign merchandise. The customers were stopped on their way to the stores and the volunteers tried to dissuade them from purchasing foreign goods. But if the reasoning and pleas of the women failed, they would lie down infront of the stores and effectively stop the customers from going in. It was however unaggressive. Picketing in Madras city was practically confined to women. In order to encourage even more women to participate in the movement, leaflets on boycott of foreign clothes were distributed. One such leaflet published by N.S. Rajaratnam of Kanchipuram said,

> "Are not the 5000 eminent women who are suffering in jail on our account members of respectable families?".[275]

As a result, foreign cloth markets in the city were gradually paralised. So the government declared picketing illegal and many picketers were arrested.

The Congress encouraged the participation of women in boycott. The Congress Working Committee resolved that all Congress and allied organisations and workers should make greater efforts to enlist the services of women in the boycott campaign and as far as possible volunteers should be drawn from the neighbourhood.[276] But due to Gandhi-Irwin pact the movement was suspended.

Picketing of Liquor Shops

Women's organisations were from the beginning for total prohibition. In order to bring into effect total prohibition, the All India Congress Committee which met in Delhi on 27th March 1929 decided to revive the picketing of liquor shops, cutting of spathes of coconut and palmyra trees and also to prevent bidding of liquor and arrack shops.[277] The meeting of the Tamil Nadu Congress Committee held at Vedaranyam on 31st August 1929 also appealed to the people to strengthen the agitation against the drink traffic and bring about total prohibition.[278] The Congress Working Committee met in Allahabad on 12-15th May 1930 once again emphasised total prohibition and called upon the Provincial Congress Committees to organise picketing of liquor and toddy shops within their jurisdiction.[279] The Civil Disobedience movement gave a fillip to the prohibition movement. In Tamil Nadu it was very vigorous in Madurai, Tirunelveli, Coimbatore and Salem districts and in many cases it developed into violence.

Women's India Association wanted legislation for prohibiting the import, manufacture and sale of liquor and all intoxicating drugs.[280] Several women's associations of Madras prepared a questionnaire to the candidates who stood for the council election. It had a question on prohibition which ran as follows: "Are you for prohibition and total abstinence from drink?" If yes, women would vote.[281] The Women's India Association also pressed for the enforcement of prohibition. One of the resolutions contained in the 'Women's Charter of Reforms' passed at Madras in December 1927 was on prohibition,

> "Women realising the ruinous effects of intoxicating drinks on the home life and the race earnestly desire that the drink evil be done away with by any and all means. They call on the government as the first reform step to decrease largely the number of licensed shops for 1928 and to enforce rigorously the existing rules for their early closing".[282]

When picketing of liquor shops was included as an item in the movement and Mahatma Gandhi had given approval for the women to participate in large numbers, there was a great response from women. Mahatma Gandhi said if the women of India took up picketing and specialise in them they could contribute more than men to the nation's freedom.[283]

Liquor shops were picketed as it was regarded as a vice. When the auction of liquor licence was done, women went there and requested the people who came there not to participate in the auction. As a result, the government revenue derived from liquor sales dwindled. At village festivals, usually there were unrestricted sale of liquor. But women prevailed upon public organisations and charities to supply free milk and fruit drinks to the merry makers thereby stopped the liquor sale.[284] Repressive orders were passed and many were arrested and put in prison.[285] At Tuticorin from 1st June 1931, seven women picketers stood at a distance of twenty to thirty yards and started picketing.[286] Because of the picketing of liquor shops Mrs. Sakuntala Iyer was arrested and imprisoned for four months. At Tiruppur two well known women Mrs. Padmavathi Ammal, wife of V.V.S. Iyer and Mrs. Asher Padmavathi also went to jail.

In the North Arcot district Nagammal and Pushpavathivammal, while taking part in the boycott of toddy shops movement, were arrested and kept in the Thirupathur Jail for fifteen days. Since they refused to apologise they were sentenced to three months imprisonment and a fine of Rs. 25/- and were kept in the Vellore jail.[287] These women fearlessly surrounded drink shops and often successfully appealed to the addicts to give up the habits.

Towards the later stage of the campaign, *vanar senas* (Monkey Army) functioned in several part of Tamil Nadu.[288] Women played a prominent part by organising young people into what was called the *vanar senas*. This organisation sowed the seeds of patriotism in the minds of young boys and girls.

Women were found in almost all fields of activities. They set out at dawn even before the sun was up, walked through streets unfurling their banners, singing devotional and national songs. They held mammoth demonstrations in defiance of prohibitory orders. They led processions and when obstructed sat on the road with cool composure.[289]

The movements for the boycott of foreign clothes and the prohibition of intoxicating liquors and drinks were undoubtedly a great boost to the moral and economic well being of millions of Indians. The foreign clothes undermined the economic foundations of the nation and threw millions out of employment. Drinks and drugs sap the moral well being of those who were given to the habit. The distress in each case was felt in the house and therefore by the women. The moral results of the two reforms were obviously great. The political result was also great. Prohibition of intoxicating drinks and drugs meant the loss of twenty five crores of revenue to the Government. Boycott of foreign clothes meant the saving of atleast sixty crores of India's millions.[290]

Boycott of Schools

The role of students in the Civil Disobedience movement was very considerable inspite of the government regulation against that. The Tamilnadu Congress Committee meeting at Coimbatore, on 18th August 1930 passed a resolution to picket colleges and enrol students as volunteers in the movement.[291] T.V. Swaminatha Sastri, opened an ashram at Tiruchirappalli with the object of providing loding and training to volunteers for picketing colleges and polling booths. The Congress also prepared leaflets exhorting the students to quit the colleges and join the movement. The Youth League under the Presidentship of Rukmini Lakshmipathi worked tremendously to win over the students towards political programme.[292] As a result many students left their studies. The visit of Miss Slade,[293] a woman volunteer of the Sabarmathi Ashram to Madras gave a fillip to students activities.[294] She visited Tiruchirapalli on 22nd August 1930 and appealed to the students to give up their studies and join the Congress. For about a fortnight after the advent of Miss Slade, a vigorous propaganda was carried on in Tiruchirapalli by the members of Tamilnadu Congress Committee under the leadership of Dr. Pichimuthu Ammal of Madurai, the then President of the Tamil Nadu Congress Committee. On 3rd September 1930, Dr. Pichaimuthu Ammal and others began to picket the colleges. Students and teachers were prevented from entering into their colleges by the volunteers lying across the gates. It was repeated on the next day also. Immediately thirty nine persons who picketed the colleges were arrested and were sentenced to various terms of imprisonment.[295] As a mark of protest students from Queen Mary's College boycotted the classes.[296]

On 2nd July 1930, 107 students from National College, Tiruchirapalli and sixty three students from Government Brenner College, Tellichery participated in the movement.[297] On 4th September, eighty one per cent of the students, on the next day 137 students, on 6th, eighty per cent, on the next day sixty per cent and on 8th September forty five per cent of the students of St. Joseph's College, Tiruchirapalli participated in the movement. On 23rd October out of the 700 students of the Loyolla College, Madras, 200 students participated in the Civil Disobedience movement. Many students were arrested and fines were levied on them.[298] Some students, who were not content with merely boycotting their respective schools, picketed other schools in Madras.[299] In the Madras Presidency itself there were 856 youths and Juveniles below twenty one years were sentenced for offences in connection with the Civil Disobedience movement till 9th December 1930. Out of that, 497 were sent to Borstal schools and 359 students to certified schools. Thirty two of them were below fifteen years of age and they were sent to certified schools and one below twelve years sent to certified school was soon released.[300] Madurai sent many students to prison.[301]

Padmavathi Ammal, and others violating the orders, saluted national flag and were arrested and imprisoned.[302] By 15th November 1930, the total number of satyagraha prisoners in the Madras Presidency jails were 2,966 including thirty one Muslims and fifty others. Out of these forty three were women and twenty three were juveniles under seventeen years of age.[303] Anticipating that many women and young boys would be arrested in connection with the Civil Disobedience movement, the government directed the district magistrates to report any noticeable tendency on the part of these classes to participate and also to recommend any special measures for dealing with them.[304] Till then, the government had followed the policy of leaving or ignoring women and young boys as far as possible. After that, the government discouraged the women by arresting them. A new special jail for women was also opened in 1930 at Vellore. It was first of its kind in India.[305] This jail had accommodation for 237 prisoners who could be housed according to their classification.[306]

Even though repressive measures were adopted by the government they were unable to suppress the movement. Then the government decided to have a settlement with the Congress. On 25th January 1931, Lord Irwin, the then Viceroy released Mahatma Gandhi unconditionally along with other members of the Congress.[307] It resulted in the Gandhi-Irwin Pact signed on 5th March 1931. The Congress agreed to participate in the second Round Table Conference to be held in London, and to suspend the Civil Disobedience movement, whereas the government agreed to release unconditionally all political prisoners except those concerned with terrorist activities and withdraw all repressive ordinances.

The agreement was approved in the Karachi Congress session held in March 1931.[308] Even though the Civil Disobedience movement was suspended, the Karachi Congress session laid special emphasise on the need for peaceful picketing and intensification of the boycott of foreign clothes by increasing khadi propaganda.

After the pact, the movement had ceased a little, and there was laxity in picketing though the pact allowed peaceful picketing. The result was import of British cloth into India increased. So inorder to intensify foreign cloth boycott and to supply khadi yarn and clothes, the Tamilnadu Congress Committee in March 1931 formed a Boycott Committee with S. Ambujammal as one of its members. The Tamil Nadu Youth

Conference under the presidency of Rukmini Lakshmipathi passed a resolution to boycott all foreign goods especially British goods. It also advocated the severance of the British connection.[309]

A strong appeal was made by Durgabai Amma at Vellore which contained the following observations among others:

> "Swaraj will be attained only if lakhs of people render sacrifice. It was because women took part in large numbers in the last struggle that this government came down. So prepare yourselves for the next struggle. But do not think that things will stop with imprisonment and beating with lathis. The authorities will charge with bayonets and shoot you with revolvers and machine guns. You should remain undaunted even if they take you to the gallows and carry on your work valiantly relying cheerfully upon non-violence".[310]

At Coimbatore also in a public meeting she made a spirited speech encouraging women to come to the forefront of the war and not to be afraid of canon and guns.[311] Women were asked to come forward to join the struggle for freedom. Picketing in Madras was confined to women only. Now, Durgabai Amma and Margaret E. Cousins took the lead. About sixty women joined the movement there and they picketed foreign cloth shops at Madras almost daily. Women had donated their bangles, nose rings and bracelets to the national fund. One satyagrahi from Madras, Meena Krishnaswamy who met Mahatma Gandhi at the young age of eleven donated her ornaments to him towards *Harijan* fund. After that she never wore gold ornaments.[312] In Madras in the month of April 1931 alone, thirteen women were arrested in connection with the picketing of foreign cloth shops.[313] In Madurai Padamasini Ammal, Thayammal and Sitalakshmi Ammal carried on continuous propaganda advocating the boycott of foreign goods. Picketing was successfully conducted there by Dr. Pichaimuthu Ammal. Nearly fifty women under her leadership participated in the movement.[314]

Women also started peaceful picketing in front of the toddy shops. As a result the daily sales had considerably gone down. Toddy shop auction for that year also failed to attract many vendors.[315] Picketing was attempted in many districts but it remained non-violent.[316] Tamil newspapers made strong appeals to the women of Tamil Nadu to participate in the movement irrespective of whether Mahatma Gandhi permitted it or not. *Sutandira Sangu* wrote "picketing of toddy shops should be carried on vigorously in villages and picketing of foreign clothes in towns by the women and students".[317] Almost all the national dailies supported the movement. Women's India Association carried on continuous propaganda infavour of prohibition. It welcomed the prohibition movement started by C. Rajagopalachari.[318]

Since the government violated the pact, Mahatma Gandhi revived the movement in 1932 with more vigor. Immediately Mahatma Gandhi was arrested. It resulted in reviving the movement every where. In Madurai itself altogether thirty women were arrested and imprisoned including Padmasini Ammal, Thayammal, Sitalakshmi Ammal, Kondalakshmi Ammal and K.T. Kamala.[319] The arrest of A.Vaidyanatha Iyer of the Madurai Bar in 1932 was signalised by a public hartal resulting in the arrest and imprisonment of Mrs. Sundararaman, Mrs. Subbaraman and Dr. Pichaimuthu Ammal. Akilandammal, wife of Vaidyanatha Iyer was also arrested once.[320]

In January 1932 Dr. Ms. Sakuntala Iyer and two others arranged a meeting at Madras and appealed to the people to boycott foreign clothes and join the movement. On 4th February she was arrested while distributing leaflets.[321] She was released only on 4th February 1933 after serving the full term of one year. The soul stirring national songs rendered by K.P. Sundarambal, D.K. Pattammal and other women singers served as an impetus to all and prepared them for any sacrifice for the sake of independence.

At Gudivada on 21st February 1932, two women picketers A. Ushamani and T. Kausalya Devi were sprayed with water for about twenty minutes until they fell unconscious and were removed to the hospital by the police. S. Ambujammal along with other women picketed the foreign cloth shops at Rattan Bazar. To prevent them drainage water was sprayed on them through rubber tubes.[322] Even then they continued the movement until they were arrested. Both Ambujammal and Gnanammal were given six months imprisonment and Rs. 250/- as fine for violating the law. Sonabai, wife of Srinivasan, a freedom fighter from Coimbatore was arrested for participating in the Civil Disobedience movement in 1932. She was imprisoned at Vellore jail for six months.[323]

From the Coimbatore district alone, the following women were arrested and imprisoned for participating in the freedom movement. Mrs. P.D. Asher, Mrs. B.S. Sundaram and her mother-in-law from Tirupur, Mrs. T. Ranghavachari, Mrs. K. Subramaniam and Mrs. C.A. Ayyamuthur from Coimbatore, Mrs. S.A. Narayana Sastry from Satty, Mrs. Savithri Ammal from Udumalpet, Srimathi Bagavathy Amma and Mrs. Rajan Iyer from Pollachi.

M. Kodhainayaki, W/o V.M. Parthasarathi Iyengar, was also arrested and sentenced to six months imprisonment under section 17(1) of 1908. She was sent to the State jail for women at Vellore. Mahatma Gandhi said until arrest everyone should continue the movement. At Madurai, Ahilandathammal, Lakshmi Bharathi, Soundaram Ramachandran, Mrs. Krishnaswami, Mrs. Ramaswami were arrested and imprisoned.[324] The government tried to combat this upsurge by arrests, ill-treatment and making prison life intolerable. When practically all men leaders were in jail, women became dictators of war councils set up to direct the day to day activities.[325]

Jawaharlal Nehru was surprised at the participation of the women and remarked:

> "Most of us menfolk were in prison, and then a remarkable thing happened. Our women came to the front and took charge of the struggle. Women had always been there ofcourse, but now there was an avalanche of them, which took not only the British government but their own menfolk by surprise. Here were these women, women of the upper or middle classes, leading sheltered lives in their homes, peasant women, working class women, rich women, poor women, pointing out in their tens of thousands in defiance of government order and police lathi...".[326]

Inorder to promote khadi for the successful boycott of foreign clothes, Krishnabai Nimbkar, the then Secretary of the Women's India Association and Ammu Swaminathan, an active member of the Women's India Association worked hard for months together to start a Swadeshi Emporium at Madras. Its aim was to divert the eighty crores of rupees spend for the import of foreign goods to be made available for the poor who were suffering from unemployment, low wages, bad and insanitary housing, ill-health and mass illiteracy. The Women's India Association had also undertaken the mission of swadeshi, which naturally in its complete synthesis meant swaraj.

Because of all these efforts, a lot of foreign cloth shops were sealed by the merchants themselves. So, the government arrested many women though peaceful picketing was allowed. Because of the repressive measures the movement began to decline.

Then the Tamil Nadu Congress Committee held a secret meeting on 1st August 1933. There C. Rajagopalachari emphasised Mahatma Gandhi's wish that individual civil disobedience should be carried on openly. But the opinion was divided. Many Congressmen lost faith in direct agitation and wanted to enter the council under the proposed new constitution. They held a private meeting convened by

S. Satyamurthi and decided to revive the Swaraj Party to start constitutional agitation.[327] When the majority opinion was against Civil Disobedience movement, Mahatma Gandhi suspended it in May 1934. In return, the government cancelled the repressive ordinances and released the political prisoners.[328]

The treatment of women political prisoners was far from satisfactory. Their customs were simply ignored. In the Vellore jail, authorities removed their bangles and the *kumkum* from the forehead of the married women.[329] In the south *kumkum* was a religious symbol of marriage. Married women never go out with out bangles.[330] At Tellicherry, the Joint Magistrate ordered Mrs. Surendranath Prabhu's *tali* to be removed for paying the fine and when she protested, ordered the constable to remove the same by force. Later, he apologised to the government.[331]

Many women political prisoners were kept in 'C' class jail along with the criminals. For example Lakshmi Ammal wife of Dr. Sankara Iyer was placed as a 'C' class prisoner in 1932, but later the government placed her in 'A' class. Srinivasan from Coimbatore informed that his wife Sonabai was treated as a 'C' class prisoner since she belonged to the middle class family. Because of that she lost her health and after two months medical treatment only she recovered.[332] Women 'C' class prisoners in the Vellore jail had been denied even the bare necessities of life, and for trivial or imaginary faults two women political prisoners had been transferred from the women jail Vellore to the Madurai jail and were made to live with the criminals. As a result of that, one of the women political prisoners on her release was found to be wrecked in her physic and mind. Only two meals were given to them. The beds were dirty, oil given for bath was not sufficient, food was not hygiene. Nearly hundred women had to use one toilet. On Sundays from evening four to morning five they were kept locked in the rooms. They had to break stones, weave wollen etc.[333] It is apt to quote an extract from the experience of a woman prisoner that had appeared in the *Indian Social Reporter*, reprinted in *Stri-Dharma*,

> "Long term imprisonment and hard labour irrespective of their health, habits and education have been their lot. Too frequent transfers from one jail to another and that too at unearthly hours and in the strictest secrecy as to the destination were calculated to instil dread of the unknown into the hearts of the women..."[334]

The Vellore jail overflowed with women satyagrahis during 1930-32. By the end of February 1933, there were 557 men and forty women prisoners of Civil Disobedience movement in jails in the Madras Presidency.[335]

Mahatma Gandhi was very much surprised on seeing the activities of women. He wrote to Women's India Association:

> "the manifestation of energy, devotion and sacrifice which thousands of women made during the last satyagraha in India was nothing short of a miracle --- Women have set a noble example to men by abstaining from claiming special privileges. I would like to have their blessings in order that I may not fail to represent the cause that has been entrusted to my hands".[336]

An important feature of the freedom struggle in Tamilnadu in the 1930s was the impetus it had given to the women. Even the government could not help noting that the feminine element was conspicuous during this movement. Women's India Association also supported the Civil Disobedience movement. Many of the women political workers who dared prison and lathis came from its ranks.

Individual Satyagraha

At the out break of the II world war England proclaimed India to be at war with Germany without consulting the Congress ministries. As a mark of protest, the Congress ministries resigned and obstructed the people from rendering any help in the war effort. To intensity its campaign Mahatma Gandhi launched an Individual Satyagraha. The campaign was inaugurated on 7th October 1940 when Vino Babe had offered satyagraha as the first satyagrahi. The procedure of the satyagraha was simple. On being selected by Mahatma Gandhi, a satyagrahi had to go to his own Congress committee area, home town or village and formally notify the magistrate of his intention to break the law and give the date, time and place of his satyagraha. He was not expected to organise demonstrations on the occasion. His duty was to explain to those present the slogans,

> "Do not give money to the war fund, do not give men for the war, do not give materials for the war".

This he should continue until arrest and on release from jail or when not arrested for breaking the law in this respect, a selected satyagrahi should repeat again and again his offering of satyagraha.[337] The Individual Satyagraha was organised in almost all parts of the Madras Presidency. Every where Congress committees were formed, anti-war posters were displayed.[338] The authorities in the Madras Presidency dealt rather severely with Congressmen offering satyagraha. Many were arrested. It did not deter women and many joined the satyagraha and courted arrest. To start with, the satyagraha was offered in Madras city. Later on it was extended to other districts.

T.S.S. Rajan, launched the campaign of Individual Satyagraha in Madras. He was arrested and sentenced to one year imprisonment and a fine of Rs.1000/- or indefault two months further imprisonment. Rukmini Lakshmipathi followed him in offering satyagraha on 21st November 1940. She was also arrested and sentenced to one year imprisonment. Before arrest she told,

> "Let the women in India follow the leadership of Mahatma Gandhi and maintain the honour and dignity of our Motherland".[339]

For distributing anti-war pamphlets or shouting anti-war slogans, in December 1940 Radhabai Subbarayan and in the early part of 1941 M. Kamaladevi Arya, T. Thirupurasundari Ammal, Santa Bai, A.C. Jayalakshmi Ammal, Sitalakshmi Ammal, Devaki Ammal and Thayarammal were arrested and imprisoned.[340] Mrs.K.K. Subhanna Gounder and Mrs. V.C. Palaniswami Gounder from Coimbatore who took part in the Individual Satyagraha were not sentenced to imprisonment though they were kept in remand for a whole day.[341]

From Madurai, K.P. Janaki Ammal was arrested for anti-war propaganda which earned her the distinction of being the first woman in South India to be arrested for this offence. She was the founder President of the All India Democratic Women's Association, Tamil Nadu. She invited Subash Chandra Bose to Madurai in the year 1938 and escorted to various meetings there.[342] Ahilandammal and Alamelu Sundara Rajan were also arrested for shouting anti-war slogans and Satyagraha in January 1941.[343] From Coimbatore, Mrs. Padmavathy Asher, Mrs. S.A. Narayana Sastry, Mrs. T. Raghavachari, Mrs. K. Subramaniam, Mrs. Amma Baghavathi, Mrs. C.P. Ayyamuthu, Mrs. Savithri Ammal and Lakshmi took part in the movement and went to jail. Besides, Mrs. K.K. Subhanna Gounder and Mrs. V.C. Palani Swami Gounder took part in the Individual Satyagraha.[344] The first Satyagrahis to start on the march to Delhi were Mr. and Mrs. Perumal from Vellore on 15th February 1941.[345]

From January to March 1941 one woman each from Chengleput, and Tirunelveli three each from Tiruchirapalli, North Arcot, South Arcot and Ramnad were arrested for anti-war slogans and distributing anti-war leaflets. They were given punishments according to the nature of the crime ranging from imprisonment till the rising of the court to six months simple imprisonment and a fine or three months rigorous imprisonment under Defence of India Rules. Thus women were arrested in large numbers from virtually every districts of Tamil Nadu for anti-war lectures or distributing anti-war leaflets or anti-war slogans. Many of these women once came out from jail also continued their activities. Meetings were conducted during the occasions of their release to stir enthusiasm among women.[346] As a result there were isolated instances of satyagraha.[347] In Salem, a students organisation was opened by Miss. Parvati Subbarayan, on that occasion she criticised the British Government and induced the students to go against the government.[348] The movement of 1940-41 was an experiment in a purer or strictly restricted form of civil disobedience without the element of political drama which characterised the mass satyagraha movement.

Quit India Movement

In 1942, with the Quit India Movement numerous women again joined the agitation and courted incarceration. Mahatma Gandhi had informed the people that Quit India Movement would be short and swift. There would be mass participation of the people. Each one would be his or her own guide. The government would resort to brutal and ruthless repression. People would have to face the challenge non-violently in a spirit of 'Do or Die'. In his stirring message to the nation on the morning of 9th August, Mahatma Gandhi exhorted the *Satyagrahis* to seek and face death then only the nation would survive.

The same day Mahatma Gandhi and other members of the working committee and many other prominent Congress leaders were arrested by the government. The Tamilnadu Congress Committee was declared an unlawful association and its office was sealed. Local Congress committees were also declared illegal.[349] The Quit India Movement was practically leaderless as all senior members of the Congress had been put in jail. However when the news of their arrests spread, spontaneous hartals, protest meetings and strikes took place all over the country. Women joined in taking out processions, holding meeting, demonstrations and organising strikes. In Tamil Nadu, when leaders were arrested, Rukmini Lakshmipathi became the acting President of the Tamil Nadu Congress Committee and took the initiative to keep the organisation alive.

The most significant event during the Quit India Movement was the participation of women students. They played a spirited role in accelerating the national struggle. Students of the Queen Mary's College, Women's Christian College, etc., abstained from classes and organised hartals, processions and picketing.[350] Women students of Annamalai University along with men students played an integral part in the movement.

On 14th August 1942 Kamala Devi Arya was arrested for distributing leaflets.[351] Mrs.Soundaram Ramachandran helped the families of the people who were in jail in connection with this movement.[352] Hundreds of labourers from the Buckingham and Carnatic mills struck work. Anthony Ammal and Petchiammal from Coimbatore participated in the Pankajam mill strike which was part of the movement. They were arrested and lodged in Coimbatore Jail for six months and then in the Vellore jail for three months. Kuttiammal and Cholaiammal from Coimbatore were arrested and imprisoned when they broke the railway line at Singanallur with nearly 100 women workers.[353] Meena Krishnaswamy from Madurai, Narayana Ammal from Ramnad, Anchalai Ammal from South Arcot were arrested and imprisoned for shouting anti-war slogans and distributing leaflets. They were kept in various jails. Ambujammal started the Voluntary Corps of Madras. It played a very important role in helping the refugees with food and shelter.

The movement continued even in 1943. Independence Day was celebrated through out India in January 1943. In Madras, the National Flag was hoisted by Radhabai Subbarayan and the song of *Vande mataram* was sung on that occasion. Immediately Radhabai Subbarayan and Damayanti were arrested and sentenced to three months imprisonment. Ammu Swaminathan and Manjubhashini organised students strike on 19th February 1943 and they were arrested and imprisoned for one year. As a result, the strength in colleges reduced.[354] During the anniversary of Quit India Movement, women *Satyagrahis* took out processions and distributed leaflets asking the shop keepers to observe hartal.[355] Rukmini Lakshmipathi continued to play a remarkable role in the Congress politics till the end.

Women in the Indian National Army

While thousands of women joined the freedom movement responding to Mahatma Gandhi's call, there were a few who could not accept his creed on non-violence. Notable among them was Lakshmi Swaminathan, daughter of Ammu Swaminathan of Madras. She joined the Indian Independence League formed in January 1942 at Kuala Lumpur to fight for India's freedom, Later, its name was changed into Indian National Army. Many Indian women in East Asia joined the Indian National Army, assisted in the preparation and collection of bandages, first field dressing, collection of funds and articles required by the troops and inspiring young men and women to do their duty in the critical hours.

In March 1943, a women's section of the Indian National Army was started and Indian women in Malaya, Thailand and Burma enlisted themselves as volunteers. Mrs. M.K. Chidambaram was elected as Chair person and Ms. Saraswathy as Secretary of the Women's Section of the Indian Independence League. Lakshmi Swaminathan became the Secretary at the headquarters.[356] In July Subhas Chandra Bose addressed a meeting and his call to women to share the burden of the battle for freedom brought new spirit into the movement. As a result a Women's Regiment popularly known as the Jhansi Rani Regiment was started with Lakshmi Swaminathan as its captain.

Another remarkable but invisible woman of Tamilnadu who played a remarkable role in the Indian National Army was Govindammal. Originally she was from North Arcot district but her parents went to Malaysia for business purpose. There she attended the meeting addressed by Subhas Chandra Bose. He asked for men and women volunteers to share the burden of fighting for freedom. It caught the imagination of Govindammal and she not only joined the Indian National Army, but also donated her six sovereign bangles and an acre of rubber plantation owned by her to the Army. She was an important personality in the Janshi Rani Regiment. Subhas Chandra Bose only 100 women volunteers first to be given training in shooting. Govindammal was the one among the hundred. She was a very sincere worker in the regiment. Appreciating her sincerity, Subhas Chandra Bose had given her the title of 'Londs Naik'. Until 1945 she worked in the Army.[357] Nearly seventy five per cent of the women in the Indian National Army were from Tamil Nadu.

Lakshmi Swaminathan was the commander of the Jhansi Rani Regiment and also the Minister of Social Welfare and Medicine in the Azad Hind Cabinet. As the Commander, she was designated as Lt. Colonel. In the dramatic interview with Subhas Chandra Bose just prior to her assuming leadership, he asked her whether she was prepared to sacrifice her medical practice and devote all her time to the formation of the regiment, immediately she had given her complete willingness to do so. In the next morning she was found planning and organising her regiment.[358] In an interview with *Domei* she expressed her confidence in obtaining enough women for the regiment and for the red cross and nursing staff "We shall get enough volunteers and even more." Regarding the regiment, she said, "it will not work behind the lines, but right in the front. Subhas' appeal to the Indian women had been taken in the best of spirit by them. In his Bangkok address he said,

"I am sure that the presence of our sisters in the fighting

> ranks and in Red Cross units will be a powerful incentive to those wavering. It is not unprecedented experience to have our sisters fighting in a national emergency".[359]

In order to assist in the further enlistment of volunteers, Captain Lakshmi Swaminathan visited various parts of Asia and encouraged her sisters to join up in the fight to free India from the shackles of western imperialism. When the Indian National Army collapsed she did not surrender to the British. But she was captured and was later placed under arrest. Her regiment was disbanded in 1945 and most of the girls were sent away to Singapore from Rangoon, Lakshmi Swaminathan was sent to Rangoon Jail.[360] In the next year she was released. Then she came to Madras and addressed a number of meetings. An organisation under the name of "The Friends of the Indonesian Republic" was inaugurated at the well attended public meeting held at Madras on 10th May 1946. Its president was Lt. Col. Lakshmi Swaminathan.[361]

It is evident that the saga of women's participation in the national movement in Tamil Nadu began in 1916. After that in all forms of political activities women took part. They led the satyagrahas, braved police lathies, went to prison and challenged the right of the British to rule our country. It is apt to quote from *Viswakarnataka* published in 26 April 1937:

> "In India's fight for freedom the heroism of the women and the suffering they underwent attracted the attention of the whole world. Did not Mahatma Gandhi say that to the women belongs the honour of having raised India several steps higher in her march towards freedom".

References

1. *Swadesamitran*, 25 March 1915 (MNR).
2. *New India*, 2 January 1915.
3. Demi Official Fortnightly Report from the Govt. of Madras to the Govt. of India, 29 September, 1915. (Hereafter FR)

4. G.A. Natesan and Co. (ed.), *Congress Resolutions*, p. 403.
5. Within the Congress, there were two groups - Moderates and Nationalists. The Bombay Congress session held in December 1915 authorized the AICC and the All India Muslim League Committee to frame a scheme of reform on the basis of the resolution on Self Government passed in that Congress session. They were asked to submit the same on or before Ist September 1916 [G.A. Natesan and Co. (ed.), *Congress Resolutions*, pp. 210, 212].
6. *New India*, 4 January 1916.
7. Annie Besant, *The Future of Indian Politics*, p. 144
8. FR, 16 September 1916.
9. *Ibid.*; Annie Besant, *National Home Rule League: Why Founded and How?*, pp. 8-9.
10. *New India*, 4 December 1916.
11. Letter from the Acting Chief Secretary, Govt. of Madras to the Govt. of India, 23 June, 1917, Home in *Home Rule movement, 1914-20* (TNA) [Here after HRM], pp. 375-77.
12. *Report of the Indian National Congress*, (hereafter RINC) Lucknow, 1916, pp. 70-71.
13. G.O. No. 150, Pub., 27 March 1919; T. Varadarajulu Naidu, *The Justice Movement, 1917*, p. 1.
14. *Justice Party Golden Jubilee Souvenir*, p. 1.
15. *The Hindu*, 20 December 1916; S.Saraswathi, *Minorities in the Madras State*, pp. 201-02.
16. *New India*, 21 December 1916; Eugene F. Irschick, *Politics and Social Conflict in South India*, p. 49.
17. *New India*, 20 December 1916; T. Varadarajulu Naidu, *The Justice Movement, 1917*, p. 1.
18. *Madras Year Book, 1923*, p. 239; T. Varadarajulu Naidu, *The Justice Movement, 1917*, p. 1.
19. "Statement by V. Chakkarai Chetti and P. Chenchiah, delegates of the Madras Presidency Association" in *Joint Select Committee on the Government of India Bill*, Vol. III, Appendices (London,. 1919), Appendix-O, pp. 84-85.
20. Eugene F. Irschick, *Politics and Social Conflict in South India*, p. 60.
21. Thiru Vi.Ka., *thiru.vi.ka valgai kuripukkal*, pp. 258-59.
22. *New India*, 22 September 1917; E.Sa. Visswanathan, "E.V. Ramaswami Naicker and the Tamil Nadu Congress" *Journal of Indian History*, April 1976, part I., Vol. LIV, p. 178.
23. G.O. No. 273, Pub., 23 March 1918.
24. *RINC*, Lucknow, 1916, p. 77; Jamnadas Dwarkadas, *Political Memoirs*, p. 15.

25. Subramanian, "The Home Rule League and Mrs.Annie Besant" in N.R.Ray (ed.), *Public Associations in India,* p. 275; S.Vijayalakshmi, "Healing the Breach and the Home Rule Movement" in B.N. Pande (ed.), *A Centenary History of the Indian National Congress, 1885-1919,* Vol. I, p. 482.
26. *New India,* 18 September 1918.
27. FR, 2 February, 1917; P. Chakravarthy, "Emergence of Justice Party" *Journal of Indian History,* April & August 1977, part. I, II, Vol. LV, p. 300.
28. FR, 16 February 1917.
29. G.O. No. 744, Pub., 9 June 1917.
30. Eugene F. Irschick, *Politics and Social Conflict in South India,* p. 37.
31. *Ibid.,* p. 363.
32. G.O. No. 559, Home (Education), 1 May 1917; HRM, 1914-20, p. 277.
33. *New India,* 1 June 1917
34. G.O. No. 774, Pub. (Confl.), 7 June 1917.
35. Home Rule Files (6) in HRM, 1914-20, p. 343; G. No. 744, Pub. (Confl.), 7 June 1917.
36. G.O. No. 785, Pub. (Confl.), 14 June 1971
37. Circular instructions from the acting Chief Secretary, Govt. of Madras to the District Magistrates, Pub. (Confl.), Ootachamund, 19 August 1917, D.O.No.3191 W/l in HRM, 1914-20, p. 453; RAMP, 1917-18 p. ix.
38. *RAMP,* 1918-19, p. ix
39. B.R. Nanda, *Builders of Modern India: Motilal Nehru,* p. 82
40. *The Hindu,* 11 June 1917
41. H.N. Pandit, *Fragments of History: India's Freedom Movement and After,* p. 21
42. S.Vijayalakshmi, "Healing the Breach and the Home rule Movement", p. 489.
43. *New India,* 10 July 1917.
44. FR, 2 July 1917; FR 5 October 1917.
45. *Sampad Abhydaya,* 14 August 1917 (MNR).
46. *Swadesmitran ; Hindu Nesan,* 10 August 1917, p. 2188 (MNR).
47. *Desamata,* 15 August 1917, p. 2239 (MNR).
48. *Sampad Abhydaya,* 14 August 1917, p. 2238 (MNR)
49. FR, 5 October 1917.
50. FR, 17 July 1917.
51. Letter from the Chief Secretary, Govt. of Madras to the Secretary, Govt. of India, Pub., 31 July 1917 in HRM, 1914-20, p. 435.
52. *New India,* 2 August 1917.

53. FR, 17 August 1917.
54. *New India*, 10 August 1917.
55. FR, 1 September 1917.
56. *New India*, 16 August 1917.
57. G.O. No. 948, Pub. (Press, Confl.), 19 October, 1918; *India in 1917-18*, p. 36.
58. *India in* 1917-18, p. 37.
59. Rangaswami Parthasarathy, *A Hundred years of the Hindu*, p. 213.
60. Manmohan Kaur, *Women in India's Freedom Struggle*, p. 127.
61. *New India*, 24 August 1917.
62. *Ibid.*, 30 August 1917; FR, 1 September 1917.
63. FR, 18 September 1917.
64. G.O. No. 917, Pub. (Confl.), 5 October 1918.
65. *New India*, 16 September 1917; *RAMP, 1917-18*, p. ix.
66. FR, 5 October 1917.
67. FR, 18 October 1917.
68. *Stri-Dharma*, July-August 1930, p. 285.
69. Annie Besant, *Birth of New India*, pp. 10-12.
70. *New India*, 28, November 1917; *Joint Select Committee*, Appendix B, p. 9.
71. *Justice*, 29 November 1917.
72. *RINC*, Calcutta, 1917, p. 19; *EINC*, 1916-20, Vol. VII, p. 357.
73. Radha Kumar, *The History of Doing*, p. 57.
74. *New India*, 28, November 1917; *Joint Select Committee*, Appendix B, p. 9.
75. Letter from Yaqub Hasan and Moulana Abdur Subhan Sahib Bahadur, the honorary Secretaries, Madras Presidency Muslim League to the Chief Secretary to the Govt. of Madras in G.O. No. 948, Pub. (Press, Confl.), 19 October, 1918.
76. G.O. No. 122, L and M., 17 October 1919.
77. Letter from Chidambaranatha Mudaliar, President Ist annual conference, Madras Presidency Association to the Private Secretary, Govt. of Madras in G.O. No. 273, Pub., 23 March 1918.
78. G.O. No. 273, Pub., 23 March 1918.
79. FR, 18 May 1918; P. S. Sivaswami Iyer, L.A. Govindaraghava Iyer, Presidents of the Madras Provincial Congress Committee, G.A. Natesan, editor of the Indian Review and a few others.
80. *New India*, 21 July 1918.
81. FR, 18 July; 20 August 1918.
82. The Mont-Ford Reform Scheme proposed to establish in the provinces of British India a system of dyarchy or dual government. Under that system the Provincial administration was to be divided

into two parts namely the reserved subjects to be administered by the Governor and his Executive Council, and the transferred subjects to be administered by the Governor and his Ministers (A.C. Kapur, Constitutional History of India, p. 205).

83. *New India*, 7 April 1919; FR, 2 April 1919; Moderates included L.A. Govindaraghava Iyer and G.A. Natesan, former Presidents of the MPCC and Home Rulers like B.P. Wadia and C.P. Ramaswami Iyer both of whom had been Secretaries of the Home Rule League. (FR. 2 April 1919).
84. By the Rowlatt Act, the accused would not be given the privilege to defend himself. It was commented by Motilal Nehru as 'no power, no appeal, no argument' (G.O. No. 318, Pub.2 July 1919; *The Hindu*, 8 March 1919; B.C. Bamford, *Histories of Non-Cooperation and Khilafat Movements* (Confl.), p. 3).
85. G.O. No. 222, Pub. (Confl.), 24 April 1919; Report of the Indian Central Committee, p. 40.
86. G.O. No. 222, Pub. (Confl.), 24 April 1919; USSF, No. 407 (Secret), 6 May 1923.
87. *The Hindu*, 31 March 1919; Extract from the Fortnightly Report of the Commissioner of Police, Madras, 25 March 1919 in G.O. No. 222, Pub. (Confl.), 24 April 1919; *New India*, 31 March 1919.
88. Extracts from the fortnightly report of the Commissioner of Police, Madras, 25 March 1919, G.O. No. 222, Pub., 24 April 1919.
89. *The Hindu*, 10 March 1919; *Desabhaktan*, 31 March 1919, p. 548 (MNR).
90. *The Hindu*, 24 March 1919.
91. G.O. No.222, Pub. (Confl.), 24 April 1919; G.O. No. 318, Pub., 2 June 1919; *New India*, 7 April 1919.
92. *New India*, 15 April 1919.
93. *RINC*, Amritsar, 1919, p. 176; *Swadesamitran*, 2 January 1920; *Navasakti*, 3 January 1920.
94. *India in 1920*, p. 41.
95. *Collected works of Mahatma Gandhi* (hereafter CWMG), August 1919-January 1920, vol. XVI, p. vi; *Desabhaktan*, 5 August 1920, p. 928 (MNR).
96. *Sampad Abhyudaya*, 20 May 1920, p. 621 (MNR).
97. *Desabhaktan*, 18 February 1920, p. 222; 29 April 1920, p. 534. (MNR).
98. *CWMG*, January - June 1920, Vol. XVII, p. 413.
99. *Young India*, 2 June 1920.
100. Vijay Agnew, *Elite Women in Indian Politics*, p. 35
101. *Desabhimani*, 18 March 1921, p. 471 (MNR).
102. *Ibid.*, 3 April 1921, p. 499 (MNR).

103. *RINC*, Allahabad, 1888, p. 9.
104. *PMLC*, August 1924, Vol. XVX, pp. 303, 448.
105. *Report on the Madras Abkari Department for the year 1919-20*, pp. 2-4; G.O. No. 2688, Revenue, 8 November 1920.
106. *Navasakti*, 28 March 1921.
107. David Arnold, *The Congress in Tamilnad*, pp. 64-65.
108. FR, 1 March 1921; 1 November 1921.
109. B.S. Baliga, *Compendium on Temperance and Prohibition in Madras*, p. 60.
110. USSF. No. 407 (Secret), 6 May 1926.
111. Excise supplied 9.8 per cent of the revenue of the Madras Government in 1902-03 and 21.77 per cent in 1920-21 for more than in any other province, (Report on the Administration of the Abkari Revenue of the Madras Presidency, 1920-21, p. 3).
112. *Tamil Nadu*, 25 December 1921, p. 21; *Swadesamitran*, 13 February 1922, p. 177 (MNR).
113. K. Veeramani (compil.), *Periyar on Women's Rights*, p. XIII.
114. A.Eraiyan, *suyamariyathai chudarozhikal*, (Self-respecters) p. 3
115. *Young India*, 27 July 1920, 17 March 1927.
116. *New India*, 2 April 1919.
117. *Young India*, 15 September 1920; *EINC*, 1916-20, Vol. VII, p. 58.
118. USSF. No. 328 (Secret), 15 November 1921; *EINC*, 1921-24, Vol. VIII, pp. 378-79
119. Harijan, 13 April 1940; *Census of India, 1961, Handlooms in Madras State*, Vol. IX, part XI-A, p. 128.
120. Tilak Swaraj Fund was created in memory of Tilak for the purpose of financing the non-cooperation movement. (*EINC*, 1921-24, Vol. VIII, p. 663)
121. Vijaya Ramaswamy, *Textiles and Weavers in Medieval South India*, p. 1.
122. *Memorandum of the Progress of the Madras Presidency*, p. 52
123. B.S. Baliga, *Compendium on History of the Handlom industry in Madras*, p. 2.
124. *Memorandum of the Progress of the Madras Presidency*, p. 54.
125. Claude Markovits, *Indian Business and Nationalist Politics: The Indigenous Capitalist Class and the rise of the Congress Party*, pp. 33-34.
126. Eugene F. Irschick, *Tamil Revivalism in the 1930s*, p. 129.
127. H.R. Pate, *Madras District Gazetteers, Tinnevelly*, Vol. I, p. 358.
128. F.R.Hemingway, *Madras District Gazetteers, Tanjore*, p. 117.
129. B.S.Baliga, *Gazetteer of India, Madurai District*, p. 174.
130. E.Sa.Visswanathan, *The Political Career of E.V. Ramaswami Naicker*, pp. 140-41.

131. USSF. No.328 (Secret), 15 November 1921.
132. *Young India*, 20 April 1922.
133. *Sutandiram*, 26 October 1924, p. 1440 (MNR).
134. *Navasakti*, 30 March 1923.
135. *All India Spinners Association Annual Report, 1925-26*, p. 1; A.Benjamin, "Relevance of Gandhiji's Economic Ideas in the first half of the Twentieth century; A case study", *Journal of Indian History*, December 1969, Part III, Vol. XIII, p. 531.
136. *RAMP, 1923-24*, p. xi.
137. A. Arunachalam, *Khadi Economics: A few aspects*, p. 137.
138. *Navasakti*, 21 November 1924.
139. *Young India*, 20 March, 1924.
140. *Swadessamitran*, 23 June 1926, p. 823 (MNR).
141. *Young India*, 13 March 1924; *Navasakti*, 26 March 1924.
142. *Young India*, 24 May 1924.
143. Spinning franchise meant that those who wanted to become member of the Congress Committee or organizations should contribute 2000 yards of evenly hand spun yarn of his or her own spinning or in case of illness or any such other causes a like quantity of yarn spun by any other person. It was open to every one to contribute the full quota for the whole year at a time (*Young India*, 13 November 1924; *Indian Quarterly Register*, July-December 1925, p. 17; *RINC*, Belgaum, 1924, p. 39; *Young India*, 5 February 1925; *EINC, 1921-24*, Vol. VIII, p. 647).
144. *EINC*, 1925-29, Vol. IX, pp. 39-40.
145. *Indian Review*, January 1925, p. 82.
146. *Navasakti*, 23 January 1925.
147. *Ibid.*, 11 September 1925.
148. The Bharath Ashram was started by Subramania Siva, the Great Nationalist of Madurai District in 1921 at Madurai to train youngmen to the service of Motherland. After the arrest of him Srinivasa Varadhan of Madurai looked after the ashram. (Statement of Srinivasa Varadhan, Madurai, 8 June, 1955 *in Personal Statement of Political Personalities* (hereafter PSPP), pp. 1-2).
149. *Statemeit of Srinivasa Varadan*, 8 June 1955 in PSPP, pp. 2-5.
150. *Madura Jilla thiyahigal malar*, p. 39.
151. *Young India*, 4 December 1924
152. *Ibid.*, 18 December 1924.
153. FR, 17 September 1923.
154. *All India Spinners Association Annual Report*, 1925-26, p. 3 in G.O.No.506, Pub., I June 1927.
155. *Census of India, 1961, Handlooms in Madras State*, Vol. IX, Part XI-A, p. 130.

156. *Young India*, 1 October 1925; 'Report of the AICC for the year 1925' *Indian Quarterly Register*, July-December 1925, p. 27.
157. *Young India*, 24 January 1929.
158. B.K. Ahluwalia and Shashi Ahluwalia, *Rajaji and Gandhi*, p. 63.
159. *Young India*, 25 June 1925.
160. Christopher John Baker, *The Politics of South India, 1920-37*, p. 251.
161. *Young India*, 25 June 1925.
162. *Ibid.*, 24 January 1929.
163. *Young India*, 13 October 1925; FR, 2 September; October, 1927.
164. In order to commemorate the Rowlatt Satyagaraha of 6th - 13th April 1919, Gandhi suggested that every year the period between 6th - 13th April would be celebrated as the National Week. These celebrations had been held yearly since 1920 (Programme of the National Week in CDM, 1930-35 (SRRF); *Young India*, 31 March 1920.
165. FR, 17 April 1928.
166. Government Servants Conduct Rules in G.O. No. 284, Pub., 4 March 1925.
167. G.O. No. 506, Pub., 1 June 1927; G.O. No. 1111, Pub., 9 November 1927; *The Hindu*, 26 February, 1927.
168. *PMLC*, March 1928, Vol. XVI, p. 487.
169. *Al-Ammen*, 6 June 1926, p. 838 (MNR).
170. *PMLC*, January & February 1929, Vol. xxvi, pp. 548; *Congress*, 21 September 1926, p. 1263 (MNR).
171. *Young India*, 27 May 1926.
172. FR, 20 January 1921.
173. FR, 1 March 1922.
174. *Statement of Srinivasa Varadhan*, Madurai, 8 June 1955, *PSPP*, pp. 3, 7.
175. Neill aged 47 was one of the commanders of the British army during the Sepoy Mutiny. Embarking from Madras for Calcutta with the Madras Fusiliers on 18 May 1857 Neill took part in the defence of Benaras, Allahabad and Cawnpur and fell on 25th December 1857. He committed inhuman atrocities on old men, women and children. He didn't even spare "helplesswomen with sucking infants at their breasts" says Holmes. The words inscribed about the general on the pedestal of the statue which runs : "James George Smith Neill ... A brave resolute, self reliant soldier universally acknowledged as the first who stemmed the torrent of rebellion in Bengal, he fell gloriously at the relief of Lucknow, September 25, 1857". Appreciating his service during the mutiny, a statue of Neill was installed by the government at Mount Road, Madras) (Surendranath Sen, *Eighteen Fifty Seven*, p. 150).

176. G.O. No. 248, Pub., 13 March 1928; *The Hindu*, 16 August 1927, p. 1 (MNR); FR, 16 August 1927; *RAMP*, 1927-28, p. XV; Statement of Srinivasa Varadhan, pp. 7-8.
177. Though her name was Amma Kannu Ammal, Gandhi called her Leelavathi. From that time onwards she was called Leelavathi.
178. G.O. No. 2952, Public Works, 7 December 1927; *Navasakti*, 7 September 1927.
179. FR, 16 September 1927
180. *The Hindu*, 20 October 1927.
181. FR, 16 November 1927.
182. *PMLC.*, Vol. XXXVIII, October-November 1927, p. 421.
183. *Navasakti*, 21 September 1927.
184. G.O. No. 2602, Public Works, 13 July 1937; G.O. No. 2616, Local Self Government, 13 December 1937.
185. The Congressmen who wanted to enter into the council and continue constitutional agitation from within were called "Swarajists".
186. *The Hindu*, 28 November 1927.
187. *Young India*, 3 January 1928.
188. FR, 7 January 3 February 1928; B.S. Baliga, *Tanjore District Hand Book*, pp. 103-104.
189. *New India*, 17 November 1927.
190. *The Hindu*, 26 January 1928.
191. *Ibid.*, 28 January 1928.
192. *The Hindu*, 2 February 1928.
193. USSF. No. 651, 27 September 1929.
194. *PMLC*, January 1928, Vol. XXXIX, p. 309; *RAMP*, 1927-28, p. XII.
195. *PMLC*, January 1928, Vol. XXXIX, p. 314.
196. FR, 3 February 1928.
197. *RAMP*, 1927-28, p. X; FR, 17 February 1928; *The Hindu*, 4 February 1928.
198. *RAMP*, 1927-28, p. X; FR, 17 February 1928.
199. *Navasakti*, 29 February 1928; FR, 2 March 1928.
200. FR, 17 March 1928.
201. USSF. No. 615 (secret) 27 March 1929.
202. Ragamì, *viduthalai veerankanai Rukmini Lakshmipathi* (Woman Freedom Fighter Rukmini Lakshmipathi), p. 64.
203. *Stri-Dharma*, September 1930, p. 489.
204. *Stri-Dharma*, 2 February 1928.
205. Ragami, *viduthalai veerankanai Rukmini Lakshmipathi*, p. 64.
206. *Ibid.*
207. CWMG., March-June 1930, Vol. XLII, pp. 15, 58.
208. *Young India*, 9 January 1930; *Andhra Patrika*, 1 January 1930, p. 13. (MNR).

209. *Young India*, 8 May 1930.
210. G.O. No. 354, Law (Confl.) 8 June 1930.
211. *Stri-Dharma*, June 1930, p. 336.
212. *Ibid.*, July 1931, p. 422.
213. *Ibid.*, July-August 1930, p. 385.
214. FR, 4 June 1930.
215. *Shri-Dharma*, July 1931, p. 422.
216. Salt laws provided for the government monopoly over salt.
217. *Indian Ladies Magazine*, July 1930, p. 610.
218. *Shri-Dharma*, April 1930, p. 28.
219. *Indian Ladies Magazine*, July 1930, p. 610.
220. *Sutandira Sanghu*, 26 March 1930.
221. *The Hindu*, 4 June 1931.
222. Eugene. F. Irschick, *Tamil Revivalism in the 1930s*, p. 119.
223. T.V. Kalyana Sundara Mudaliar who left the Congress in 1926, at the request of C. Rajagopalachari rejoined the Congress in 1930 (*Navasakti*, 25 January 1930).
224. *The Hindu*, 4 June 1931; CDM, 1930-31 (Confl.), p. 156.
225. G.O. No. 952, Pub. (Confl.), 16 September 1931.
226. *CDM*, 1930-31 (Confl.), Appendix III, pp. 157, 176.
227. *USSF*. No. 661 (Secret), 9 April 1930.
228. G.O.No.668, Pub. (Confl.), 28 May 1930; USSF, No. 683-A (Secret), 30 April 1930.
229. *The Hindu*, 11 April 1930; *Young India*, 15 May 1930; Fortieth Anniversary of India's Independence: Vedaranyam Salt Yatra Re enatched 13-28 April 1988, *Indian Express*, 27 April 1988; *The Hindu*, 28 April 1988.
230. USSF, No. 683-A (Secret), 30 April 1930.
231. G.O.No.952, Pub. (Confl.), 16 September 1931; *The Hindu*, 28 April 1988; The Statement of P. K. Narayan, *PSPP*, p. 26.
232. The Hindu, 4 June 1931; G.O. No. 952, Pub. (Confl.), 16 September 1931.
233. *Young India*, 15 May, 1930 *Kudi Arasu*, 4 May 1930.
234. G.O.No.668, Pub. (Confl.), 28 May 1930.
235. *Young India*, 15 May 1930; *Kudi Arasu*, 4 May 1930.
236. *Tamil Nadu Conference Committee Report* (1929-31 in G.O. No. 952, Pub. (Confl.), 16 September 1931.
237. *Young India*, 15 May 1930.
238. Rukmini Lakshmipathi took a leading part in the CDM. As the President of the Madras Youth League, she attended the Lahore Congress and learnt the spirit underlying the movement in North India. This had its reactions on the political section of the local

organisation. At her instigation resolutions were passed at a meeting of the Madras Youth League on 20th January 1930 approving of the declaration of complete independence and the boycott of legislatures (FR, 3 February 1930).

239. *Indian Ladies Magazine*, July 1930, p. 610.
240. *Young India*, 22 May 1930, p. 199.
241. G.O. No. 952, Pub. (Confl.), 16 September 1931; CDM 1930-31, Appendix - III, p. 165.
242. FR, 4 June 1930.
243. *Young India*, 22 May 1930, p. 190.
244. She came under the influence of Mahatma Gandhi at the age of twelve, left school and took up his constructive work.
245. Madras Police Offence, 13 April 1930, Strictly Confl. USSF NO. 683 (A) 30 April 1930.
246. *The Hindu*, 16 April 1930.
247. *Ibid.*, 21, 22 April 1930.
248. G.O.No. 952, Pub. (Confl.), 16 September 1931; *The Hindu*, 4 June 1931, *Congress*, 22 April 1930, p. 715, (MNR).
249. FR, 6 May 1930.
250. USSF No. 683 (A) (secret) 30 April 1930.
251. *Young India*, 8 May 1930, p. 186.
252. Aparna Basu, "The Role of Women in the Freedom Struggle" in B.R. Nanda (ed.), *Indian Women: From Purdah to Modernity*, p. 26.
253. T.B.Russel, District Magistrate, North Arcot District, 6 January 1931, in CDM 1930-31, p. 67 (TNA).
254. FR, 5 June 1930; *Young India*, 5 June 1930; *PMLC*, November 1930 - January 1931, pp. 147-49.
255. T.B. Russel, District Magistrate, North Arcot, 6 January 1931 in CDM 1930-31, p. 67.
256. J.Hussian Khan, District Magistrate, Chengleput, 4 January 1931 in CDM 1930-31, p. 81.
257. CDM Diary of the Chengleput District, in CDM 1930-31, Appendix I.
258. Raj Pruthi and Bela Rani Sharma, *Encyclopaedia of Women, Society and Culture*, Vol. 2, pp. 164-65.
259. *Young India*, 11 August 1921.
260. *Bharati*, November - December 1931, p. 87. (MNR).
261. *Stri-Dharma*, July 1937, p. 422.
262. *Indian Ladies Magazine*, July 1930, p. 612 ; CDM Diary of the Chengleput District, in CDM 1930-31, Appendix-I.
263. *Stri-Dharma*, June 1930, p. 340.
264. USSR No.705 (Secret) 29 August 1930 ; G.O.No.672, Pub.,12 June 1930.

265. *RAMP, 1929-30*, p. XIV.
266. *The Hindu*, 4 February 2001.
267. S.P. Sen, (ed.), *Dictionary of National Biography*, Vol. I, pp. 20-22.
268. *Anandavikadan*, 19 November 1964, (Ambujammal's Interview).
269. *Young India*, 5 June 1930.
270. G.O. No. 952, Pub. (Confl.), 16 September 1931 ; *The Hindu*, 4 June 1931, Congress, 22 April 1930, p. 715, (MNR).
271. *Mathrubhumi*, 12 December 1930, p. 11 (MNR).
272. G.O. No. 952, Pub. (Confl.), 16 September 1931; *The Hindu*, 4 June 1931; *Navasakti*, 11 February 1931; Young India, 19 February 1931.
273. G.O. No. 2602, Law, 11 July 1932.
274. *Andhra Prabha*, 3 March 1931, p. 366 (MNR).
275. *Dravidian*, 12 January 1931, p. 127. (MNR)
276. USSF, 725, 10 March 1931; *The Hindu*, 19 May 1931.
277. *Kudi Arasu*, 7 April 1929.
278. *Indian Quarterly Register*, July-December 1929, p. 366; *Andhra Patrika*, 31 August 1929, p. 1263 (MNR).
279. *EINC*, 1930-35, Vol. X, p. 56.
280. *Indian Ladies Magazine*, October 1929, p. 144.
281. *Shri-Dharma*, May 1929, p. 302.
282. *Ibid.*, p. 303.
283. Tara Ali Baig, *Women of India*, p. 22.
284. *Ibid.*
285. G.O. No. 2414, L&M (Confl.), 17 June, 1930.
286. G.O. No. 785, Pub. (Confl.), 30 July 1931.
287. *Suthanthiraporil vada arcot mavattam*, (North Arcot District in Freedom Movement).
288. G.O. No. 952, Pub. (Confl.), 16 September 1931.
289. S. Ambujammal, naan kanda bharatham (The Bharat I have seen), p. 52.
290. *Stri-Dharma*, May 1930, pp. 303-304.
291. *Navasakti*, 10 September 1930.
292. G.O. Nos. 215-16, Pub., 2 March 1931; *Navasakti*, 20 July 1930.
293. Miss Slade alias Mira Behn was one among those from all over the world who were drawn to Gandhi's cause. She was the daughter of an English admiral Madeleine Slade. From the moment of her arrival at the Sabarmathi Ashram, she was known only as Mirabehn, the name conferred on her by Gandhi
294. G.O. Nos. 215-16, Pub., 2 March 1931.
295. S.Ranganathan, District Magistrate, Tirichirapalli, 5 January 1931, CDM 1930-31, p. 14.
296. USSF, No.699, G.1939.

297. *The Hindu*, 4 July 1930.
298. CDM, 1930-35 (SRRF).
299. *Azad Hind*, 17 September 1930, p. 1413 (MNR).
300. G.O. No. 363, Pub. (Jail, Confl.), 13 April 1931.
301. G.O. No. 450, Pub. (Confl.), 10 January 1931.
302. *Navasakti*, 31 December 1930; *Dravidian*, 2 December 1930. (MNR)
303. S.R. Bakshi, *Gandhi and Civil Disobedience Movement*. p. 101.
304. Instructions issued, D.O. No. 123, S, 8 April 1930 in the CDM, 1930-31, p. 34.
305. *RAMP*, 1929-30.
306. Ibid., 1930-31, p. 42; USSF No. 716, 6 November 1930.
307. *Young India*, 5 February 1931; *Indian Annual Register*, January-June 1930, p. 75.
308. *Indian Annual Register*, January - June 1930, p. 82.
309. G.O. No. 844, Pub., 6 June 1932.
310. *Dravidian*, 18 June 1931, p. 886. (MNR).
311. Ibid, 6 June 1931, p. 843 (MNR).
312. Interview with Meena Krishnaswamy, 12 August 1993 (at MTWU, Madras).
313. G.O. No. 558, Pub., 15 May 1931.
314. *Madurai Jilla thiyahigal malar* (Madurai District Martyrs Issue), p. 48.
315. *Stri-Dharma*, October 1931, p. 646.
316. FR, 2 May 1931.
317. *Sutandira Sangu*, 10 June 1931, p. 849 and 3 January 1932, p. 77. (MNR).
318. Report of the Women's India Association, 1936-37, 1937-38, pp. 29-33.
319. *Madurai Jilla thiyahigal malar*, p. 48.
320. B.S. Baliga, *Gazetteer of India, Madras, Madurai*, p. 81.
321. *Stri-Dharma*, 1932, p. 355.
322. Interview with Dalavai, a veteran freedom fighter on 12 August 1993 (at MTWU, Madras).
323. Interview with Srinivasan, husband of Sonabai, a veteran freedom fighter, Coimbatore, 10 October 1993.
324. *Madurai jilla thiyahigal malar*, pp. 48-50.
325. *Stri-Dharma*, 1930, p. 355.
326. Joanna Liddle and Rama Joshi, *Daughters of Independence*, p. 34.
327. FR, 22 August 1933.
328. G.O.No. 460, Pub., 5 May 1934; G.O. No. 409, Pub., 11 June 1934; *Indian Annual Register*, January-June 1934, p. 286; July- December 1934, p. 49.

329. *PMLC*, Vol. LXII, August 1932, p. 43.
330. *Stri-Dharma*, 1932, p. 297.
331. *PMLC*, Vol. LXI, March 1932, p. 113.
332. Interview with Srinivasan, husband of Sonabai, a veteran freedom fighter, Coimbatore, 10 October 1993.
333. G.O. No. 507, Pub., 15 June 1933.
334. *Stri-Dharma*, March-August 1932, p. 531.
335. *Sutandira Sangu*, 3 April 1933.
336. *Stri-Dharma*, November 1931, p. 27.
337. B.N. Pande(ed.) *A Centenary History of the Indian National Congress 1885-1985*, Vol. III, 1935-1947, pp. 407-8.
338. Saroja Sundararajan, *March to Freedom in Madras Presidency 1916-1947*, p. 575.
339. *Indian Express*, 9 December, 1940.
340. FR, 3 February, 25 Febuary, 4 March, 3 April, 18 May 1941.
341. PSPP, p. 38.
342. Mythily Sivaraman, "Remarkable Political Activist", *The Hindu* 29 March 1992.
343. FR, 3 February, 25 February, 4 March, 3 April, 18 May 1941.
344. *PSPP*, pp. 4-5; FR 3 February 1941.
345. *Indian Express*, 24 February 1941.
346. FR, 19 April 1941.
347. FR, 23 December 1941.
348. FR, 4 March 1942.
349. *Dinamani*, 17 August 1942.
350. *The Hindu*, 13 August 1942.
351. Ibid., 17 August 1942.
352. N.Narayanan Velu Pillai, *navayuga navamanigal*, (Nine women), p. 73.
353. Interview with Srinivasan, husband of Sonabai, veteran freedom fighter, Coimbatore, 10 October 1993.
354. FR, 8 March 1943; Ambujambal, "Manjubashini", in Butchi Arumugam, et.al., *Some Illustrious Women...*, p. 40.
355. FR, 21 August 1943.
356. ManmohanKaur, *Women in India's Freedom...*, p. 229.
357. Interview of Govindammal published in the *Ananda Vikandan*, 23 January 1994.
358. Ravindra Kumar, *The Selected works of Subhas Chandra Bose, 1936-1946*, Vol. II, p. 51.
359. *Ibid.*, p. 52.
360. Manmohankaur, *Women in India's Freedom...*, p. 229.
361. FR, 8 April 1946.

Four

Progress of Girls and Women's Education

After his Gettysburg oration some one asked Abraham Lincoln in which University he had his education "At my mother's knee" was his prompt reply.

"If a woman is educated the whole family is educated". But women's education was for ages conspicuous by its absence. The tradition of highly educated women in early times conserved in literature had become almost a thing of the past. The only class who seemed to have been taught to read was the dancing girls attached to the temples in South India and some Vaishnava women devotees of Bengal. Girls education on any adequate scale began only in the later part of the nineteenth century. It was the first legitimate offspring of feminism. The christian missionaries were the first to take interest in girls education. Public opinion had also started gathering momentum in favour of educating girls though the orthodox sections of the community opposed it.

Christian education for girls in South India began at Tranquebar in the early eighteenth century. Schools opened by German missionaries were attended by girls though few in number along with boys. The first Anglo-Indian girls school St. Mary's Charity school was opened in 1715 at Madras where thirty poor protestant children were educated with diet and education gratis.[1] Schools for Eurasians had long flourished in Madras. Before the close of the eighteenth century missionary education in Madras had obtained state aid and thus established the claims of private effort to the recognition of the state.[2]

After the passing of the Charter Act of 1813 many missionaries came to South India with their wives. Many educated unmarried women also came out as missionaries. At the renewal of the Charter Act in 1833, missionaries from other countries were also permitted to work in India. This had great influence in the development of education in general and girls education in particular. In 1832, Mrs.Drew from LMS Mission opened a girls school in Vepery, Madras from which the Bentinck school had developed. In 1841 Mrs. Braidwood of the Scottish Presbyterian mission began the education of three girls from high caste in Royapuram, Madras. In 1849, German Lutheran missionaries in Madras opened classes for girls in a church at Purasaiwalkam.[3] In 1821 Vepery School Committee opened a native girls school at Madras. S. Sathianadhan, stated that the most remarkable feature of the Vepery School was the large proportion of girls attending them.[4] The nine students at the school of the Free Church of Scottland in 1843 had increased to about 700 in 1854.[5] The girls educated in mission schools frequently belonged to christian or low caste families. It was Rev. John Anderson, the first Scottish Presbyterian missionary in Madras considered that the education of girls especially girls from high castes was more important than that of boys. He was the founder of the Madras Christian College School and was also the pioneer of higher education in the Madras Presidency.[6]

Next to Madras, Tirunelveli attracted the attention of the missionaries. James Hough of CMS mission opened twelve schools including three for girls in Tirunelveli in 1816. A girls school was opened at Palayamcottai in 1823 by Mrs. Rhenius of the same mission. The girls school at Nazareth became the first school for Indian girls to be recognised as a high school by the Madras Department of Public Instruction.[7] By 1854 there were probably 7000 girls at schools conducted by missionary societies and although bulk of these were native christians, there were also considerable proportion of Hindus.[8]

In most of these schools there were provisions for training in small scale industries like tape making, cloth making, mat weaving, rope making, sewing, basket making, knitting and gardening. Thus christian missionaries played a notable part in imparting education among girls in the Madras Presidency.

However attempts had also been made from time to time by the government and the public to improve the educational condition of girls. With a view to initiating educational reforms Sir Thomas Munroe, the then Governor of Madras started an educational enquiry. The report submitted by him in 1826 showed that out of the total population of 1,34,76,923 ; 1,84,110 boys and 4,540 girls were in attendance at about 12,000 schools.[9] All these girls were dancing girls.

With the exception of institutions run by European missionaries all existing schools were run and managed by the people themselves. After the enquiry, a few government schools were established although the number of their pupils was but small they served as useful models. Missionary schools had also been set up in many districts and were encouraged by the state.[10] Thus by 1850, a good foundation of education had been laid. However very little could be achieved in respect of female education till the publication of the Charles Wood's Despatch in 1854.

Education after 1854

The development of the education of girls and women from 1854 to the independence had been a long and difficult business. Indian educational policy was based on Charles Wood's Despatch of 1854. It was the first official proclamation pleading for the encouragement of women's education. It wanted the government to give women's education in India its "frank and cordial support". As a result many schools were started by both christian missionaries and Hindu reformers.[11]

After that schools for girls were included among those to which grants-in-aid were to be given. Recognised schools were inspected by government and received grants-in-aid. Mission schools came little by little to be incorporated into the educational system of the presidency as it was largely through them that the education of girls was promoted.[12] By 1859 there were fortyfour girls schools aided by government with 2,077 pupils and eighty girls schools unconnected with government with 4,906 pupils. Among them 107 were mission schools and five run by the natives and twelve by others.[13] The Indian Education Commission reported that in 1881 among the 1,57,49,588 women population of the Madras Presidency only 39,104 were under instruction. That is women under instruction was one in 403 and women who could read and write but not under instruction was one in 166.[14] The department figures indicate that the proportion of the actual school going population to every 1,000 of the population in 1881 was 12.6 boys and two girls.[15] Though the number of girls under instruction was still lamentably small, it was far satisfactory because during the decade ending March 1881 it rose to more than thrice.

Inspite of the recommendations of the Charles Wood's Despatch, some schools did not receive grants-in-aid. Unaided secondary schools for girls were confined to Madras and Bengal only. Thus girls education had made a certain amount of progress independently of the state and chiefly under missionary management many of which received aid from the government before 1881.

The Madras Government assumed direct responsibility for girls education only in 1881. In order to promote girls education effectively, the government in 1881 appointed Mrs. Isabel Brander, the first headmistress of the Presidency Training School as the Inspectress of Girls Schools in the Madras Presidency. She was the first woman Inspectress in India. From that date Madras had taken the lead among the provincial governments in the education of Indian girls.[16] Owing to her influence the number of girls under instruction in recognised schools in the presidency rose from 32,341 in 1881 to 1,04,988 in 1893.[17] Girls also joined boys schools. The presence of young girls in boys schools did no great violence to native feeling. In Madras alone it increased from 14,000 in 1881-82 to 22,000 in 1885-86. Of the increase in the number of girls nearly two-third were in the boys schools and only one-third in the girls schools proper.[18] Madras ranked highest in the census returns of 1881 among the provinces of India with regard to female education.

The Indian Education Commission (1882) recommended for aid all female schools or orphanages, whether on a religious basis or not, so far as they produced any secular results such as a knowledge of reading or writing. The conditions of aid to girls schools should be easier than to boys schools and the rates higher especially in the case of those established for poor or low caste girls. The standards of instruction for primary girls schools be simpler than those for boys schools and be drawn up with special references to the requirements of home life and to the occupations open to women. Special aids should be given wherever necessary to girls schools that make provision for boarders. Keeping in mind the condition of this country, the commission recommended for separate girls schools other than infant schools[19]

Matriculation education was imparted to women only from 1888. Until then no institution had begun to provide instruction for women in the matriculation course of the university. But a special examination called the Higher Examination for women was instituted with the object of carrying their education beyond the middle standard. Schools preparing their pupils for that examination were classed as high schools. In 1881-82, fiftyfive candidates presented themselves for the examination and twenty four passed. In 1884-85, sixty two candidates appeared for the examination from twentysix schools and twenty two passed.[20] A matriculation class was opened for the first time in the Female Normal School, Nazareth as early as 1888. Five girls were successful. To this school belonged the honour of having passed the first native women candidates. In the next few years other schools sent girls for the matriculation examination such as Sarah Tucker High School, Palayamcottai in 1890, the UPCSM Boarding School, Madras in 1892 and the London Mission Girls School, Madras in 1896. Women missionaries of the Scottish mission and the Arcot mission opened Day schools for high caste Hindu girls. They also grew in numbers and popularity. But only the exceptional girls went to high schools. The support while at school and in later life presented a serious problem for other girls. To solve that problem lace making classes were opened in Travancore, Tirunelveli and Tiruchirapalli followed by different industrial schools. These schools did much good in fostering a spirit of self help and industry.[21]

The need for women teachers became evident when girls education was first advocated and girls schools were started. So efforts were made to start training schools for women. The christian community was the first to desire its women to take up professional careers. The Christian Vernacular Education Society (1858) helped the training of women teachers in many ways. They opened a Teachers Training School at Dindigul where elementary school teachers were trained. In 1858, the Sarah Tucker Female School opened a department of training classes. In 1870 a training class was started inconnection with the day school managed by the Scottish mission in the city of Madras. In the same year a Government Female Normal School later known as the Presidency Training School was opened in Madras. By 1884-85, there were twelve training schools for mistresses with 291 students, all these schools were aided.[22] By 1892-93, the number of training schools for women in the Madras Presidency rose to seventeen with 342 pupils. Among them four were under government control. St. John's Female Training Institution, Nazareth and the Sarah Tucker Institution occupied prominent position.[23]

At first it was the christians and reformed Hindus sent their girls to schools. Muslims and other orthodox communities did not allow their girls to go to schools. Normally Muslim girls were taught in the zenanas by elderly women scholars or Muslim widows. They taught them recitation of Quran and the fundamental principles of Islam. That was an informal type which was imparted in the private houses. In order to impart formal education to such women side by side with the teaching given in Hindu Girls Day Schools, teaching was also given through the system of home education classes. The wives of the missionaries took the initiative in opening zenana classes for educating young women. They visited a number of houses for home teaching. In Madras alone in the year 1881 they visited 2,029 houses. The agencies which started education among Muslim girls were the National Indian Association, the Free Church Mission and the Church of England Zenana Mission. Among them the Madras branch of the National Indian Association alone availed of the government aid for home education. Others did not, probably for the reason that the rules were somewhat difficult to carryout. Hence rules were revised and made easier. This system was suited to the conditions and circumstances of the country and calculated to be of immense help to the progress of women.[24] However zenana education was not so extensively developed or apparently so much required as in some other provinces. May be because the seclusion of women of the better classes was less and it was easier for girls to obtain a considerable amount of education at school.[25]

The following table shows the per centage of pupils, literates and illiterates for each religion.

Religion	*Pupils*		*Literate*		*Illiterate*	
	Male	*Female*	*Male*	*Female*	*Male*	*Female*
Hindus	3.15	0.22	11.32	0.48	85.53	99.30
Muslims	4.22	0.59	14.04	1.04	81.74	98.37
Christians	7.43	5.63	17.96	7.12	74.61	89.25

Source: *Census of India, 1891*, Vol. XIII, *Madras*, p. 173.

As regards female literacy the christians were far ahead of other creeds. The Muslim females show the next best result at that time.

Although liberal encouragements had been offered, the response from Hindu and Muslim communities for the higher education of girls was discouraging. No Muslim or Hindu girl had matriculated at the Madras University in the nineteenth century.

On the whole there was an increase in the girl's education in the Madras Presidency by the turn of the twentieth century. It was 98,471 in 1892 and 1,16,747 in 1897 and it increased to 1,30,432 in 1902 and 1,64,706 in 1907. It is true that the increase of 34,274 between the years 1902 and 1907 was more than double comparing to the previous quinquennium, but hardly any Hindu or Muslim girls reached the high school stage.[26] Viewed by religion and in relation to the total population formal education of girls of all religions had increased, Hindu women by five per thousand Muslim women by three and Christian women by thirty two per thousand. As regards the total religious community, it was only Christian literate women were of appreciable account. They numbered 106 per thousand in contrast to the eleven per thousand of Hindus and Muslims. Women literates in general had increased at the rate of eighty one per thousand.[27] It is to be noted that there was a tremendous increase not only in the number of schools meant for girls, but also in their enrolment in the early twentieth century.

The following table clearly indicates the number of girls institutions and the girls enrolled.

Year	*No. of Girls Institutions*	*Girls enrolled*	*Total Girl Students*
1916	1,734	1,31,068	2,93,617
1921	2,556	1,71,831	3,58,402
1926	3,416	2,24,536	4,86,662

Source: Memoranda of the Administration of the Madras Presidency, p. 1206.

These progress had not been as satisfactory and as rapid as was desired. In 1916 the per centage of students reading in all classes to the total population was 3.1, it was only 3.4 in 1921 and 4.2 in 1926.

The per centage of boys and girls reading in all classes separately is given in the following table :

Year	*Boys*	*Girls*
1916	5.2	1.0
1921	5.5	1.2
1926	6.9	1.4

Source: *Memoranda ...*, p. 1206.

The table shows that the per centage of girls at schools increased very slowly indeed. It was one per cent in 1916 and in ten years it had increased only to 1.4 per cent.

It is noteworthy that the objection to the co-education of girls and boys gradually disappeared. It is evident from the fact that the number of girls reading in boys schools increased by 40.4 per cent as against an increase of only 14.7 per cent between 1916 and 1924 in girls schools.[28] The girls reading in boys elementary schools rose from 1,82,700 in 1921 to 2,81,317 in 1927 and that of girls studying in all grades of schools rose from 1,97,517 in 1922 to 2,98,632 in 1927.[29] But comparing to the education of the boys, the education of girls was very backward. This is due to the fact that, besides child marriage and indifferent attitude on the part of the parents, the educational facilities offered for girls were far from satisfactory. The result was that the girls lagged very much behind boys. Hence Women's India Association, continued to press for compulsory education and other facilities. It had its impact on the government policies. The Madras Elementary Education Act, 1920 inaugurated a new era in the history of elementary education. It made provisions for compulsory primary education. Added to that in 1921 dyarchy came in and education became a transferred subject passing into the hands of Indian provincial ministers responsible to the elected legislative councils. In the Madras Presidency the Justice Party formed Ministry in 1921.

The following measures were adopted to improve the education of girls. Between 1916 and 1926 girls were admitted into all classes of instructions and colleges at half rates of fees. A deputy directress of public instruction was appointed to correlate and direct all the activities of girls education. The inspecting agency for girls in all grades of institutions were largely increased and a woman specialist in physical training was appointed. Special scholarships were instituted for Hindu widows and the number of scholarships tenable by girls in college and primary schools were increased. The number of trained women teachers were increased and additional facilities were provided for the training of women teachers.[30] In 1924, an educational survey was conducted in the Madras Presidency and as a result a large number of schoolless centres were provided with schools. Between 1921 and 26, the government handed over the management of all government primary schools for girls except those in the agency tracts to local boards.[31] These local boards were not serious in introducing compulsory education but levied taxation for educational purposes.[32]

After the election in 1926 Swarajists took over the administration. S.Muthulakshmi Reddy became the Deputy speaker of the Madras Legislative Council. She did a lot for the uplift of women through the council. Through frequent interpellations in the council she urged the council to exempt poor girls from payment of school fees upto III standard. She also urged the government for the sanction of scholarships so as to enable the poor girls of all communities to have the benefit of higher education.[33] The Women's Charter of Reform passed on the Women's Day at Madras in 1927 demanded that compulsory primary education be provided for every one including Muslim girls.[34] As a result compulsory elementary education was introduced for everyone excluding Muslim girls in seven division of the corporation in the city of Madras in 1926-27.[35] In the next year it was extended to many areas. In the same year the government sanctioned the opening of 590 new elementary schools for girls in schoolless centres with a population of 2000 and above to improve the conditions of girls education.[36].

After discussing the general question of women's education at a conference of women in educational services, the government sanctioned the opening of five new training schools. With that the number of training schools for women rose to twenty one.[37] A Central Advisory Committee for Women's Education had been constituted and separate advisory committees had been formed for all the secondary schools.[38] In order to make women's education more effective, the Madras Government nominated Ms. J. Joseph from the Women's India Association as a representative for its newly formed Advisory Committee on Women's Education. Women's India Association also played a notable role in improving women's education.[39] The branches of the Women's India Association conducted schools and special classes at various places. By 1930 the scheme of compulsory primary education was implemented throughout the presidency.[40]

Inspite of the pressure from the Women's India Association, Muslim girls were excluded from the scheme of compulsory primary education because of the strict opposition from both the muslim public and the press.[41] Hence they were in the backward state and was a serious obstacle to the progress of that community. Muslim women did not attend the missionary schools because of the *purdah*. Hence S. Muthulakshmi Reddy demanded that a hostel should be constructed for the muslim women studying in the Hobart Training School, the only secondary school in the presidency for the Muslim women. For other women in *purdah* she wanted the government to provide with conveyance. All India Women's Conference also urged upon the desirability of extending the scheme of compulsory education to Muslim girls in Madras. Because of the continuous propaganda by the Women's India Association, Muslims themselves later started demanding the extension of compulsory education to them. The All India Muslim Conference also passed a resolution infavour of compulsory education.[42]

Women's India Association had given a number of scholarships from time to time to deserving girls for their higher courses of study in other institutions. The association had also instituted a fund towards the education of Adi-dravida girls. When the government ordered to withdraw fee concession and fee remissions to poor girls and to backward communities, the association, not only held a public meeting to protest against the order but also went on deputation to the Hon'ble Minister of Education and the Director of Public Insttruction and submitted a memorandum. As a result the order was repealed.[43]

Because of S. Muthulakshmi Reddy's involvement in women's education, she was selected by the government as a member of the Hartog Education Commission.[44] She was the only woman member of that committee. It reported,

> "Despite the growing increase in girls education the measures taken to promote it have been inadequate--- in the interest of the advance of Indian Education as a whole, priority should now be given to the claims of girls in every scheme of education".

It added that

> "until a system of infant classes staffed by trained women is established in India, education will remain unsound at its very foundation".[45]

The second point was not applicable to Madras because in Madras trained women teachers were available. But the facilities afforded for the girls education was too insufficient compared to the demand. It is surprising to note that in

Madras and Punjab in the quinquennium (1927-32) the per centage of girls enrolment was for the first time greater than that of the boys.[46] Philip Hartog reported that Madras led both in the per centage of girls at school and of trained women teachers.[47] There was a tremendous increase in the women's literacy in the Madras Presidency. It had been only 2.5 per cent in 1931 and it increased to 6.3 per cent in 1946 making an increase of 150 per cent. The desire for the education of girls was there and the demand augmented every year. For example the number of women and girls reading in all types of institutions for Indians in the year 1943-44 was 11,78,671, within a year it increased to 12,05,968.[48] The number of girls receiving instructions in elementary schools touched the figure of 11,51,186 in 1942 as against half a million two decades ago.[49]

The remarkable increase in the number of Hindu girls attending secondary schools had been in the part the result of the passing of the Sarda Act. There was a rush of girls into the primary schools for boys. It is because of the new system initiated in 1936 by requiring that in existing boys schools in areas where there was no girls schools twenty five per centage of the seats should be given to the girls of local areas and that in new boys schools in such areas at least a third of the strength should consist of girls.[50] The expansion in girls education had necessitated the opening of many new schools. Many convent schools had been opened by Roman Catholic nuns. As a result college education also gained momentum.

In the beginning there were no women graduate teachers in the schools and the burden of teaching and supervision fell on the women missionaries. In the 1940s in the majority of christian girls schools there were no women missionaries at all and the full responsibility rested on the Indian headmistresses and their Indian women colleagues. It was because of the rapid spread of higher education.

College Education

The 1890s marked the dawn of a new era in women's higher education in the Madras Presidency. Colleges were opened for women. As early as 1895 Tiruvelveli showed its leadership in girls education by opening the Sarah Tucker College by Miss. Askwith. The Sarah Tucker Institution, one of the earliest started in South India in 1858 for the education of women was raised to a second grade college and was affliated to the University of Madras in 1895.[51] After that small college departments were added to eight large secondary schools including the St. Marys Presentation Convent College at Madras.[52] In the year 1901 - 02, one woman obtained degree in the Madras University.[53] S.Muthulakshmi Reddy was refused admission in the Pudukottai Men's College. Then she apealed to His Highness, the Maharaja who was a westernised gentleman. He immediately passed an order that the girls who had passed matriculation should be given a chance for higher education and a trial of three months might be given as an experiment.

The years from 1911 to 1926 saw the birth of a number of women's colleges all over the country. In 1912, two intermediate colleges for Europeans were opened by catholic sisters in Madras. In 1914 Queen Marys College, the first government college for women was started in Madras. In the next year with the co-operation of six American and six British missionary societies, Women's Christian College, Madras was opened.[54] For a long time there was a limited demand for higher education that even those three colleges did not have sufficient number of students in them. In 1916, there were only 151 women students of whom fourteen were in medical colleges, by 1920-21 the total number of women scholars had increased to 330 including twenty five in medical colleges.[55] In 1921 the government started the Lady Willingdon Training College. It was here the Hindu widows were trained. In 1923 St. Christophers Training College was opened with the support of four British and four American missionary societies with twelve students.[56]

The following table indicates the number of students in the Arts colleges for Indian women in the Madras Presidency.

Sl. No.	*Women's Colleges*	*Strength in 1921-22*	*Strength in 1926-27*
1.	Queen Marys College for Women, Madras	178	178
2.	Women's Christian College, Madras	125	136
3.	Holycross College for Women, Teppakulam	-	14
4.	Sarah Tucker College, Palayamcottai	10	28
5.	St.Anns College for Women, Mangalore	22	60
	Total	335	416*

* There were besides seventy two women students were studying in Indian colleges intended for men.

Source: RPIMP, 1926 - 27 and for the quinquennium 1921-22 to 1926-27, Vol. II, p. 114.

In 1926 there were five arts colleges for women and two training colleges and the total number of scholars was 575 including forty six in medical colleges and forty one in training colleges. There was also a corresponding increase in the number of girls reading in colleges intended for men from thirty five in 1921 to seventy two in 1927.[57] Soon the necessity of a women's university was felt. S.Muthulakshmi Reddy in the Madras Legislative Council asked for a women's university on the lines of the women's university at Bombay.[58] It is significant to note that in the year 1933 - 34 among the ninety four Muslim students in the professional colleges, at least three were women.[59] In 1942 girls undergoing university courses numbered 210.[60] A remarkable number of women from depressed classes also attended the arts colleges. In 1944 - 45 Lady Hope Municipal College for women was opened at Guntur. With that the number of arts colleges for women became six.[61] There was an all round increase in the enrolment of students in colleges. In the professional colleges also the number of women scholars increased from 478 to 554 within a year from 1943-44 to 1944-45.[62] The process of building colleges for women went on so steadily that by 1947 there were seven arts colleges for women with the strength of 1,585 besides 1961 women attending men's colleges and there were seventy five women attending Sanskrit College.[63] In addition a considerable number of women studied in professional colleges also. The number of women who passed the examinations of the Madras University in 1927 was 358 and in 1947 it was 2,779. It increased nearly eight times with in two decades. Madras University had from the first been liberal in its attitude towards women, in admitting them to all courses of study and to seats on university bodies. Radhabai Subbarayan was elected as senator of the Madras University in open competition with men in 1925.[64] Mrs. Mona Hensman had been a nominated member of the Madras University Senate since 1930 and she had been elected four times in succession to the Syndicate of the university.[65] Many students from these colleges became teachers and girls schools were immensely strengthened by the presence of well educated women on the staff.

Professional Courses

A distinct trend towards specialised education besides general education was noticeable. Women joined medical and law colleges. Medical education for women was sought as early as the seventies and eighties of the nineteenth century, not so much to provide women with a medical career but to afford relief to the ailing women who could not consult men doctors. The system of seclusion had not only been a hindrance to women's freedom but it made them suffer a great deal when they were ill, for there were no women doctors to attend them. In fact it was this suffering that persuaded women to take to medical careers and their services became invaluable. Christian missionaries pioneered in introducing medical service to Indian women.

It is remarkable, a few progressive women were prepared to study with men to receive medical training in Madras. The Madras Medical College[66], had opened its portals to women as early as 1875, at a time when only one hospital, the Royal Free Hospital in London was prepared to give clinical instruction to women.[67] Even before that medical schools were thrown open to women in Madras. These medical schools were intended to give medical education below that which was required for a University degree.

Dr. Balfour, the Surgeon General of Madras advocated medical education for women in 1872. He proposed two courses, first a two years training programme at the Women and Children's Hospital and the second was a separate class for girls at the men's medical college. The Director of Public Instruction turned down the proposal thinking that it was entirely premature. However after a couple of years he brought up the question again and this time it was strongly supported by Dr. Furnell, the Principal of the Madras Medical College.[68] In 1875 the Government of Madras sanctioned the admission of women students in to the medical college. In the same year for the first time four women students of European and Anglo-Indian decent were admitted in the Madras Medical College. They were Ms. Mary Scharlieb, Ms. S. Mitchell, Miss. D. White and Miss. M. Beale. They would qualify for the degree of the Madras University or for a certificate subject themselves to a training at the college and at the hospitals for a period of three years, the first of which to be pre-collegiate and other two academic with clinical instruction at the hospitals.[69] Since the Bengal Government had not permitted the women to study medicine, two women Ellen D. Abreu and Abala Das who had passed the Fine Arts and the entrance examinations respectively joined the Madras Medical college in 1881 with the scholarships from the Bengal Government. Thus Madras became a pioneer in the medical education of women. Upto 1883 women students from Bengal who had passed the qualifying examination of the University but were nevertheless refused admission to Calcutta Medical College were compelled to pursue their medical studies in Madras. By the resolution of 2nd June 1883, women candidates were declared admissible to the Medical College of Calcutta provided they had duly passed the First Arts examination as required in the case of men. The following is the extract from the resolution: "the Lieutenant Governor learns to his regret that some Bengali ladies fully qualified by educational attainments for admission to the college have had to be taken themselves to the more liberal presidency of Madras, there to prosecute their medical studies from which the council of Calcutta Medical College had excluded them. The Lieutenant Governor therefore considers it his duty to support this movement, and he looks on the objections which have been made to it on the grounds of the difficulty of teaching mixed classes as unsubstantial and absolute. Experience gained in Europe, in America and in Madras has shown that mixed colleges can be taught without any bad results, while the aptitude of women for the study and profession of medicine is in his opinion no longer open to discussion or doubt." The Lieutenant Governor also sanctioned a special scholarship of Rs. 20/- per month tenable for five years, for all women candidates without restriction, who after passing the First Arts examination elected to join the Medical College. The Government of Bombay in May 1883 decided that a Class should be opened in the Grant Medical College at first for non-University women students and after the lapse of five years for those alone who had passed the licentiate examination. Upto 1884 - 85, in Madras and Bombay no native woman candidate had passed the entrance examination of the University nor was there any institution in which they could be taught to that standard.[70]

It is to be remembered that even before the Indian women began going to colleges for general education, medical classes were started for them. Miss Ramsbotham qualified for the work of a medical practitioner in the year 1883-84. In that year among the eighty eight medical students three were women.[71] In the following year there were five women students in the Madras Medical College, seventeen in the Grant Medical College in Bombay and three in the Calcutta Medical College.[72] A.M. Van Ingen, a student of the Madras Medical College passed the L.M.S. degree of the Madras University in 1885. She was the first woman graduate of the Madras University. Mrs. Scharliebs, one of the earliest students of the Madras Medical College, later became the first woman to take the M.D. degree of London University (1888) and the first woman to be appointed as physician in the Royal Free Hospital, London in 1902. Krupabai Sathianadhan was a student of the Madras Medical College. She was the first South Indian woman to join the Medical college. Though she stood first she had to discontinue her studies on account of her ill-health.[73] To encourage women to join medical course Countess Dufferin Fund was created. From that Fund, scholarships were given to eligible women. It was open to women of any nationality and it carried a monthly stipend of Rs. 25/- tenable for four years. The candidates had to produce certificates of age and qualification and satisfactory testimonial of character. The successful candidates were required to enter into an agreement to serve when qualified the boards for a term of five years. The Madras branch of the Countess Dufferin Fund Committee had the power to suspend or withdraw a scholarship if the holder of it misbehaved in any way or was likely to prove ineffective. In 1886 the Fund supported six women students in Madras Medical college eighteen in Bombay's Grant Medical College and three in Calcutta Medical College. Krupabai Sathianadhan Medical Scholarship was also instituted for women to perceive medical education.[74] This scholarship was open to women who were native of India other than Europeans or Eurasians who were desirous of qualifying for the medical profession in the Apothecary of higher grades. The amount of scholarship was Rs. 25/- per month tenable for a period of the course for which the candidate was selected. As a result gradually the strength of women in the medical colleges increased. By 1886, there were fifteen medical schools in India. Like the medical schools in the Madras Presidency, other medical schools were also thrown open to women before 1886[75]. In the school department of the Madras Medical College there were 308 students under instruction in the year 1893-94. Before the College Board of Examination eighteen students including twelve women appeared for the final examination and eleven students including six women appeared for the primary examination of the diploma of Apothecary and all passed. In the Medical college there were eighty two students in the M.B. & C.M. section and there were fortynine including five women in the L.M.S. section in the same year.[76] In the next year the students strength in the medical college fell from 82 to 72. Twenty including one woman student were in the M.B. & C.M section and thirty two including three women students were in the L.M.S. section. Nine students including a native christian woman obtained British diplomas.[77]

S. Muthulakshmi Reddy joined the Medical college in 1907. She was inspired by the photograph of two women dressed in the graduate gown appeared in magazine. She too longed to become a graduate. At that time there was no hostel for girls other than christian hostels and her parents were not prepared to admit her there. So they rented a house where she could stay and pursue her medical studies. She was a very good student and stood first in the exams and passed the M.B & C.M. the highest medical degree in 1912. She earned so many medals and honours that Col. Giffard, the famous gynic surgeon who presided over the college day celebration related that it was a red letter day in the annals of the Madras Medical College that a Hindu woman had taken the highest University medical degree with distinction, medals and honours.[78]

In the year 1908-9, there were 220 students under

instruction in the Madras Medical College. Among them thirteen were women. In the school department of the medical college there were at the close of the year fiftynine apothecary students including nineteen women.[79] In the year 1916 there were fourteen women students in the medical college, within five years in 1921, the number of women students in the medical college increased to twenty five and in 1923 it was thirty eight. It showed a gradual progress and in 1926 there were forty six women students in the medical colleges.[80] The Apothecary class for women students ceased from Ist July 1923 and a separate medical school for women was opened at Madras on Ist July 1923. A woman tutor was appointed in 1926 at the Madras Medical College to teach women students who were backward in their studies. L.M.S. degree was abolished in 1925.[81] In the year 1928 - 29, there were 161 women students in the medical schools and seventy four women in the medical college and nine women students appeared for examination and five passed.[82]

By 1945 Madras Medical College had on its rolls 1014 students of whom 788 including 194 women were in the MBBS course. In the year 1945, in the Stanley Medical College seventy two students were admitted, among them fifteen were women. In the same year, there were 346 students including forty four women studied in the schools of Indian Medicine.[83]

The first christian medical training school for women in South India was opened by Dr. Ida Sophia Scudder. The Christian Medical College and Hospital today is the outcome of the effort of this single woman. Born in 1870, Ida Sophia Scudder visited her missinary parents at Ranipet in South India in 1890. One eventful night she was asked to help three young women from different families struggling in difficult childbirth. Being without training at that time Ida herself could do nothing. She offered the help of her missionary father who was also a medical doctor. However to her amazement, the men responded saying "what! take a man into my house to care for my wife? It is better that she should die than another man should look upon her face". Custom prevented them from accepting the help of a male doctor. The next morning Ida found out that all the three women had died. Ida Sophia Scudder believed that it was a calling and a challenge set before her by God to begin a ministry to the health needs of the people of India, particularly women and children.

She went back to America, entered medical training and in 1899 graduated from Cornell University Medical College as one of the first group of women students. She specialised in obstetrics and gynecology and returned to India in 1900 and opened one bed clinic in her father's bungalow at Vellore. Women patients began to multiply everyday and over 5000 patients were treated in the year 1901. Then a new hospital for women and children with forty beds was opened in 1902 with the help of the generous donation of $ 10,000 offered by Mr. Schell, the president of the New York Metropolitan Bank in memery of his wife Mary Taber Schell. The hospital was named as Mary Tabel Schell hospital after the name of its donar.[84] Then she realised that the women of India themselves should be trained to help in medical works. She started a School of Nursing for women in 1909 which was upgraded to a College of Nursing in 1946.[85] In 1918 she founded at Vellore the medical school for women which was raised to MBBS standard in 1942 and became the great co-operative christian enterprise, the Christian Medical College, Vellore (CMC). In 1947, this exclusively women's college was thrown open to men students also.[86] Today CMC offers ninety recognised training programmes for both men and women in allied health, nursing and medical field.[87] In 1923 a separate medical school for women was opened at Madras.[88] Miss Mithan Tata d/o Herabai Tata (the first secretary of the Bombay branch of the Women's Media Association) was the first Indian woman barrister and was allowed to practice law.[89]

Inspite of the restriction that women could not practice

law, some women joined law colleges and secured degrees. During the quinquennium 1922-27, for the first time in India seven women came out as successful lawyers. Among them two were from Madras.[90]

Though girls' education made some progress it was not as much as it was needed or at the desired rate yet inspite of the fact that in addition to general educational institutions for both the sexes special institutions for women were being encouraged. It was because the money spent on girls education was far short of what was necessary. Regarding the expenditure on women's education it was only 17.2 per cent of the total expenditure on education.[91] The entire expenditure on education for boys and girls for the year 1931-32 amounted to 5.8 per cent of total expenditure of the government and from that amount the benefit to women was wholly insufficient for the needs.[92]

Indigenous Efforts to Promote Girls Education

Indigenous efforts to secure the education of girls had been seen not only in the increase in the number of girl students but also in the number of girls schools that had been opened under Hindu managements. Some of these schools charged fees and catered to well-to-do girls from middle class homes. Some such as the industrial side of the Madras Seva Sadan and the Sri Sarada Vidyalaya gave free board and lodging and instructions to widows and destitute women with the aim of training them to be teachers, nurses, midwives, matrons and health visitors.

The Madras Seva Sadan also promoted adult education among women and made them self-reliant and self supporting and thus enabling them to earn an honourable living. Resident students were given scholarship from the funds received from the public and from the Women's India Association. The classes were mostly vocational such as lace-making, embroidery, weaving and spinning. In 1927 articles worth about Rs. 2000 were made there. The teachers also gave them lessons in vernaculars, English, music and religion. In addition to the resident students, many grown up girls and women in the neighbourhood daily came and attended the classes. The Industrial Home for women located in Mylapore gave not only protection, free boarding and lodging to a number of widows and destitute women but also trained them in useful professions. They were also taught hand spinning and handweaving, embroidery, sewing, music etc. This institution was opened to all castes and creeds.[93]

Sister Subbulakshmi

Madras did not have at that time reformers of the stature of Ranade and Gokhale to advocate women's education or Indian women like Pandita Ramabai and Ramabai Ranade to open classes for girls and women, but in all parts of India there were Hindu men who longed to have their daughters educated and who were willing to face the disapproval of their families and friends inorder to make this possible. One such man was R.V. Subramania Iyer, father of Sister Subbulakshmi. Because of him she became a pioneer among the South Indian reformers who promoted women's education.

Contrary to the customs of those days, Sister Subbulakshmi, a child widow joined the college and passed her B.A in 1911 winning first class and made history for her name appeared in the newspapers as the first Hindu woman and a widow at that time to pass the B.A examination. She founded a widows home in 1913 which later became a teachers training college. The institution grew and there were more than 100 widows studying in it. Most of them passed S.S.L.C. and were trained as teachers and nurses. Many continued their studies in Queen Marys College and passed their B.A., M.A. and L.T. degrees and became lecturers, headmistresses, inspectresses of girls schools etc.[94]

For the older widows and deserted women, Sister started the Sarada Home in 1919 and later the Sarada Vidyalaya with its own training section and model school. Then she started the Sarada Ladies Club and a Reading Room in Mylapore. She also started two schools for fisherfolk one in Madras and the other in Cuddalore. The Kalanilayam was started for the older girls and married women to study for the S.S.L.C. privately.[95] In 1929 Sister with the help of the members of the ladies club opened a model elementary school at Triplicane attached to the Sarada Vidyalaya, where trained students could practice.

The widows who studied in these institutions in their turn spread her gospel and helped other unfortunate sisters to become educated and self supporting. This was an important event in the history of social reform as well as in the history of education in the Madras Presidency.

S. Muthulakshmi Reddy

S. Muthulakshmi as a representative of the Women's India Association periodically brought legislations in the Madras Legislative Council to promote women's education. Ever since its inception, the Women's India Association had been pressing for universal free and compulsory primary education. As a legislature and as the President of the Women's India Association she urged the government to sanction grants for the private philanthropic institutions such as Women's Home of Service manned by women to help destitute women and widows of over school age and to train them so as to enable them to earn their livelihood as vocational teachers, as nurses etc. In order to meet the expenditure of the Madras Seva Sadan[96] which engaged in training women in various crafts, S.Muthulakshmi Reddy moved a resolution recommending the government to sanction special and liberal grants to it.[97] Because of her efforts, the government sanctioned scholarships for Adi-dravida girls intended to be trained in the Industrial Home for Women, Mylapore. It not only gave protection, free boarding and lodging to a number of widows and destitute women but also trained them to useful professions. They were engaged in hand spinning, hand weaving, embroidery, sewing, music etc. Thus they were made self supporting and self-reliant.[98] Besides, she forced the government to extend compulsory primary education to everyone including Muslim girls.

Because of her efforts, Women's India Association launched an adult literacy campaign in 1939 and Mangalambigai Sadasiva Iyer, Ambujammal and Swarnamal took keen interest in the work.[99]

Curriculum

While there was a consensus of opinion among the social reformers for encouraging women's education, all were not agreed as to the type of education to be imparted to women. The general opinion prevailed was against English and western education. Western education developed sentimental feminity and false individuality that were averse to the cares and responsibilities of household duties. Hence both the public as well as the press were more worried over the gulf between the purely western atmosphere of the government and mission schools and the cultural background of the Indian homes.

The general opinion expressed by the press was that the curriculum should emphasis subjects of feminine interests. It should embrace subjects of study which supply informations useful to women in their several life relations. Besides religious and moral education, simple scientific education in the laws of sanitation, hygiene and simple medicine should be taught.[100]

> "... aggregate culture which is provided should represent what in our judgement marks a good housewife an enlightened woman and a friend of progress" said Hon'ble Justice Muthuswami Iyer of Madras.[101]

Even S. Muthulakshmi Reddy had the same opinion. Since the number of girls who took to profession such as teaching, medicine etc. were very small and the majority of girls were meant for home life, the education should be such as to enable them to look after their homes in a most efficient manner.[102] She was of the view that to encourage the education of girls there should be courses in domestic sciences and that girls should not be taught the same subjects as boys. She also advocated the use of the vernacular as the medium of instruction.[103] Various women's conferences had also expressed the same opinion. All India Women's Conference called upon all education departments throughout India to make home science, a compulsory subject in women's education.[104] Some were of the view that mere elementary knowledge of reading and writing was sufficient, some sought to include industrial training in the curriculum for women with a view to enable them to earn their livelihood if they so choose. V.S. Srinivasa Sastri refuted this narrow concept of women's education and said that men and women had to advance together not only in the direction of family life, but in all directions in which human endeavour was to be made for the further progress of the country.[105] O.P. Ramaswamy Reddiar, the Premier of Madras said that the education they receive should be a harmonious blending of all that is best in the old and the new in the East and the West. It should make every woman an ideal daughter, sister, wife and mother.[106]

The popular opinion was that though men and women should have equal rights in religion, social and political matters, it was essential that there should be some difference in the system of education devised for them. The curriculum prescribed for the girls should be much simpler than that for boys.

The main object of girls education was not only to train them for clerical service or to help them to obtain independent means of livelihood, but also to make them good wives and mothers and efficient home makers.

> Women have more feeling more imagination
> and a greater spirit of sacrifice than men.
> If men have sight, women have insight
> If men are rational, women are intuitive
> If men have learning women have wisdom.[107]

References

1. K. Nora Brockway, *A Larger Way for Women : Aspects of Christian Education for Girls in South India, 1872-1948*, p. 11.
2. *Report of the Indian Education Commission, February 1882*, p. 10. (hereafter RIEC).
3. K. Nora Brockway, *A Larger Way for Women...*, pp. 37-38.
4. S.Sathianadhan, *History of Education in the Madras Presidency*, Appendix-C, p. xvii.
5. *RIEC*, p. 11.
6. C.S.Srinivasachari, *History of the City of Madras*, p. 239.
7. K. Nora Brockway, *A Larger Way for Women...*, pp. 49-50.
8. *RIEC*, p. 11.
9. Sir Philip Hartog, *Some Aspects of Indian Education : Past and Present*, p. 60; *Manual of the Administration of the Madras Presidency*, Vol. I, p. 490; B.S.Baliga, *Studies in Madras Administration*, Vol. II, p. 63.
10. *RIEC*, pp. 9-11.
11. S. Sridevi, *A Century of Indian Womanhood*, p. 72.
12. K. Nora Brockway, *A Larger Way for Women...*, p. 69.
13. *Selections from Educational Records*, Vol. I, *Educational Reports*, 1859-71, p. 89.
14. *RIEC*, Part - II, p. 523; *The Women of India and what can be done for them*, p. 20.
15. *Report of the Public Instruction of the Madras Presidency* 1881-82, p. 15 (Hereafter RPIMP); B.S. Baliga, *Studies in the Madras Administration*, Vol. II, p. 65.
16. *RIEC*, part II, P. 523.
17. S.Sathianadhan, *History of Education ...*, p. 223.
18. *The Women of India ...*, pp. 35-36.
19. *RIEC*, part II, p. 523.
20. *Review of Education in India in 1886 with special reference to the Report of the Education Commission*, p. 80.
21. K. Nora Brockway, *A Larger Way for Women ...* p. 80.
22. *Review of Education in India...*, p. 240.
23. *RPIMP, 1892-93*, p. 35.
24. *Ibid.*, 1883-84, p. 93.
25. *RIEC*, part II, p. 523.
26. *Progress of Education in India 1897-1902*, Vol. I, pp. 301-19.
27. *Census of India, 1911, Vol. XII, Madras*, part I, p. 120.
28. *Memoranda of the Administration of the Madras Presidency*, p. 1206.
29. *Ibid.*, p. 1164.
30. *Ibid.*, p. 1207.

31. *Ibid.*, pp. 1164, 1207.
32. *RAMP*, 1926-27, pp. 199-200.
33. S.Muthulakshmi Reddy, *My Experience as a Legislature*, pp. 65-66.
34. *Stri-Dharma*, January - March 1928, p. 38.
35. *RAMP , 1926-27 and for the quinquennium* , 1921 - 1922 to 1926-27, Vol. 1, p. 78.
36. *RAMP*, 1927-28, p. 1.
37. *Ibid.*, p. 182 ; 1926-27 p. 111.
38. *Ibid.*, 1928-29, p. 184.
39. *Ibid.*, 1929-30, p. 11.
40. *Stri-Dharma*, June 1930, p. 356.
41. *Azad Hind and Quami Report* opposed it by saying that women should not be made victims of any compulsory laws. Instead they advised home education by Muslim female teachers. (*Azad Hind*, 29 and 30 Nov. 1924, p. 1560; *Quami Report* 30 Nov. 1924 and 1 and 2 Dec. 1924, p. 1560 (MNR) *Mukhbiri Deccan* supported the scheme and requested the opponents to remove the defects if any in the proposed scheme and benefit by the example of sister communities *(Mukhbir-I Deccan* 10 Dec. 1924, p. 7 (MNR).
42. S.Muthulakshmi Reddy, *My Experience...*, p. 89.
43. *Report of Women's India Association, 1936-37 and 1936-38*, p. 10.
44. *Stri-Dharma*, June 1930, p. 356.
45. Philip Hartog, *Some Aspects...*, p. 57.
46. *Swarajya*, 12 January 1931, p. 61 (MNR).
47. Philip Hartog, *Some Aspects...*, p. 55-56.
48. G.O.No. 258, Education and Public Health, 6 February 1946; *RAMP*, 1944-45, p. 145.
49. *RPIMP*, 1942-43, p. 32.
50. S.Y. Krishnaswami, *Rural Problems in Madras*, p. 406.
51. *History of Higher Education in South India*, Vol. II, *Madras University*, 1857- 1957, p. 79.
52. S.Sridevi, *A Century of Indian Womanhood*, p. 77.
53. *Progress of Education in India*, 1897 - 1902, Vol. I, p. 301.
54. K. Nora Brockway, *A Larger Way for Women...*, p. 116.
55. *Memoranda.....*, p. 1206.
56. *RPIMP*, 1923 - 24, p. 24.
57. *RPIMP, 1926 - 27 and for the quinquennium 1921-22 to 1926-27*, vol.II, p. 114.
58. S. Muthulakshmi Reddy, *My Experience...*, p. 126 (Smt Nathibai Damodar Thackersay Indian Women's University popularly known as SNDT Women's University was established in 1916).
59. *RAMP, 1933 - 34*, p. 172.

60. S.Y. Krishna Swami, *Rural Problems...*, p. 400.
61. *RAMP*, 1944 - 45, pp. 145 - 46.
62. G.O. No. 258, Education and Public Health, 6 February 1946; *RPIMP*, 1944 - 45, p. 12.
63. *RAMP*, 1946 - 47, p. 1-69.
64. *Women's India Association Golden Jubilee...*, p. 4.
65. K. Nora Brockway, *A Larger Way for Women...*, pp. 130 - 132.
66. The Madras Medical College was founded as a Medical School by the Rt. Hon. Sir, Fredrick Adam K.C.B. in July 1835. It was started with ten medical apprentices and eleven Indian medical pupils in a temporary room. In the year 1850 it become Madras Medical College.
67. K. Nora Brockway, *A Larger Way for Women...*, p. 77.
68. S. Sridevi, *A Century of Indian Womanhood*, p. 77.
69. *Madras Medical College session, 1875 - 76*, p. 11.
70. Review of Education in India in 1886.., p. 44; *Asylum Press Almanac*, 1898, pp. 1080, 1089.
71. RPIMP, 1883-84, pp. 58, 87.
72. Review of the Education in India in 1886, p. 44.
73. K.Nora Brockway, *A Larger Way for Women..*, p. 78.
74. *Asylum Press Almanac*, 1898, pp. 1080, 1089.
75. *Review of Education in India in 1886*, pp 83-84.
76. *RPIMP*, 893-94, p. 53.
77. Ibid., 1849 - 95, p. 37.
78. Padma Seth, "A Farsighted Educationist" in Aparna Basu (ed.) *Dr. Muthulakshmi Reddy: The Path finder*, pp 45-46.
79. RAMP, 1908-9, pp. 20, 91-92.
80. *Memoranda...*, Vol. V, pp. 1206-7; *RPIMP*, 1923 - 24, p. 23.
81. *Memoranda...*, p. 509; *RPIMP, 1926-27, and for the quinquennium 1921-22 to 1926-27*, p. 49.
82. *RPIMP. ..*, 1928-29, pp. 57, 61.
83. *Madras in 1945*, pp. 33 - 36.
84. D. Kothandaraman "Christian Contribution to the Development of Medical Care Infrastructural Facilities in Vellore District" in *Socio-Economic History of the Vellore District*, p. 180.
85. *The Official Guide to the Christian Medical College and Hospital, Vellore, India*. p. 3.
86. K. Nora Brockway, *A Larger Way for Women..*, p. 77.
87. *The Official Guide....*, p. 3.
88. *RPIMP, 1926-27 and for the quinquennium 1921-22 to 1926-27*, Vol. I, p. 49.
89. *Women's India Association Golden Jubilee...*, p. 3.

90. *Ibid.*, p. 6; S. Sridevi, *A Century of Indian Womanhood*, pp. 108-09.
91. S. Muthulakshmi Reddy, *My Experience...*, p. 123.
92. *RAMP, 1931-32*, p. 48.
93. S.Muthulakshmi Reddy, *My Experience ....*, pp. 81-82.
94. Santha Sundari, "Sister Subbulakshmi" in Butchi Arumugam et.al., *Some Illustrious Women in India...*, p. 82.
95. *Ibid.*, p. 83; Lalitha Chandra Sekhar, "Sister Subbulakshmi" in *Women's India Association Golden Jubilee...*, (Appendix).
96. Madras Seva Sadan was started in 1923 by the Women's India Association to promote adult education among women and also to make them self reliant and self supporting and thus enabling them to earn an honourable living (*Stri-Dharma*, September 1929, p. 490).
97. *Stri-Dharma*, September 1929, p. 100; S.Muthulakshmi Reddy, *My Experience...* pp. 77-78.
98. S. Muthulakshmi Reddy, *My Experience...*, pp. 81-82.
99. *Women's India Association Golden Jubilee...*, p. 9.
100. *Dravida Patrika*, 2 January 1918, p. 27 ; *Desabhaktan*, 17 November 1920, p. 1375 ; *Navasaki*, 26 November 1920, p. 1388 ; *Tamilnadu*, 14 October 1923, p. 1320 (MNR).
101. *The Women of India...*, p. 26.
102. S. Muthulakshmi Reddy, *My experience....*, p. 126.
103. Padma Seth, "A Farsighted Educationist" ion Aparna Basu (ed.) *Dr.Muthulakshmi Reddy: The Path finder*, p. 45.
104. *Stri-Dharma*, November 1931, p. 25.
105. *Indian Quarterly Register*, Vol. I, January - June 1929, p. 422.
106. *Madras Information*, January 1949.
107. *Ibid.*

Five

Movement for Social Reform

An important aspect of the women's movement was the agitation against certain social customs and practices which stood in the way of the advancement of women. Some of them were child marriage, *devadasi* system and prostitution. They were the worst systems which ruined the life of the women in the state. As the educated Indians came to be acquainted with European liberalism, they were inspired to reflect upon their own value system and to examine the inequalities, injustices and oppression of their own culture. This introspection stimulated a strong movement for social reform. The removal of evil practices and customs that led to suffering for women figured prominently in the agenda for social reform. The lead given by men in the nineteenth century was taken up by women in the early part of twentieth century. Women's India Association united all the enlightened women and inspired them to fight for progressive social legislations abolishing these evils.

Abolition of Child Marriage

Among the numerous customs prevalent in India, early marriage was the worst of all. This practice was institutionalised by the Hindu society for several centuries. It stroke at the root of all development, physical, intellectual and spiritual and destroyed the individuality of the women of the country. Associated with early marriage was other evils of early maternity, frequent maternity, premature motherhood, maternal and infantile mortality and the saddest consequence of all was the large number of virgin widows, who for no fault of their own were made to undergo many hardships in society. It was also responsible for the large per centage of illiteracy and the slow spread of higher education among Indian women. It was not only very harmful to the health and happiness of our young children, but it was also a sad commentary on our civilisation. Such severe handicaps no doubt undermined our society and retarded its progress.

The Government legislation to improve the situation of minor girls resulted in the first Age of Consent Bill passed in 1860 which made sexual intercourse with a girl less than ten years a rape. In 1891 the government passed an amendment raising the age of consent to twelve in both marital and extra-marital cases. It was done to protect female children from immature prostitution and from premature cohabitation.[1]

Madras was one of the provinces where the custom of early marriage was prevalent only among certain castes. It was less among the Tamil people whom the Dravidian influence had been dominant than the Telugu population. Marriage before maturity and perpetual widowhood were the institutions foreign to the Dravidian races. This was abundantly proved by the statistics for the hill tribes and such castes as the Kallan, Maravan, Shanan, Pallan, Paraiyan, Vellala as well as the principal castes of Malabar. Among the bulk of these castes, the marriage relations was originally a very loose one and it developed into polyandry and freedom of divorce. Among the Telugus the dissolution of the marriage tie was generally much more difficult, this shows the greater influence of brahmanical customs there rather than any original divergence of practice.[2] Among the Kallars of Tanjore divorced women were not outcasted, such women could contract honorable marriage. Sometimes a woman having many children was allowed to seek a second husband on condition of paying the first husband her marriage expenses.[3] Among the Idayars (Shepherd Castes) in some districts widows were married by the husband's brothers. Potter caste (Cusavar) also allowed their widows to marry. Teeyars of Kerala sometimes had one wife between several brothers and plurality of wives and divorce were common among them. Paraiya castes married at any age and widows were permitted to marry and concubinage of widows were common. Weaving castes, (3.44 per cent) sanctioned widow marriage and concubinage of widows.[4] Though the child marriage, denial of widow marriage and divorce were generally regarded as a characteristic of the Brahmins, certain sections of the non-Brahmin Hindus in course of time imitated these customs.

THE DISTRIBUTION OF AGE OF 10,000 MARRIED WOMEN AND 10,000 WIDOWS IN TYPICAL CASTES IN THE YEAR 1891

Caste	*10,000 Married Women*				*10,000 Widows*			
	0-9	*10-14*	*15-39*	*40 & above*	*0-9*	*10-14*	*15-39*	*40 & above*
1	2	3	4	5	6	7	8	9
Tamil Castes								
Brahmins	387	1525	6383	1705	21	108	2926	6951
Kallan	61	204	7734	2001	5	5	2044	7945
Maravan	57	164	7604	2172	5	7	1837	8151
Vellala	62	280	7646	2003	5	12	2554	7429
Pallavan	50	175	7709	2066	5	7	1923	8964
Palli	93	350	7868	1680	7	12	2244	7737
Paraiyan	80	332	7756	1832	5	13	2304	7678
Shanan	52	186	7715	2047	5	7	2475	7515
Telugu Castes								
Velama	1055	1444	6101	1406	83	111	2641	7165
Kalingi	1197	1667	5792	1344	125	263	2770	6842
Kapu	458	934	7136	1472	23	69	2926	6982
Mala	326	828	7324	1522	25	62	2723	7190
Komati	514	1550	6315	1621	23	118	3192	6667
Kamsala	621	1409	6373	1597	34	140	3342	6484
Mangala	474	1049	6956	1527	30	35	3064	6821
Tsakala	489	1012	6986	1513	20	75	2993	6972
Madiga	369	841	7350	1440	21	66	3017	6896
Malayalam Castes								
Nayar	14	361	7941	1684	3	6	1771	8230
Cheruman	14	282	8008	1696	11	3	1936	8050
Tiyan	19	351	8056	1574	5	9	2019	7967
Mappilla	27	354	8127	1499	9	16	2340	7635

Source: *Census of India, 1891, Vol. XIII, Madras*, p. 150.

The table indicates that among the Tamils, the Brahmins had the highest number of child marriage and naturally child widows. For the whole presidency the average proportion of Brahmins was only 3.94 per cent of the Hindu population.[5] The widows of Brahmins were not permitted to remarry nor was concubinage tolerated as a caste practice. Their marriage system required that every girl should be married before puberty, prohibited the remarriage of widows and allowed dissolution of marriage only on the ground of adultery of the wife. This system though differing so essentially from that of the Dravidians had been adopted in its entirety by many Telugu and a few other castes, and there was hardly a caste or tribe in which its influence had not been felt to some extent. If some members of the inferior castes became wealthy they at once endeavoured to obtain the services of the Brahmin priests and to introduce their customs into their families. A sub-division of these castes in which these customs were enforced and the whole caste was in time affected to a greater or lesser extent. In nearly every considerable caste there was some sub-divisions which enforced the marriage of girls before puberty and prohibited the marriage of widows.[6] The artisan castes who constituted 2.98 per cent of the Hindu population and the accountant castes (0.37 per cent) never tolerated widow marriage or concubinage.[7] The Kapus, a non-Brahmin caste had the highest per centage of girls married below the age of five in the whole of India. Among them for every 1000 girls, fifty girls were married below five and 338 were in between five and twelve. In the Madras Presidency among every 1000 girls, 177 Komatis, sixty two Tamil Brahmins, 220 Telugu Brahmins, thirty eight Adi-dravidas were married between the age of five and twelve.[8] In India as per the Census Report of 1921 there were 218,463 girls married under the age of five, and 20,16,687 between the ages of five and ten and 63,30,207 betwen ages of ten and fifteen.[9]

In the Bengal Presidency out of every 1000 Hindu girls

between five and nine years of age, 271 were married and eleven were widows.[10] The all India average of girls affected by early marriage was 42.2 per cent. Among the Hindus the average child marriage was 48.4 per cent and Muslims 37 per cent. In the Madras Presidency it was 24.3 per cent, with Hindus 26.7 per cent and Muslims 22 per cent. The per centage was high at Central Provinces and Berar with an average of 56.9 per cent. Among them 62.8 per cent were Hindus and 31.8 per cent were Muslims. Comparing with the Hindus, child marriage was less among Muslims.[11] Because of the child marriage, there were lot of child widows. During that time there were 612 Hindu widows who were babies not even one year old and a total of 12,016 widows were under five years of age. The number of Hindu widows between five and ten years of age were 85,580, and those between ten and fifteen years were 2,33,533. The total number of widows under ten were 97,596 and under fifteen were 3,31,129. Majority of the child widows were prevented by Hindu customs and usage from remarrying.[12]

The abolition of child marriage had been advocated both in the press and on the public platforms from the nineteenth century. Many Brahmins of the Madras Presidency had also shown desire for reform. In 1903 they started a special association called the Hindu Marriage Reform League at Madras with branches all over to promote post-puberty marriage.[13] In order to discuss the question of post-puberty marriages, conferences were convened by pandits in April 1912 at Kancheepuram and in December 1912 at Tiruvadu. There the opinions of the pandits were taken. Many pandits said that the sastras permitted post-puberty marriages under certain circumstances for a period of three or four years after puberty. Only a few pandits said that the sastras prohibited post-puberty marriages.[14] In 1913, Annie Besant arranged a lecture on the evils of child marriage given by the Justice T.Sadasiva Iyer. He emphasised that the father had no right to give his daughter in marriage till the girl completed her sixteen years and no male could marry before he completed his studies. Marriages should take place after the puberty of the bride and should legally take place only then, though conditional gift by the father might take place before. Till consummation, the bride and bridegroom would not become united in *gotras, pinda* and *sutaka,* and hence there was no real widowhood of the bride, if the bridegroom happened to die before consummation , just after mere oral gift of the bride by her father. He submitted that the future of India as a nation depended on the abolition of child marriage amongst the people.[15] Because of all these efforts, people became aware of the evils of child marriage. Still the orthodox sections cling to the view that a Brahmin would be acting irreligiously if he did not marry his daughters before puberty. They declared that post-puberty marriages were invalid and children born to them became illegitimate. In the case of non-Brahmins there was no question as to the legality of post-puberty marriages and many of them conducted such marriages only.

In order to validate post-puberty marriages among Brahmins, V.S. Srinivasa Sastri introduced a bill known as Hindu Post Puberty Marriage Bill in 1914 in the Madras Legislature. The bill was circulated among the leading personalities and important officials. Majority of the Brahmins opposed the bill on the ground that pre-puberty marriages would only increase the number of virgin widows. But post-puberty marriages would increase the number of unmarried girls who would never get married at all. Since the agitation against the bill was so great that the measure was finally withdrawn.[16] One of the objectives of the Women's India Association was to put a stop to the practice of child marriage. Periodically it organised meetings in different parts of the country and urged the government and legislatures to enact laws to eradicate this evil. In 1924 Women's India Association and its branches together sent a memorandum supporting Sir

Hari Singh Gour's legislative attempt in the Imperial Legislative Council to raise the age of consent for girls to fourteen within marital relations and fifteen outside. Along with Women's India Association, Women Graduate Association and the Seva Sadans of Madras supported the bill. Both Tamil and Telugu papers wrote articles strongly in praise of the bill.[17] But the government did not support it though the whole assembly was in favour of it.

In the next year itself Sir Hari Singh Gour decided to bring the bill under the better title 'Children Protection Bill'. It was designed to absolutely protect infants below thirteen years, protect them against strangers upto the age of fifteen, and to protect the girl wife against her husband's injurious approaches upto the age of fourteen. The bill extended the definition of rape to girls not exceeding thirteen years of age. Sexual intercourse with a girl below fifteen was made punishable in the case of strangers with imprisonment upto two years with or without a fine and sexual intercourse by a husband with a wife below fourteen was punishable with one year imprisonment with or without fine. It aimed at protecting girls against unlawful intercourse even by their husbands. When the news of the proposed bill reached, leading women of Madras under Mangalambigai arranged a meeting to support the bill. Even the Women's India Association brought the matter to the notice of the international organisations such as World Young Women's Christian Association and the International Suffrage Alliance.[18] This time though the orthodox members opposed the bill, the government passed an amendment in the Indian Penal Code raising the age of consent within marriage to thirteen and outside to fourteen.[19]

Women did not stop with that, they demanded that the age of consent should be raised to sixteen. Even the Women's India Association passed a resolution to that effect.[20] Again in 1927, Sir Hari Singh Gour brought forward an amendment raising the age of consent within marital relations to fifteen and outside to sixteen. The whole assembly was in favour of it, but the government thought it better to consult the people of India and a committee of enquiry was promised. Because of the series of efforts, the government constituted a committee of enquiry called 'the Age of Consent Committee' under Sir Morepant Vishvanath Joshi in 1928 to seek public opinion. On behalf of all the women's associations Ms.Brijlal Nehru was chosen as one of its members.[21] The work of the committee attracted the largest attention in the Madras Presidency and more than 300 out of about 1200 written statements received by them were from the Madras Presidency. Nearly fifty out of eighty witnesses examined by the committee were Brahmins. But contrary to their expectation, the Brahmins in Madras supported post-puberty marriages. Pre-puberty consummations were not common in this province. The practice of consummation soon after puberty was however extensively prevalent among them. Mantha Suryanarayana, a Brahmin and the former member of the Madras Legislative Council stated that, 'garbhadhan' ceremony was performed among Brahmins and Vaisyas on the fourth day after puberty as was the rule, and marriage was consummated that night.[22]

The enquiry of the committee revealed that there were three opinions prevailed in the Madras Presidency regarding child marriage. The first category consisted of orthodox people who did not want any age limit fixed for marriage. They held that marriage should be performed before puberty and consummation might be postponed. According to them the sastras should not be violated at any cost. The second category was the people who were already performing marriages after puberty and they therefore felt that it was unfair to cast a doubt on the legality of such marriages. But the fact was that the attainment of puberty was not revealed in such cases.[23]

There was a large group of Brahmin witnesses who felt that a marriage law was essential and that the age of consent should be advanced. Women's organisations also expressed similar opinion. But most of them especially Sister Subbulakshmi and Mangalambigai advocated sixteen as the minimum age of marriage for girls whereas a group of Brahmin women under Srirangamma had given a pathetic account of the conditions of girl wives and advocated eighteen as the minimum age of marriage.[24] Evidences given proved that majority of the Hindus in the Madras Presidency wanted to fix the minimum age for marriage. As far as Muslim community was concerned they did not want to apply marriage law to them, since this evil was not much prevalent among them and there were definite rules in their religious books governing marriage, divorce and succession.[25]

After analysing all these opinions, the committee made two recommendations; (1) The age of consent within and outside marriage be raised to fifteen and eighteen respectively. Sexual relation below that age be made a cognisable offence; (2) Inorder to deal most effectively with the evil of early marriage and early consummation, law should be enacted fixing the minimum age of marriage of girls at fourteen years.[26] It was a remarkably courageous and convincing document. But various women's organisations in Tamil Nadu demanded that the age of consent for girls should be raised to sixteen and nineteen within and outside marital relations.[27].

Rao Bahadur Harbilas Sarda introduced 'the Hindu Child Marriage Bill' in the Legislative Assembly in September 1927 proposing to make the marriage of a Hindu girl under twelve and a Hindu boy under fifteen invalid. The primary object of the bill was to put a stop to child widows. The bill was first sent to ascertain public opinion and then referred to a select committee.[28] Though the women's organisations in Tamilnadu supported Sarda bill, they demanded that the marriage of girls and boys be raised to sixteen and twenty one respectively. They said, "nothing short of these ages will satisfy us. We ask our friends not to advertise to the whole world that India thinks twelve the right age at which the girls should be married.

We appeal to them not to strengthen the present evil of child marriage by giving ratification and honour to this age of twelve for girls just as this time when those very same social reformers are striving to raise the age of consent to fourteen and sixteen. In the light of the public opinion the select committee amended Sarda bill raising the marriage age of girls and boys to fourteen and eighteen respectively.[29] The Women's organisations in Tamil Nadu appealed to the Viceroy and the members of the Legislative Assembly to enact the measures into law and requested the Viceroy to nominate Ms. Rameshwari Nehru and Mrs. Hamid Ali, on behalf of them to participate in the discussion of the Sarda bill in the Assembly.[30]

S. Muthulakshmi Reddy also sought permission from the Government of India to introduce her bill in the Madras Legislative Council for the prevention of child marriage of girls below fourteen years and boys below eighteen years. Supporting S. Muthulakshmi Reddy's attempt for the abolition of child marriage, Dr. Ida Sophia Scudder of Vellore wrote that she had many disastrous results of child marriage and said "I would probably have never studied medicine and would not have come back to India had it not been for three child wives, none of them over fourteen who died during one night. I was powerless to help ... another girl of thirteen or fourteen came to me to be repaired for vesico vaginal fistula. She was like an innocent child and found it hard to understand what had happened to her". It was because of child marriage. Dr.Kugler, a woman who had spent forty five years of medical service wrote "It was in 1883 that I first arrived in India and my work as a physician among the women and children has afforded me very many opportunities of seeing the evils resulting from child marriage. I have often operated upon child mothers who have been seriously injured in child birth and I have seen many young mothers so injured that they could not again function as wives... I could give many instances that I have seen of the deletratious effect of child marriage and enforced widowhood. I could also write much of the terrible infant mortality that makes India occupy so low a position in the health records of the world... My own conviction is that if India is to develop she must have the courage of her conviction and be prepared to suffer for the carrying of them into effect".[31] The government replied her to S. Muthulakshmi Reddy to wait for the finalisation of Sarda bill. Then she constantly organised meetings of women both in the city and outside and also wrote articles in the press in favour of Sarda bill. Inorder to get the support of the local council members for the Sarda bill in the assembly, she drafted a child marriage resolution signed by a number of Brahmin and non-Brahmin members and moved in the Madras Legislative Council recommending the government of Madras to communicate to the Government of India the opinion of the Madras Legislative Council to raise the marriageable age of boys and girls to atleast twenty one years and sixteen years respectively. She said "if we want to grow into a strong, robust and a self respecting nation, if we want to reach our full physical and mental height the system of child marriage must go because science and experienced observation tell us that a girl becomes a woman only after the age of sixteen and a boy his manhood only after twenty one years".[32]

Apart from the Government, the ex-Minister Sir A.P. Patro spoke strongly against it, whereas many members spoke supporting the motion. Justifying her attempt S. Muthulakshmi Reddy pointed out that the child marriage evil was more serious and urgent than the other evils such as *sati* and infanticide (for which the government had already enacted measures to stop them) because it involved life long suffering as a child wife, child mother and very often as a child widow. It also affected the health and happiness of millions of Indian girls and thereby the future race. Therefore she appealed to all sections of the house to support that motion to save millions of our girls from a life of premature wifehood, premature motherhood and enforced widowhood. The motion was put to the House and declared carried. It was then communicated to the Government of India.[33] All the women's associations sent a joint memorandum and appeal to the Viceroy and the members of the assembly requesting to pass the bill into law.[34] They pointed out in the memorandum, "We see the suffering caused by the injustice of binding two young children in a bond which even death does not break. What right have the elders to deprive the boys and girls of their freedom and happy days of carefree childhood? Why ruin their health? Why not give opportunities to educate them? Why burden their young shoulders with responsibilities of family life of bearing children when they themselves are in need of being cared for by their parents".[35] The educated and enlightened women of all communities unanimously agreed on the urgent need for legislation to prevent child marriage. But the orthodox centres like Tiruchirapalli and Tanjore expressed strong opposition to the bill. Agitations were held and conferences were convened by the Brahmins to condemn the bill.[36]

The bill when it was sent out for eliciting public opinion was warmly received in the country and the total number of opinion received amounted to 167. Among them 128 being infavour of the bill. The bill though backed by opinions outside could not get the support of those in the legislative assembly. Mr. Acharya's amendment to postpone the consideration of the bill till the report of the Age of Consent Committee became available was carried by fifty three to thirty four votes amidst cries of "Shame, Shame".[37] After the Age of Consent Committee report was submitted, Rao Bahadur Harbilas Sarda again introduced the bill and was passed by sixty seven to fourteen votes on 1st October 1929.[38] It was called the 'Child Marriage Restraint Act'. It prohibited the marriage of girls under fourteen and of boys under eighteen.[39] The orthodox Hindus and a section of the Muslims did their best to get rid of the Sarda Act. But all their efforts were in vain and the Act came into force.[40] In order to thank those who had helped in the passing of the Child Marriage Bill and to express feelings of relief and happiness, under the auspices of the Women's India Association, the Indian Ladies Samaj, the Mother's Union, South Indian Brahmo Samaj and the Madras Muslim Ladies Association, a public meeting of the women was held under the Presidentship of Mangalambigai at Egmore. S. Muthulakshmi Reddy, Ms. Paul Appasami, Rukmini Lakshmipathi, Ms. Bhagirathi, Ms. Meenakshi, Ms.Malathi Patwardhan and Ms.Lakshmi Amma spoke expressing the great relief that piece of legislation would bring to the anxious parents in India.[41] It was largely owing to the efforts and support of the women's organisations that the Sarda Act was passed.

The women's organisations promoted this legislation at every stage. They generated propaganda against child marriage, commented on the proposed bills, petitioned, met with the Joshi Committee, lobbied to secure the passage of the Child Marriage Restraint Act and worked after its passage for keeping it in tact. Resolutions were passed by the Women's India Association and many other associations thanking Rao Bahadur Harbilas Sarda, the members of the Legislative Assembly, the Government and all those who had helped towards the passing of the Act.

Passing of the Sarda Bill excited keen controversy in the Madras Presidency ranging from its description as, "a land mark in the history of British legislation in India".[42] Local newspapers such as the *Tamil Nadu, the Dravidian*, and the *Viswabandhu* expressed their full support.[43] The *Viswabandhu* remarked that since the majority of the selected representatives of the public themselves demanded that such a measure should be enacted, the government had in no way acted against the spirit of the Queen's Proclamation of 1857.[44] The *Kesari* raised strong objections to the foreign government's interference in the social customs of the people based on religious scriptures.[45] The *Saiphul Islam* condemned this law to be contrary to the Islamic faith and declared that the action of the government in compelling the Muslims to approve of it would amount to an interference with their religion.[46] The Brahmins of Tanjore felt that they were let down by the Congress politicians.[47]

The orthodox Hindus and Muslims wanted them to be excluded from its operation. The All India Sanathana Dharma conference went to the extent of passing a resolution asking all orthodox persons to celebrate the marriages of their children subsequent to 1st April and thus disobey the provisions of the Sarda Act.[48] The orthodox Brahmins did not keep quite. Rao Bahadur Krishnama Achariyar, a member of the Legislative Assembly announced his intention to introduce in the Assembly a bill to amend the Sarda Act to exempt the Brahmins, the Vaisyas and the Saurashtras from the operation of the Act. Immediately it evoked strong opposition from Tamil press. *Tamilnadu* severely criticised such amendment.[49] The Women's India Association, Madras communicated this news to all its branches and requested the government not to go back on their own verdict.[50] The Women's India Association, Rangoon in response to the communication called a meeting on 29th September 1931 and passed the resolution strongly protesting against the proposed amendment. It also appealed to the Viceroy and the Government of India not to support such amendment.[51]

The government also did not take interest in implementing the Act. People also frequently disregarded the Act inspite of the effort of the Women's India Association to keep the Act in tact. Even prominent persons such as V.U. Srinivasa Aiyangar, an ex-High Court Judge, and C. Vijayaraghava Achariyar, an ex-President of the Indian National Congress and a prominent advocate conducted marriages of girls of their families below fourteen years old.[52] During the six months between the passing of the Act and the enforcement, the number of children led into matrimony was probably more than three million girls and two million boys.[53] There were hectic celebrations of pre-puberty marriages all over the presidency.[54] The Sarda Act has been described in many parts of India as 'practically a dead letter'.[55] The women's organisations continuously appealed to the government to keep the Act in tact. It also repeatedly called upon the public to strictly obey the provisions of the Act. It held meetings periodically to educate the public regarding the evils of child marriage. But the Government of India did not proceed with further legislation and left the reformed legislatures to deal with these problems.

The Government of Madras did not give effect to the Age of Consent Committee's recommendation on the age of consent, as the Child Marriage Restraint Act, a comparatively milder measure had met with opposition from the Muslims and the orthodox Hindus.[56]

Since the Hindu law allowed polygamy, the society had not derived much benefit from the age of consent bill. The parents of the girls never refused to send their daughters to their husbands for fear that the boys might be remarried. There is no doubt that the Sarda Act had good results in fortifying those parents who in their hearts disapproved of child marriage. A remarkable increase in the number of unmarried Hindu girls attending secondary schools in later years had been in part the result of the passing of this Act.

Devadasis

The term *devadasis* meant dancing girls dedicated to temple services. They were the well known class in South India and were employed by the kings for certain kinds of services in the temples and were engaged as temple dancers. From generation to generation this was their profession and a daughter of a *devadasi* must become a *devadasi.* Every temple of repute in South India had its troop of these sacred women.

Every day they had to attend *deeparadhana* in front of the deity at sunset, singing hymns in praise of the deities, dancing before the idol and follow with the processional deity carrying the holy light and by singing and dancing.[57] References are there in the inscriptions of King Rajaraja and other Chola Kings in the Tanjore district regarding the temple dancers. King Kulothunga III appointed dancing masters in the temple to teach lessons on gestures.[58]

Regarding the origin of this custom Annie Besant wrote, "there was a band of pure virgin devotees attached to the ancient Hindu temples. They used to preach religion like other religious teachers to the common people that resort to the temple for their daily worship. In those days they were held in high esteem and respect and were very well looked after. They would spend their time in doing religious service to the Gods and devotees of the temple as the word *dasi* itself signifies. They would follow the procession of Gods dressed in the simplest *sanyasi* garbs and singing pious hymns suitable to the occasion".[59] They formed part and parcel of the worship of God in the Hindu temples and were an order of pure virgin ascetics wearing the simplest clothes, partaking only of the food they got from the temples, personal purity, rectitude of conduct and a vow of celibacy were the essentials enforced of the *devadasis*.[60]

The causes for dedicating girls to the God were numerous. In order to obtain a safe delivery expectant mothers would often vow to dedicate their child if it was a girl to the service of God. Among the weavers of Tirukalungkundrum, in the Chengleput District, the eldest daughter of every family was devoted to the temple.[61] If any female child fell ill some parents would vow to God to dedicate her as a *devadasi*.[62] Among the Kaikolan musicians of Coimbatore at least one girl in every family should be set apart for temple service, and she should be instructed in music and dancing.[63]

The actual dedication was made by following some religious ceremonies. Before attaining puberty the girl meant for dedication was taken to the temple and was initiated into certain ceremonies. The priest would keep the clothes and *tali* at the feet of the idol in the temple. The girl would be seated facing the idol and in the inner sanctuary the priest would perform the marriage rituals. Then the priest or a man of her caste would tie the *tali* kept before the idol on behalf of the God or his representative, the sword on the neck of the girl.[64] Symbolically she was united in marriage with a God and it was her chief duty to dance and sing before Him to please Him.

As the *dasi* could never become a widow, the beads in her *tali* were considered to bring good luck to women who wore them. And some people sent the *tali* required for their marriage to the *dasi*, who would prepare the string for the *tali* by attaching to it black beads from her own *tali*. In order to ward off evil omens, the *dasi* was deputed to walk at the head of the Hindu marriage processions. It was believed that the *dasi* to whom widowhood was unknown possessed the power of warding off the evil effects of inauspicious omens.[65] *Devadasis* were the only women in India who enjoyed the privilege of learning to read, to dance and to sing.[66] As per the Census Report of 1881, the number of women dancers in the Madras Presidency was 11,573.[67]

For the duties the *devadasis* discharged in the temple, they were paid by the temple depending on the wealth of the temple. Sometimes houses and lands belonging to the temple were placed at their disposal.[68] In certain cases they were awarded *inams* in the form of lands and revenue. They had no hereditary right to the post but only for the service during their life time. Service tenure in the temple devolved from the mother to the daughters provided the latter had been dedicated as usual to the deity. If one had no heirs, she could adopt a girl at her choice and appoint her as her successor.[69] They could even adopt two girls and there was no ceremony needed for its validity.[70] As the prevalent belief was that this adoption of the girl by the *devadasi* could improve the condition of the former, near relatives of the *devadasis* were always willing to give their daughters for adoption. If there were none in their families for adoption young girls of other families would be adopted and dedicated as *devadasis*. The adopted girls name would be duly entered in the temple registers and would be recognised as the successor of the adoptive mothers.[71]

Originated with the noblest and the highest motives, this institution had gradually degenerated into something highly objectionable. The high ideals degenerated and demoralised. They became the paid female servants of the temples either because of the inadequacy of their emoluments or other causes. They led a worldly life and developed into women of loose morals. Instead of living within the temples, these women were settled in houses erected on separate free holdings granted to them.[72] They supplemented their income by selling their favours in as profitable manner as possible. They were held always ready at a price for the use of men pilgrims during their devotional sojourns in the temple precincts.[73] Stripped off the aura of religion and the obligation of temple service, they lost even the reverence that they had received from devotees as the servant of Gods.[74] They became common prostitutes and the law recognised them as such. The most pathetic nature of this custom was that the training for the immoral work began for these girls even from their childhood, at an age when they could not think and act for themselves. Well tutored in the art of evil trade from childhood they were taken to the temple and made to undergo a form of nominal marriage with a sword or with an idol which ceremony prohibited them from lawful marriage afterwards.[75] In theory life long virginity was assigned to them in practice they were no more virgin than were devotees of Gods. The ceremony of dedication precluded matrimony, but it was in no way a prelude to the difficult discipline of voluntary celibacy. The dedicated girls thus became either openly or secretly prostitutes.

The promiscuous life of the *devadasis* were not considered as a serious matter in the society until the later part of the nineteenth century, since it was attached to Hindu religion. The government tried to put some restrictions to prevent the adoption of girls by the *devadasis* for prostitution by enforcing the existing laws.[76] The then law made both the seller and buyer of a minor girl for purposes of prostitution punishable under section 372 and 373 of the Indian Penal Code. The language of sections 372 and 373 of the penal code was no doubt very wide and as observed by Mr. Mayne "if these two sections are vigorously applied to the relations and patrons of the dancing girl or prostitute caste of India, half the population may be put into jail whenever it is thought desirable". But the judicial interpretation placed upon these sections were not consistent. According to some the positive intent at the time of dedication or adoption must be affirmatively proved by cogent evidence despite the admitted existence of evil results in every caste. The only object of adoption of girls by the dancing women would be to have successors to their profession.[77] Thereafter adoption was usually carried on secretly with the consent of both partners. On considering them responsible for spreading the venereal disease and wanted to bring them under control, the government implemented the Contagious Diseases Act of 1868.[78] Even then they were not able to stop this practice.

With the spread of modern education this system was recognised as a social evil and steps were taken to curtail that practice. It was unanimously decided in 1905 by the Executive committee of the Prince and Princess of Wales Reception Fund that there should be no performance by the *devadasi* girls at the entertainment to be given to the Royal Highness at Madras.[79] Since the law should not permit the existence of such evil as early as 1912 three different bills were introduced in the legislatures respectively by Mudhalkari, Dadabhoy and Madge to protect the minor girls from dedication.[80] The three bills were circulated to local governments together with the government's comments. Basing on the replies the government also prepared and introduced another bill for the same purpose in 1913. The bill was referred to the Select Committee which modified sections 372 and 373 to prevent the disposal of the minor girls (below 16 years) for the purpose of prostitution or illicit intercourse with any person or for any unlawful and immoral purposes. This report was then circulated to local governments. But the question of legislation was postponed in view of its controversial nature and also because of the I world war.[81] Thus four bills to suppress this evil directly or indirectly were brought during 1912-1914.

In 1922 Hari Singh Gour brought a resolution recommending legislation to prohibit the traffic of minor girls for immoral purposes ostensibly intended as *devadasis*. It was adopted by the Assembly.[82] As a result in February 1924, a bill amending section 372 and 373 Indian Penal Code was introduced to rescue and protect young girls under eighteen years living in circumstances calculated to lead to prostitution. The bill became Act XVIII of 1924. It prohibited selling, buying or hiring of any person under the age of eighteen for the purpose of prostitution or illicit intercourse or for any unlawful and immoral purposes. As regards *devadasis* in view of the religious significance of the system, the mere employment as *devadasi* was not to constitute an offence under the bill unless such employment was proved to be for the purpose of prostitution.[83] Since this act did not directly mean *devadasis*, and also influenced by Ms Mayo's book "Mother India" and the agitation against this custom at Madras, Hon' V. Ramadass Pantulu in 1927 moved a resolution in the Council of State at Simla for introducing a legislation to prohibit the practice of dedicating minor girls to the temple as *devadasis*. The government did not accept the resolution as it stood and before introducing any resolution public opinion must be sought and so he withdrew the resolution.[84]

During 1920s and 1930s S. Muthulakshmi Reddy took a lead to abolish the *devadasi* system. Her membership in the Madras Legislative Council gave her sufficient opportunity to uphold her views against this system. She took a vow that she should never rest till she got the pernicious custom eradicated from this land.

Since the penal code then prohibited girls below eighteen years to be so dedicated, the parents or guardians successfully evaded the law by having performed the ceremony after that age. Though after eighteen years they were at liberty to choose the life before them, they were not in a position to do so because they were taught from childhood to look upon this practice as their caste duty of *dharma* and the God would be displeased otherwise. Out of their ignorance even after they attained majority they would choose a life of shame.[85] The irony of fate was that the age limit fixed in the penal code served to legalise dedication which was identical with prostitution. The only thing was that the girls destined for dedication had to appear before the magistrate and to give a declaration stating their willingness and their age, if they said that they reached eighteen years, then they would be given permission.[86]

It was felt legislative enactment was necessary in the Madras Presidency for dealing with the *devadasi* system. It forced S. Muthulakshmi Reddy to move a resolution in the Madras Legislative Council on 4th November 1927. It recommended the Government of Madras to undertake a legislation or if that was impracticable to recommend to the Government of India to undertake a legislation at a very early date to put a stop to the practice of dedicating young girls or young women to Hindu temples, which had generally resulted in exposing them to an immoral life.[87] She appealed for its passage on the ground that it was a reform which could rescue thousands of young innocent children from a life of immorality and vice, from life long invalidation, suffering diseases and death resulting from infection with venereal diseases. If removed from these circumstances the girls, "would become virtuous and legal wives, affectionate mothers and useful citizens". She was at pains to explain that "these women do not belong to the brothel class and that they are only the victims of tradition, custom or a mistaken religious fervour and that there is no innate tendency in them to vice".[88]

The resolution evoked complex responses. When the people came to know about the bill, they had started sending innumerable letters of sympathy and support to S. Muthulakshmi Reddy requesting her to go on with her work. She had all sympathy and support from the press, the platform and the public. Many public bodies such as the district municipalities and local boards, and mass gathering of men and women had sent her their approval. *Devadasi* associations through out the presidency conducted meetings demanding legislation to put an end to the dedication of girls to Hindu Temples. Twelve *devadasi* women's associations, fifteen *devadasi* community men associations, and fifteen women's associations sent representation to her supporting her efforts to abolish this evil custom.[89] K.R. Karant, C.V. Venkataramana Aiyangar, C.N. Muthuranga Mudaliar and Anjanayulu of the Congress Party, A.B. Shetty, Syed Ibrahim, U. Munusamy Pillai and S.W. Dorairaja of the Ministerial Group and M. Krishnan Nair, the Deputy Leader of the Justice party supported the motion. The then law Minister Sir. C.P. Ramaswamy Aiyar on behalf of the Government, while appreciating the motion pointed out certain difficulties in giving practical effect to the motion.[90] On the otherhand a few *devadasis* who were actually in the trade and were being profited by such a life tried to impress upon the government and the public that her bill had not much support behind it.[91] Very few *devadasi* associations protested against the resolution on the ground that it was an ancient custom and usage of the community and especially their religion and it had nothing to do with prostitution. *Devadasis* of the Sri Ranganathaswami temple, Madras on 8th December 1927 wrote a protest letter to the Minister as follows. "We submit most emphatically that the dedication of girls and women to Hindu temples is a very old religious institution now forming part of the daily religious worship in Hindu temples. Such an institution is supported by the sastras, the *agamas* which were the authorities for the daily rites to be performed in the temples. These *agamas* prescribe that the part taken by *devadasis* in the worship of the temple should be performed by them and by the female children born to these families.[92] Some Congressmen insisted that the *devadasi* system was essential for the preservation of the fine arts. It was also seen as part of the attack on religion being mounted on by the non-brahmins. When S. Muthulakshmi Reddy met S. Satyamurthi to get his support, he did not support her. Such impossible stand being taken made her wrote with disgust that persons like S. Satyamurthi attended the important meetings of the select committee more to safeguard the interests of the brothel prostitutes, the brothel keepers and the prostitute *devadasis*. Then she approached E.V. Ramaswami Naicker who had publicly supported the bill.[93]

The Government of Madras without trying to solve the problem simply communicated the resolution to the Government of India. It was then referred to a select committee. It took a year almost for her to obtain sanction to introduce that bill in the Madras Legislative Council. In the meantime S. Muthulakshmi Reddy collected all informations regarding the operation of the system.[94]

The main problem involved in the abolition of the *devadasi* system was the holding of *inam* lands by the *devadasi* community for the enjoyment of which they had to perform services in the temples. These *inams* were resumable in case service was not rendered.[95] So when the women grew old, in order to retain the *inams* by satisfying the trustees, young girls were brought up for the service. Therefore the only remedy to root out the evil was to enfranchise the service *inams* and grant them *pattas* thereby free them from the obligation of service.[96] In order to enfranchise the *inam* lands and make them its owner S. Muthulakshmi Reddy brought an amendment to the Hindu Religious Endowment Act in 1929.[97] It was passed as the Madras Hindu Religious Endowments (Amendment) Act 1929.[98] The *Navayuga* and the *Prajamitra* had given expression to their heart felt exultation over the passing of this piece of legislation.[99] This social reform indirectly by enfranchising the *inams* and stopping the award, removed the inducement to dedication of girls to temples. It had wiped off a stain on the reputation of the Hindu temples in the presidency and had put an end to a despicable custom which had been started by men ostensibly in the name of religion but actually for the gratification which had ruined the life of many a number of women.

This act had been applied only to the women and not to the men who were assistance to the *devadasis*. The *devadasi* service was a joint performance by both men and women even though the women were the chief. It consisted partly of dancing performed by women and partly of fiddling, drumming and scruti performed by men. So the *devadasi* reform associations sent many representations to her saying that unless the whole *inam* enjoyed by both women and men for their joint service was enfranchised, the evil custom could not be eradicated. If men were not enfranchised and freed from the obligation of service in the temple, they would train women only for that service for fear that they might loose the benefit of those *inams*.[100]

This act dealt with the *inam* holding *devadasis* only. There were other *devadasis* who dedicated a large number of girls to Hindu temples by going through the *pottugattu* or similar ceremony in Hindu temples even after the age of eighteen. There was no religion for that. Those woman did it purposely with a view to make those girls lead an immoral life. There was a class of *devadasis* outside the temples who dedicated their girls not for service in the temples but with the sole object of making them trade on the vice. The Hindu Religious Endowment Act also did not include certain temples within its operation. e.g. the Madras temples and also the temples getting a very small income of Rs. 300/- or so.[101] Hence it was realised that there was an urgent need for another legislation to eradicate the practice among the above groups.

Since the public opinion was infavour of the abolition of the custom and in response to the appeal of several associations and hundreds of enlightened members of the community of *devadasis* themselves, S. Muthulakshmi Reddy, brought forward another bill in september 1929 to free them with two fold purposes, firstly to declare the dedication of girls to Hindu temples illegal and to prohibit such dedication, secondly to punish the persons taking part in the ceremony of dedication.[102] This bill in addition to making the dedication illegal, had another provision as regards their marriages to the effect that marriages which took place after dedication should be validated. She requested her bill to be referred to a select committee.[103] It received the public support also. The second provincial Self Respect conference held on 7-11th May 1930, passed the following resolution among others, "Resolved to introduce and support the bill seeking to abolish the *devadasi* system in the Madras Presidency"[104] Since S. Muthulaskshmi Reddy had resigned before the passing of that legislation, she had to fight for it from out side the legislature only.

Mysore State had abolished the practice of dedication to the temples as early as 1909.[105] When the Maharaja of Mysore was called upon to put a stop to this custom, he appointed a committee of *pandits* to find out whether this custom had any sanction in religion. They pronounced in one voice that there was not a single text to show that the custom had any religious sanction. So the ruler issued an order to prohibit the *devadasis* from performing any temple services.[106] The States of

Travancore and Cochin abolished it in their state temples in 1930.[107] In 1934 the Bombay government abolished it.[108] The All India Women's Conference held at Madras appealed to the Hindu Religious Endowment Board of Madras to call upon all trustees of the temple under its jurisdiction totally to eradicate the *devadasi* service and the ceremony of dedication of girls in such temples by issuing an order.[109] In the meantime the bill which had been sent out for eliciting public opinion had returned with full measure of public support. But the government had delayed it.[110] After that the campaign took a more radical and democratic form demanding that the *devadasis* right to their property be protected and their children entitled to the same rights as those born legitimately. Muvalur Ramamirthammal's book *dasikal mosavalai* (The Tricks/Ploys of the *Devadasis* 1936) was a turning point in the movement. The reform campaigns forced the *devadasis* to acknowledge the moral supremacy of married life.[111]

When the temples released the devadasis from service, a lot of them were brought to the Ladies Samaj.[112] Almost all of them got married and settled into a respectable life. The Samaj discontinued the service in 1937. There after S. Muthulakshmi Reddy wrote, "There was no need for giving help to these special group of girls as such families became used to a new life of respectability and got merged into the general society".

The *Devadasis* Bill prohibiting temple dedication first introduced by S. Muthulakshmi Reddy, got passed in its complete form only in 1947. Its first enactment in 1929 was only partial and after that she had to fight for it from outside the legislature. By then the Justice Party lost interest in it, and the Congress Government under C. Rajagopalachari on later years was indifferent to it. S. Muthulakshmi Reddy wrote in her *Autobiography* that C. Rajagopalachari who was called a radical politician was a social reactionary.[113] The Madras *Devadasis* (Prevention of Dedication) Act 1947 prohibited the dedication of women to temples as it had led the women concerned adopting a life of prostitution in a large number of cases. Section 3(3) of the Act provided as follows:

> "Dancing by a woman with or without *kumbharathi* (the ceremony of *devadasi* dedication) in the precincts of any temple or other religious institution or in any procession of a Hindu deity, idol, or object of worship... or at any festival or ceremony... is hereby declared unlawful".[114]

Suppression of Immoral Traffic in Women and Children

Traffic in women and children was one of the vilest forms of slavery and the worst form of exploiting the week, ignorant and the helpless by an organised gang of traffickers. Its extreme secrecy made it almost impossible to expose the organisers and to secure her release. It resulted in the mental, physical and moral degradation of women. This inhuman slavery condemned the innocent victims who were very often girls, destitutes and neglected children to a life of unspeakable horror and misery.

There were more than 600 brothels in the Madras city alone and hundreds of minor girls were forced to live in such brothels. Because of the absence of any control by legislation and the consequent increased supply of women and young girls from the mofussals by pimps, procurers and souteneurs, the brothels were filled up.[115] These brothels in the city openly advertised vice, allured young men from the path of virtue and encouraged depravity among them. The venereal disease which claimed a large per centage of people as its victims had its origin only in the brothels.[116] In some cases innocent children of about eight or nine years of age were being dragged into brothels and made to live in the most harrowing conditions. The diabolical treatment meted out to them in brothels was heart rendering and blood curdling.[117]

The main cause for this evil was poverty. The enquiries conducted by the League of Nations from time to time in different countries as well as the Madras Vigilance Association's survey supported the same fact.[118] Other contributory causes were *devadasi* system, society's attitude towards girls, child widows, absence of widow marriages, and denial of property to women.[119] In the Madras Presidency trade in girls were openly carried on by the brokers. Brokers bought the poor girls on the false promise that they would be married by the rich persons. There were none to see how these girls were disposed of by the brokers. Most of them were made to lead a life of prostitution.[120] Girls were even exported to Burma and other places for immoral purposes from Madras by pimps and prostitutes.[121]

The Act V, 1924 of the Government of India only raised the age limit for selling and buying of minor girls for purposes of prostitution from sixteen to eighteen.[122] But these rules were successfully evaded by those people.[123] Hence the existing law was not able to do much. Because of false modesty, this question had not been placed before the public until the third decade of the twentieth century. The meeting of the Women's India Association held at Bombay demanded the removal of brothels. It organised a meeting at Madras on 13th December 1924 to here Miss.Edith Gray of Chicago on the theme "Traffic in women and children". It inspired many people who got desire to better the condition of these women. She travelled all over the world investigated this question and her lecture supplied valuable information. It was ultimately a question which affected not only the unfortunate women, but the health of the society.[124]

As a result, the Madras Vigilance Association was formed at Madras in 1925 to draw together men and women who had at heart the moral welfare of the community and especially to further the following functions; to secure the recognition of the fact that there was one moral law which was the same for men and women, to carry on rescue and preventive work in the Madras Presidency to suppress traffic in women and girls and especially to take all possible measures for the protection of girls under eighteen years of age, to establish and maintain rescue homes, to work for the abolition of brothels and prostitution, and to promote the enactment of laws that would further morality, purity and above objects and to oppose any legislation that would suggest any regulation of brothels, segregated areas or compulsory examination of women, to prevent the publication and sale of indecent and obscene books or pictures or the display of objectionable cinemas, films, theatrical performances and advertisements to suppress such evils. Above all it aimed at educating the public through meetings, publishing and distributing literatures and by any other possible means.[125] Another voluntary organisation, the Madras Children's Aid Society, Kilpauk was started by a non-official agency in 1926 and had since grown into a full blown institution with junior and senior certified schools for girls, a remand home or temporary shelter for girls and boys and the boy's own club. The government paid for the maintenance of girls in the home and for the staff as it did in the case of other certified schools in the Madras Presidency.[126] Legislative steps were also taken to abolish this evil practice.

The Madras Vigilance Association under the direction and guidance of the Rev. E.H.M.Waller, Lord Bishop of Madras had carried on intensive study and investigation into the conditions of brothels in the city of Madras since its inception.[127] After the investigation, Madras Vigilance Association and Women's India Association met eight times and spent considerable time to prepare the draft bill for the suppression of brothels and immoral traffic of women in Madras. Ms. K.V. Shesha Aiyangar with the help of the Women's India Association played a major role in the drafting of the bill. After framing the bill, they took effective measures to introduce the same in the Madras Legislative Council. In order to get the popular support, Women's India Association organised propaganda meetings in different places. Articles on its evils were published in *Stri-Dharma*.[128] Not receiving any reply from the government, a combined deputation of the Madras Vigilance Association and Women's India Association met the then Law Member Sir C.P. Ramaswamy Iyer. He suggested that it would be better if it was brought into the council by a private member. Since S. Muthulakshmi Reddy was in charge of another bill, on behalf of her, K.R.Venkatarama Iyer introduced the bill on 5th September 1928.[129] Later she made the following amendment to the bill, 'substitute' "prostitute" is a person on either sex who uses the body for promiscuous sexual intercourse, under conditions of hire" for "prostitute means a woman who offers her body to indiscriminate sexual intercourse for hire".[130] She applied the term 'prostitute' to both the sexes. Then it was referred to the Select Committee. The Women's India Association and Madras Vigilance Association appealed to the public to lend their support to pass the bill. Owing to the constant agitation set up by both the organisations through the press and the platforms, the public had become convinced of the need for the control and suppression of this commercialised vice through legislation. Finally the bill was passed by the Madras Legislative Council in 1930.[131] It was known as the Madras Suppression of Immoral Traffic Act. S.Muthulakshmi Reddy and Dorothy Jinarajadasa had worked so strenuously to get the bill passed. As per the act "prostitution means indiscriminate sexual intercourse for hire". This act was applicable to the whole of the Madras Presidency and was intended to make better provision for the suppression of brothels and of traffic in women and girls and for other purposes of a like nature. It made it an offence to keep, manage or assist in the management of a brothel and had given power to a magistrate on information to order entry into a brothel and remove all minor girls from there. The works of the Madras and Bombay branches of the Women's India Association in co-operation with the vigilance societies had been valuable in securing legislation for the abolition of brothel and the establishment of rescue homes.[132]

Though the press expressed favourably towards the passing of this social legislation they were of opinion that unless due facilities were afforded for the reclamation, the Act might not accomplish its purpose.[133] Both the members of the Self Respect Movement as well as the Moderates in the Congress were in full praise of the Act, but pleaded to the government to establish rescue homes to rehabilitate women rescued from brothel houses. The Self Respect Movement questioned; "Why is prostitution attributed to women alone? This showed the practice of permanent subjugation of women by men in the society". It added, "The word prostitution has been used to mean that women are pleasure objects to men, hence slaves. This is an impediment to women's liberty. This should go. Does the society brand men as prostitutes?".[134] On behalf of the Self Respect Movement books were also published depicting the hypocrisy of men and the helpless condition of women who indulged themselves in prostitution.

Inspite of all these efforts, the act was not put into practice.[135] The government refused to shoulder the responsibility for setting up rescue homes for the young girls rescued. It was not possible for those women to re-enter the community from where they had cut themselves because of their immoral practices.[136] Criticising the attitude of the government, *India* wrote, "should not venereal disease which is one of the deadly disease to which the people of this world become victims be get rid of from the country".[137] Abolition of brothels even if possible would not be effective unless the women turned out of these places could be trained in some useful work and absorbed into normal life. This would mean a net work of organisations subsidised and financed by the state and regular campaign of war against the evil itself.

Fortunately many organisations in the city were interested in welfare and vigilance activities. The Madras Vigilance Association and Women's India Association collected donations to construct rescue homes thereby shared the responsibility of rescuing girls and women from the brothels.[138] The Salvation Army and other non governmental agencies came forward to admit such girls irrespective of caste and creeds. The Madras Children's Aid Society, gave shelter and suitable training to those women to make them self reliant.[139] The organisations even sent voluntary women workers to rescue girls. The Women's India Association even forced Sir George Stanly, the then Governor of Madras to ask the people as well as the government to donate liberally to establish rescue homes.[140] In practice the Government of Madras had not enforced the act and decided to amend the Act to apply it only to the Madras city.[141]

The proposed amendment was subject to severe criticism both by the press as well as leading women's organisations such as the All India Women's Conference and the Women's India Association. If the Act was applicable to the city alone, the prostitutes and procurers would move to adjacent cities and so it could not be got rid of.[142] In order to prevent the amendment, a deputation of the Women's India Association consisting of S. Muthulakshmi Reddy, Ms. K.C. Acharya, Margaret E. Cousins, Rajivibai, Ms. Shiva Rao and Visalakshmi met the Home Member and requested the Government to apply the act to the entire province. They also promised their help for the successful operation of the Act and wanted for its immediate enforcement.[143] Inspite of all these efforts, the Act was amended and was passed in October 1931 applying it to the Madras city alone. After that also the government did not take any interest in it, saying that there were no separate courts to try young girls rescued from brothels and rescue homes or other facilities required in this connection. It left the matter to the public charitable institutions.[144] The *Mathrubhumi* wrote "The puerility of this plea causes a smile and the heartlessness of it intense pain to us".[145]

The Women's India Association and Madras Vigilance Association were not silent. They continued to press for the application of the legislation to the entire province. Because of their incessant efforts, the Act was extended to various places one by one. By the end of 1932 it was extended to the towns of Tiruchirapalli, Madurai and Srirangam[146] and later to Calicut.[147] In 1936 it was applied to the Mayavaram and Chidambaram municipalities. In Chidambaram though individual prostitution was quite common, yet such prostitutes were afraid of soliciting openly as they used to do prior to the application of the Act.[148] Thus it came into force gradually one place after another in the Madras Presidency.

Whatever the actions taken, the evil continued to exist. Hence in March 1938 the Act was further amended and the Madras Suppression of Immoral Traffic (Amendment) Bill 1938 was passed. It penalised the third party living on the earnings of prostitution or habitually in the company of a person living in prostitution or directing her movement.[149] But it exempted the *devadasis*. The exempting clause was attacked by the Women's India Association. It came to know the nature of the amendment that excluded certain clause of people from the operation of the act only through Ms. Hensman, the only woman member in the Madras Upper House. In order to prevent it from becoming act, the Women's India Association took various steps. It organised several public meetings and sent its protests and resolutions to the press and to the government and also submitted a memorandum to the government. It passed the following resolutions: 1. that all laws and all education should tend towards the promotion of purity and a high moral standard of sex relationship. 2. that nobody especially a family consisting of mother, grand mother, father, grand father etc. should be allowed to live on the earnings of prostitution by their own daughters, sisters and other relatives etc. and such offenders should receive deterrent punishment. 3. that the sub-clause of section 8(a) of the Madras Suppression of Immoral Traffic Bill exempting the relatives of the prostitutes belonging to any caste or community accustomed to dedicate girls to temples should be deleted. 4. that the existing statutory laws to dispense with the *devadasi* service in the Hindu temples and to prohibit dedication of girls to temples should be enforced, and a comprehensive legislation should be immediately undertaken to put down this evil and 5) that trained women welfare workers should be largely employed to help the police in the entry into and investigation of the brothels and to produce evidence to punish those who live on the earnings of prostitution. Some members of the association led by S. Muthulakshmi Reddy met the Premier C. Rajagopalachari and the Cabinet members and convinced them of the evil effect of the exempting clause. The press published all their protests. The cabinet also reconsidered the matter. On the day of discussion in the Assembly a large number of women assembled in the gallery and distributed pamphlets in support of their arguments.[150] As a result the exempting clause was deleted by the Assembly. It was a shocking that the Congress Ministry which pledged to further social purity and to redeem Indian women from the tyranny and oppression of age old customs initiated such a piece of legislation recognising *devadasis* as prostitutes and licensing them to prostitution for the maintenance of their relatives.

Again in 1940 another amendment was made. It empowered the police officers to enter into the brothels without prior order of the court to remove not only the girls under eighteen years authorised by the competent authorities but also any other girls found in the premises.[151] The Madras Act XXXV of 1947 (The Madras Suppression of Immoral Traffic Amendment Act 1947) made provision for the detention in vigilance homes for periods ranging from two to five years of women less than thirty years of age who had been found guilty of solicitation in the street or public place. These homes were to fulfil much the same function as borstal schools in relation to adolescent offenders.[152]

Though the act was brought into force in the Madras city

as early as 1930 it was not implemented by saying that there were no separate courts to try young girls rescued from brothels and no rescue homes or other facilities required in this connection. The government attributed their inability to financial stringency[153]. It was only some poor prostitutes and others ran away from Madras, but clever prostitutes remained in the city and carried on the profession, some in the name of nurse, some saying that they were mistresses of some persons and some even in the name of family women.[154]

The Madras Vigilance Association was not inactive. It had educated public opinion to realise that it was an intolerable social evil which affected the health, and the moral welfare of the society. It changed the attitude of the public from one of indifferent hostility and contempt for the victims of vice into one of active sympathy. By the end of 1933, with the help of the government and the police department, it succeeded in closing over 123 houses of ill fame without any adverse reactions of the public and with as little injury to the inmates as possible by the constant watchfulness of the workers. It had ensured that such houses closed were not reopened afterwards.

The Madras Vigilance Association assisted the victims of traffic by offering personal assistance during the house to house visitation of the women workers and also at the time of the removal of the inmates providing stipends for those who were willing to be trained to lead a moral life. It also opened Stri Sadana Rescue Home to give shelter to those women thus it had succeeded to a certain extent in preventing the continuance of the traffic.[155] It also rescued a lot of children from immoral surroundings other than brothels and sent them to the rescue home attached to the Madras Children's Aid Society. Many adults who came to the home as prevention and protection cases were suitably helped according to individual conditions and needs.[156] Some minor girls who were rescued from brothels by the Madras Vigilance Association could not be detained in the home, as these cases were not covered by the orders of court.[157]

The management of the rescue homes continued to give the girls placed under them a sound and general education with the object of finding suitable employment for them and making them fit for absorption in the normal life of the community. The girls discharged from the rescue homes would be restored to the guardians. The welfare workers also continued to do after care work by visiting and writing to the several girls who were sent out from the home. The Madras Vigilance Association spent a lot of amount for the maintenance of its homes alone.[158] The activities of the Madras Vigilance Association increased and several public meetings were held inorder to explain the usefulness of the work of the association. Vigilance associations were opened in all the places where the act was applicable.

The Women's India Association also opened a home for women at Madras in 1934 to protect such girls and women and also to educate and train them.[159] A rescue worker was appointed to the Madras Vigilance Association in 1935 to rescue large number of minor girls living in the brothels.[160] As a result of public co-operation over 105 houses of ill fame were suppressed within two years.[161] During the year 1937-38, twenty five persons were convicted for offences connected with traffic in women and children.[162] In the next year, 261 persons and from July 1937 to June 1940, altogether 249 persons were convicted for various crimes such as keeping brothels or allowing premises to be used as brothels, living on the earnings of prostitution, importing women or girls for prostitution and soliciting for purposes of prostitution. Punishment varied according to the nature of the crime ranging from the fine of Rs. 5/- to Rs. 150/- to the rigorous imprisonment for two years. It is remarkable that during the above years there were neither licensed nor recognised brothels or cases of international traffic, repatriation and deportation.[163] The working of the Act was appreciated by the pubic. Article 23 of the constitution laid down that traffic in human beings should be prohibited and any contravention of this provision would be an offence punishable in accordance with the law. To give effect to this constitutional provision, the Suppression of Immoral Traffic in Women and Girls Act 1956 was passed. It came into force throughout India on Ist May 1958.

Passing of these legislations were significant measures of success for the women. But it is a fact that these legislations did not succeed in totally eradicating these evils. Only after Independence these legislations were enforced sincerely.

References

1. "Report of the Age of Consent Committee 1928-29" in *Indian Women: Marriage and Social Status*, p. 10.
2. *Census of India*, 1891, Vol. XIII, *Madras*, p. 151.
3. B.S. Baliga, *Tanjore District Handbook*, p. 127.
4. *Manual of the Administration of the Madras Presidency*, pp. 225 - 233.
5. *Ibid.*, p. 225.
6. *Census of India*, 1891, Vol. XIII, p. 151.
7. *Manual of the Administration of the Madras Presidency*, pp. 225-233.
8. *Report of the Age of Consent Committee*, pp. 53-54.
9. *Ibid.*, p. 94.
10. *Women of India and what can be done for them*, p. 56.
11. *Report of the Age of Consent Committee*, pp. 94-95.
12. G.O. No. 3971, Law, 12 December 1927 ; *India in 1927-28*, p. 52.
13. G.O. No. 860, Pub., 3 June 1915.
14. *Report of the Age of Consent Committee*, pp. 55, 106.
15. *Wake up India* (A series of lectures delivered in Madras in 1913 to mark the beginning of an earliest movement for uplifting of India organised by Annie Besant), pp. 46-50.
16. G.O. No. 860, Pub., 3 June 1915.
17. *Stri-Dharma*, June 1924, p. 113; *The Sampad Abhudaya*, 18 March 1924, (MNR); FR, 3 October 1924.
18. *Stri-Dharma*, July 1925, pp. 147-48.
19. *Ibid.*, 1928, p. 75.
20. FR, 17 July 1926.
21. *Stri-Dharma*, 1928, p. 76.
22. Report of the *Age of Consent Committee*, pp. 54-55.
23. *Ibid.*, p. 57.
24. *Ibid.*, pp. 57-58.

25. *Darul Islam*, 25 January 1929, p. 164 (MNR).
26. "Report of the Age of Consent Committee 1928-29" in *Indian Women: Marriage and Social Status*, p. 196.
27. *Stri-Dharma,* September 1929, pp. 495-96. (Various women's organisations in Madras were WIA, Mothers Union, the Stri Sarada Ladies Union, the Indian Ladies Samaj and Women Graduates Union).
28. G.O. No. 3971, Law, 12 December 1927 ; *India in 1927-28,* p. 52 ; *Stri-Dharma*, October 1927 ; FR, 19 October 1927.
29. G.O. No. 2542, Law, 1 August 1298; *Stri-Dharma*, October 1927.
30. *Stri-Dharma*, September 1929, pp. 495-96.
31. Aparna Basu (ed.) *Dr. Muthulakshmi Reddy : The Path finder,* pp. 76-77.
32. *Ibid.*, p. 83. *Stri-Dharma*, April 1928, p. 3; S. Muthulakshmi Reddy, *My Experience...*, pp. 98-99, 236.
33. FR, 3 April 1928; S. Muthulakshmi Reddy, *My Experience...*, pp. 98-99, 236.
34. S. Muthulakshmi Reddy, *My Experience...*, pp. 99-102.
35. S. Muthulakshmi Reddy, *Autobiography,* p. 59.
36. FR, 3 September 1929.
37. *The Indian Quarterly Register*, January - June 1929, vol.I p. 167.
38. *Ibid.*, July-December 1929, vol. II, p. 138.
39. *Stri-Dharma,* September 1929, p. 497.
40. *India*, 6 June 1931, p. 830, (MNR).
41. *Stri-Dharma*, December 1929, p. 558.
42. *RAMP*, 1928-1929, p. ix.
43. *Tamil Nadu* 19 January 1931, p. 171; *Dravidian*, 21 January 1931, p. 171.
44. *Viswabandhu*, 19 December, 1930, p. 34 (MNR).
45. *Kesari*, 8 December 1929, p. 247.
46. *The Saiphul Islam*, 10 January 1931, p. 129 (MNR).
47. FR, 4 November, 1929.
48. *RAMP*, 1928-29, p. ix.
49. *Tamil Nadu,* 16 April 1931, p. 565 (MNR).
50. *Stri-Dharma,* 1932, p. 181.
51. *Ibid.*, February 1932, p. 268.
52. *Tamil Nadu*, 23 May 1931, p. 742 (MNR).
53. Nora Brockway, *A Larger Way for Women...*, p. 129.
54. FR, 3 April 1930.
55. G.O.No. 2617, Law, 13 September 1934.
56. G.O. No. 2617, Law, 13 September 1943.
57. Giri Raj Shah, *The Encyclopaedia of Women's Studies,* Vol. I, p. 208; L. Rajendran, *mahalir manam kavarntha muthulakshmi*, p. 84.
58. Projesh Banerji, *Art of Indian Dancing,* p. 18.

59. G.O. No. 4079, Law (Gen.), 20 December 1927.
60. *Stri-Dharma*, December 1941, p. 85.
61. Giri Raj Shah, *The Encyclopaedia ...*, p. 208.
62. J.A. Abbe Dubais, *Hindu Manners Customs and Ceremonies*, p. 123.
63. Santosh Chatterjee, *Devadasi (Temple Dancer)*, p. 39.
64. Santosh Chatterjee, *Devadasi (Temple Dancer)*, p. 40; Edgar Thurston, *Castes and Tribes of Southern India*, Vol. II, p. 127.
65. Santosh Chatterjee, *Devadasi*, p. 40.
66. Abbe J.A. Dubois, *Hindu Manners ...*, p. 586.
67. *The Women of India and What can be done for them*, p. 83; *Imperial Census*, Vol. II, p. 448.
68. "Traffic in women and children, System of Devadasi and child adoption among them" G.O. No. 407, Jud. (Mag.), 2 October 1924.
69. *Stri-Dharma*, December 1941, p. 85.
70. S.Venkataman, *A Treatise on Hindu Law*, p. 275.
71. "System of traffic in women and children: Systems of Devadasis and child adoption among them" G.O. No. 407, Jud. (Mag), 2 October 1924.
72. *Stri-Dharma*, December 1941, p. 85.
73. Giri Raj Shah, *The Encyclopaedia...* p. 208.
74. Prabha Rani, "In the name of humanity" in Aparna Basu, (ed.), *Dr. Muthulakshmi Reddy: The Path finder*, p. 67.
75. S. Muthulakshmi Reddy's speech in *PMLC*, November 1927, p. 416.
76. G.O. No. 629, Jud., 12 April 1904.
77. File No. 820, Judicial, February, 1922, Serial nos. 1-8 ; Home department, 1912, Judicial proceedings October 1912, No. 73/74.
78. G.O. No. 407,. Jud. (Mag.), 2 October 1924.
79. Edgar Thurston, *Castes and Tribes of Southern India*, Vol. II, (C-J), p. 133.
80. File No. 820, Judicial, February 1922, Serial Nos, 1 to 8, Home Dept. 1912, Judicial Proceedings October 1912, No. 73/74. Mr. Mudhalkars Bill.
81. Dr. H.S. Gour's Bill to amend the IPC and the code of Cr.P. C. for the purpose of prohibiting the traffic on minor girls known as devadasis for immoral purpose, Office memorandum from L.A. No. 1504, AC 13 February 1922.
82. File No. 820-22, Judicial, February 1922.
83. File No. 791, Judicial 1927, Notes, Serial Nos.1-4, Delhi, Records-2 Govt. of India, Home.
84. G.O. No. 4079, Law (Gen) 20 December 1927, File No. 791, Judicial 1927 Notes, Serial Nos. 1-4 (Delhi).
85. S. Muthulakshmi Reddy's speech in *PMLC*, November 1927, p. 416

86. Naik Maratha Mandal, *Dedication of Girls to Gods: Plea for Prohibition by Law,* p. 14.
87. G.O. No. 4079, Law, 20 December 1927.
88. Prabha Rani, "In the name of Humanity" in Aparna Basu (ed.), *Dr. Muthulakshmi Reddy: The Pathfinder,* pp. 65-66.
89. *The Awakening : Demand for Devadasi Legislation,* (Pamphlet), pp 1-5.
90. S.Muthulakshmi Reddy, *My Experience ...,* p. 57.
91. *The Awakening ...,* pp 1-5.
92. G.O. No. 4079, Law, 20 December 1927.
93. *Kudi Arasu,* 29 October 1927; C.S. Lakshmi, *The Face Behind the Mask,* p. 22.
94. G.O. No. 4079, Law. 20 December 1927; S. Muthulakshmi Reddy, *My Experience...,* pp. 57-68.
95. G.O. No. 4079, Law, 20 December 1927.
96. "A Memorial to abolish the dedication of Minor Girls to Temples: The humble representation of Kalavantalu and Shengunthar women Devadasis in Andhra and Tamilnadu", in *The awakening : Demand for Devadasi Legislation,* pp. 6-7 (Pamphlet).
97. G.O. No. 2597, Rev., 13 December 1929.
98. G.O. No. 193-94, Law (Leg.), 17 April 1929 ; G.O. No. 251, Law (Leg.), 1 June 1929.
99. *Navayuga,* 7 February 1929, p. 227, *Prajamitra,* 8 February 1929, p. 227 (MNR).
100. G.O. No. 1301, Rev., 16 January 1931.
101. S.Muthulakshmi Reddy, *My Experience...,* p. 114.
102. Fort St. George Gazette, 28 January 1930, pp. 191-93.
103. *PMLC,* January 1930, p. 993.
104. *Kudi Arasu,* 10 December 1930 ; B.S. Chandra Babu, *Social Protest in Tamil Nadu,* p. 42.
105. S. Muthulakshmi Reddy, *My Experience...,* p. 238.
106. Naik Maratha Mandal, *Dedication of Girls to Gods...,* p. 7.
107. *The Social Reformer,* 25 October 1930.
108. Radhakrishna Sharma, *Nationalism, Social reform...,* p. 243.
109. *Stri-Dharma,* November 1931, p. 26.
110. S.Muthulakshmi Reddy, *My Experience...,* p. 119.
111. Suise Tharu and K. Lalita (ed.), *Women Writing in India : 600 BC to the Present,* Vol. II, *The 20th Century,* p. 12.
112. It was founded in 1924 to protect minor girls from undesirable associations and guardianship and to educate and train them for various professions to enable them to lead an honest life. Mangalam and Varalakshmi were its President and Secretary respectively.
113. C.S. Lakshmi, *The Face Behind the Mask,* p. 22.

114. *RAMP,* 1947-48, p. 10.
115. *Stri-Dharma,* May 1931, p. 298.
116. *Ibid.,* May 1930, p. 300.
117. S. Muthulakshmi Reddy, *My Experience...,* p. 218.
118. Lakshmi Nandan Menon, "Traffic in Women and Children" in Shyam Kumari Nehru (ed.), *Our Cause,* p. 188.
119. "The Madras Council and the Immoral Traffic Act; An appeal to the Premier and to the Congress by S.Muthulakshmi Reddy" in *Report of the Women's India Association 1936-37, 37-38,* p. 22; G.O. No. 294-95, Pub., 23 March 1925.
120. *Lokapakari,* 13 August 1919, p. 2357 (MNR).
121. G.O. No. 294-95, Pub., 23 March 1925; G.O. No. 426, Jud.(Mag.), 13 March 1925.
122. G.O. No. 294-95, Pub., 23 March 1925.
123. G.O. No. 426, Jud. (Mag.), 13 March 1925.
124. *Stri-Dharma,* January 1925, p. 34.
125. *Ibid.,* March - May 1929.
126. *Ibid.,* May - June 1937, p. 284.
127. S.Muthulakshmi Reddy, *My Experience...,* p. 193.
128. *Stri-Dharma,* September 1927, p. 162.
129. *RAMP,* 1928-29, p. 28 ; *Stri-Dharma,* December 1929, p. 555; *PMLC,* Vol. XLIII, September 1928, p. 271; S. Muthulakshmi Reddy, *My Experience...,* p. 194.
130. S. Muthulakshmi Reddy, *My Experience...,* p. 202.
131. *RAMP.* 1929-30, p. 30; *Stri-Dharma,* June 1930, p. 356.
132. *Stri-Dharma,* June 1930.
133. *Swadesamitran,* 1 February 1930, p. 248; *Almanac,* 2 February 1930, p. 215, (MNR).
134. B.S. Chandra Babu, *Social Protest...,* p. 117.
135. *Triliga,* 20 January 1931, p. 173 (MNR).
136. *Swadesamitran,* 7 February 1930, p. 286 (MNR).
137. *India,* 2 June 1921, p. 788 (MNR).
138. *Stri-Dharma,* November 1930, pp. 5-6.
139. *Ibid.,* May 1931, p. 301.
140. *Ibid.,* May-June 1931, p. 618.
141. *PMLC,* Vol. LVII, August 1931, p. 220.
142. *India,* 30 July 1930, p. 1071 (MNR).
143. *Stri-Dharma,* May - June 1931, pp. 297-98.
144. *Dravidian,* 16 February 1932, p. 618 (MNR).
145. *Mathrubhumi,* 23 April 1931, p. 618 (MNR).
146. G.O. NO. 1200, Home, 4 March 1939.
147. *Stri-Dharma,* January 1934, p. 121.

148. G.O. No. 1611, Home, 22 April 1937; G.O. No. 2788, Home, 21 July 1937.
149. FR, 4 April 1938 ; *RAMP, 1938-39*, p. 4; G.O. No. 4819, Home, 29 September 1938.
150. *Report of the Women's India Association*, 1936-37, 1937-38, pp. 14,38.
151. G.O. Ms. No. 4027, Home, 30 September 1940; G.O. No. 818, Home, 18 February 1941 ; *Madras in 1940*, p. 3 ; *RAMP* 1940-41, p. 5.
152. *RAMP*, 1947-48, p. 11.
153. *Dravidian*, 16 February 1932, p. 262. (MNR).
154. *India*, 16 April 1932, p. 497 (MNR).
155. *Stri-Dharma*, January 1934, p. 121.
156. G.O. No. 986, Home, 28 February 1940.
157. G.O. No. 818, Home, 18 February 1941.
158. G.O. No. 986, Home, 28 February 1940; G.O. No. 818, Home, 18 February 1941.
159. *RAMP*, 1935-36, p. XX.
160. *Stri-Dharma*, April-May, 1936, p. 76.
161. *Ibid.*
162. G.O. No. 4717, Home, 29 September 1938.
163. G.O. No. 4826, Home, 9 September 1939; G.O. No. 4027, Home, 30 September 1940.

Six

Conclusion

It is obvious from the foregoing study that Women's movement had passed through two important phases of development within the three decades (1917 - 1947). In the first phase, women leaders campaigned against the tortures and restraints imposed on women. The operation of discriminatory laws that subjected women to legal disabilities were attacked by them. Besides, voting rights for women, compulsory primary education and eradication of social evils were demanded by them. They blamed the society for their inferior status. Women's emancipation was their priority not the nation's freedom. The second phase saw the women's question intertwined with the trends with the nationalist movement. Many women plunged into the civil disobedience movement. Infact women's movement became an integral part of nationalism. Women demanded equal adult franchise and no special reservation for them. These demands were supported by the Congress also. Engaged shoulder to shoulder with their menfolks on the long drawn out fight against the British rule, these women established a moral right to equality.

Women's India Association which led the women's movement in Tamil Nadu, made remarkable progress and achievements. The movement had been one of evolutionary rather than revolutionary. The language in which the women presented their case was one of caution never confrontation. Though women demanded equality of rights and opportunities, they never wanted to destroy the traditional family structure.

Women's movement emerged as a part of the social reform movement. The appearance of Annie Besant and Margaret E. Cousins, both western feminists, on the political arena of Tamilnadu was an important landmark in the development of public consciousness towards women's emancipation and education. It had given a fresh stimulus to the feminist movement. In fact it was Annie Besant who had given a proper direction to the women's movement in Tamilnadu.

The first offshoot of women's movement was female education. It resulted in the emergence of a number of educated women, the first cadres of the women's movement who gradually took over from men the movement and the organisation and devotedly fought against some of the injustices perpetrated on them. They not only went to universities for general education, but also pursued profession like teaching, medicine, nursing etc. Similarly professional education had also expanded. Madras Medical College was the first one in India to open its portals to women as early as 1875. Madras led the other provinces in female education. Philip Hartog in his report (1928) wrote, "Madras leads both in the per centage of girls at school and of trained women teachers." Though women demanded compulsory primary education and equal rights and opportunities for both men and women, regarding the subjects of study they were unanimous that the curriculum for girls should emphasis subjects of feminine interests. Even S. Muthulakshmi Reddy held the same opinion. Since the number of girls who took to profession such as teaching, medicine etc. were very small, and the majority of girls were meant for homelife, the education should be such as to enable them to look after their homes in a most efficient manner. The popular opinion was that though men and women should have equal rights in religion, social and political matters, it was essential that there should be some difference in the system of education devised for them. Therefore the object of girls education was not mainly to train women for jobs or to help them to obtain independent means of livelihood, but to make them good wives, mothers and efficient home makers.

Their aim was to improve their position within the established structure of the family and society and not to demand equality with men. They accepted the existing pattern of sex structured roles, but attempted to elevate their status within that frame work. They did not want to alter the conventional functions and divisions in the family. They limited their efforts to educating public opinion to proscribe oppressive convention and practices. The girls education could still be terminated at any time if a suitable marriage could be arranged. Those women who received education had done credit to their sex by leading the movements for social reforms, to prevent child marriages, to terminate the *devadasi* system etc.

The study indicates that there existed two contradictory moralities for women. On the one hand high value was set on *karpu* among women by the Hindus and the desire not to run away risk by late marriage and late consummation resulted in child marriages. Because of this system the girl child from the moment of her birth to her death underwent one continuous life long suffering as a child wife, as a child mother and very often as a child widow. The society developed a stereotyped ideals of *pativrata* which reduced women to physical, mental and spiritual slave of men. On the otherhand there developed a well established institution of prostitution. It condemned the innocent victims who were very often girls, destitutes and neglected children to a life of unspeakable horror and misery. Another allied institution was the *devadasi* system. In the name of religion, women of certain communities in Tamilnadu were dedicated to temple service and they became priests' own prostitutes. The ceremony of dedication precluded matrimony but it was in no way a prelude to the difficult discipline of voluntary celibacy. The dedicated girls became either openly or secretly prostitutes. Mahatma Gandhi said,

> "It is not right that for our lust a single sister should lead a life of shame and humiliation".

S. Muthulakshmi Reddy on behalf of the Women's India Association, brought series of legislations in the Madras Legislative Council to abolish all these evils. Passing of the legislations were infact only a partial success. The government did not take efforts to implement them.

Though Women's India Association was a non-political organ interested in promoting educational opportunities for women and improving their position by social and legal reforms it soon became an all embracing end with political demands. It became increasingly involved in the question of women's right to vote and was largely responsible for organising the suffrage movement. The right to vote was a necessary prerequisite for other desired female rights. It was infact the first equal rights movement. It was in 1917 for the first time, the women's deputation made an organised effort to press forward their political demands. The cruz of the demand of the deputation was that when franchise conditions for India were being drawn up, women be recognised as 'people' and their sex should not be made a disqualification for the exercise of the franchise. They demanded that their sex should not be listed along with lunatics, idiots, criminals, imbeciles, aliens and children while enfranchising them. The women felt deeply outraged at being treated as less than human, deprived of citizen's rights. They were also conscious of their dependence on the British Government for a change in the electoral laws. Hence they conducted campaigns to educate British public opinion on the needs of such reforms. They also started the branches of Women's India Association in Britain. Because of the incessant effort of the Women's India Association, the Madras Legislative Council had given the lead to other legislative councils in India in the matter of giving privileges to women. It was this council that first passed resolutions giving the right of franchise to women, first to nominate woman as member of the council. It was also a first instance in which a woman had been elected as a deputy president of the Legislative Council.

They thought if they had seats in the legislature, no need for them to depend entirely on men for legislative social reforms. It was infact correct. S. Muthulakshmi Reddy, who joined the legislature as women's representative brought series of legislations to uplift women, which received a large measure of support from men politicians also. The women's movement progressed as complementary to the national movement.

Because of the incessant effort of the Women's India Association, women became members of the legislatures, municipal and local boards, town councillors, honorary magistrates, university senators, lawyers, doctors, teachers etc. They also represented various commissions for India and other reform committees. S. Muthulakshmi Reddy was chosen to represent the Hartog Education Committee. Radhabai Subbarayan was selected for the Round Table Conference in London and Ammu Swaminathan and Durgabai Amma became the members of the Constituent Assembly.

Laws were passed much earlier in the Princely States with out much difficulty. Mysore state abolished the practice of dedication of girls to the temples by 1909 itself. Mysore and Travancore enfranchised its women even before the Madras Presidency. Princely state of Travancore made Dr. Poonam Lukose, as its Health Minister much earlier than the British Government permitted the Indian women to enter into the legislatures. In the Madras Presidency, with much difficulty only legislations infavour of emancipating and giving rights to women were passed. Inspite of the public opinion being infavour of them, the British Government had not implemented them sincerely. It made S. Muthulakshmi Reddy to express her fervent hope that with the securing of self-government, the Indian women would soon get rid of all these disabilities. Margaret E. Cousins wrote in *Stri-Dharma*,

> "Where men are slaves how can women be freed from the age long customs and conventions".

From then onward freedom of the country became their priority. They saw clearly the close relation between India's freedom and women's emancipation.

During the Civil Disobedience movement many leaders forged strong links between the two movements. Women abandoned their seclusion to actively participate in the Civil Disobedience movement. Rukmini Lakshmipathi led the Vedaranyam salt satyagraha and was arrested and imprisoned for one year. She was the first woman to be arrested during the Civil Disobedience movement. Durgabai Amma acted as a 'Madras City Dictator'. When leaders were arrested, the movement was carried on by women. Many women from Tamil Nadu joined the Civil Disobedience movement as equals. As a mark of protest against the arrest of Mahatma Gandhi, S. Muthulakshmi Reddy resigned her seat in the legislature, though she was a non-political person. Along with the Congress, women also boycotted the election in 1930. In the nationalist movement, the involvement of women was accepted in a natural manner and their rights were recognised without any apparent hostility or resistance. Many members of Women's India Association joined the nationalist movement and found the joy of their life in service of the motherland and at the same time they were an untiring campaigners for women's rights. Nationalism has stimulated change and involved women in roles that were new and diverse. It transformed them in the image of the emancipated women of western society.

It is obvious, regarding the franchise rights for women, two factions emerged in Tamil Nadu. One was for adult franchise and no special privileges. They adopted an equal right perspective and was supported by the Congress. The other argued for increased representation and special qualifications for women. They were supported by the British

Government. Radhabai Subbarayan, the only woman in the Franchise Sub-Committee, and the representative of the Government to discuss about women's issues in the Round Table Conference demanded that there should be a special franchise for women and a fixed proportion of women to the legislatures during the first formative years. Though she was a long standing member of the Women's India Association, it did not approve of her. On the other hand leading women of the Women's India Association repeatedly requested for adult franchise. They were opposed to the granting of any special facilities and wished women to be returned by "open door of competition". S. Muthulakshmi Reddy, who went to London on behalf of the three national women's organisations to represent them in the Joint Select Committee, made it clear that their organisations throughout stood for adult franchise which was the only logical and desirable method of fairly enfranchising the whole population. Reserved seats for women was not thought of as a favour, by S. Muthulakshmi Reddy. She considered it only a means by which the then inequalities under which women suffered would be acknowledged. Under the system of adult franchise on equal terms the theoretical equality of men and women might be maintained. Hence leading women of Madras did not want `special treatment'. The 'wifehood qualification' suggested by the series of committees was considered objectionable by them on the ground that it placed a premium on marriage and perpetuated the idea of women's dependence on men and did not recognise their independent right of suffrage. They said,

> "There could never be an equal partnership where women were not only economically dependent upon their male relations but also made to depend upon them for their citizens rights".

Women's India Association demanded uniform adult suffrage to eliminate all inequalities and discrimination. Since Women's India Association was not affiliated to any political parties, in the election, it encouraged the women to vote for the candidates who positively answer the questionnaire, (See Appendix) promising to work for women's emancipation and Swaraj.

The nationalist movement generated strength and confidence among women which helped them to organise and to fight for their own cause rather than their dependent upon the benevolent men in society to promote their cause. On independence women achieved full voting rights and their long battle against second class citizen came to an end, yet whose role was primarily at home.

APPENDIX - I

Women's Vote

The following is a questionnaire from the several women associations in Madras to the men candidates who stood for council election.

You will have women's votes if you answer in the affirmative the following questions :

1. Would you introduce and support all measures for developing the higher education for women?
2. Would you introduce and support all schemes for extending modern scientific medical relief to Indian mothers and children? e.g. children's hospital, maternity and child welfare centres, training of nurses, midwives and health visitors and medical inspection for school children?
3. Will you support Sarda Bill and the select committee report on that bill that the marriageable age of girls be raised to fourteen and that of boys to eighteen?
4. Are you for penalising marriage between minor girls and old men over seventy years?
5. Would you try your best to put down the sordid custom of buying bride grooms?
6. Are you for raising the age of consent over eighteen at least outside marital bond?
7. Would you encourage widow remarriage and take steps to remove the stigma that is attached to widows in the country?
8. Are you for the closing up of the brothels and for penalising commercialised vice?

9. Would you introduce legislation or support any legislation for the rescuing and protection of minor girls from immoral surroundings and introduce the necessary amendments in the Madras Childrens Act?
10. Are you for doing away with the present degenerated *devadasi* institution in the Hindu temples and for enacting more stringent measures for disallowing the *'pottu ceremony'* within temples for major girls also?
11. Are you for making the Hindu marriage laws just and equal between wife and husband?
12. Are you for giving inheritance rights to wives and daughters and owners and disposers of husband's and father's property?
13. Are you for prohibition and total abstinence from drink?
14. Will you introduce legislation to improve the condition of factory women and child labour in this country?
15. Are you for encouraging indigenous industries and khaddar?
16. Do you realise that untouchability, caste and communalism are a great hindrance to the attainment of India's freedom and would you work for the speedy eradication of the same?

(*Source*: *Stri-Dharma*, May 1929, p. 312).

APPENDIX - II

Questionnaire: Women's Suffrage

At present women are admitted to the suffrage on the same terms as men but as the existing qualifications are mainly based on property and the payment of taxes the number of women on the provincial electoral rolls is only a little over a quarter of a million as compared with 6½ million men. The Statutory Commission proposed that the wives and widows (if ones 25 years of age) of men entitled to vote under the property qualification should be enfranchised and that in addition an educational qualification should apply to women over twentyone as well as to men. In the Franchise Sub-Committee of the Round Table Conference it was suggested that the age limit should be twentyone for women as well as for men:

(a) Are you infavour of increasing the women's electorate in the ways suggested or would you prefer any other method?. If so what method? To what extent would you favour an increase in women's electorate?

(b) In the event of a system of group representation being established do you consider that women should be formed into groups and if so should separate groups be formed for women or should groups contain both men and women?.

(c) The suggestion has been made that any rate as a temporary measure, the legislature should co-opt women members an extent not exceeding 5% by a system of proportional representation so as to ensure some representation of women in the legislature. What are your views on the suggestions?

(*Source*: Indian Franchise Committee, vol. III: Memoranda submitted by the local governments and the provincial franchise committees in reply to the Indian Franchise committee's questionnaire, pp. 3-4).

APPENDIX - III

Women's India Association - Manifesto

A COPY OF WIA MANIFESTO TO CANDIDATES FOR EITHER THE CENTRAL OR LOCAL LEGISLATURES

The women have now to awaken to their duty for the responsible use of their votes. Every where the women of all classes and creeds have spoken with one voice and they are agreed as to what they want. We stand for every constructive effort to remove the many evils that are laying paralysing hands upon the progress, happiness and prosperity of the country and its people. We believe that injustice to women is one of the greatest of these evils. The ignorance, illiteracy, lack of the commonest amenities and opportunities for a healthy social life, the legal and social inequalities last but not least the unequal moral standard putting all blame and punishment on the woman and ignoring or condoning the same vice in a man, these are at the root of all our backward and retrograde customs and condition. We, therefore stand for equality and justice and fair dealing between men and women. This will be the first step towards progress, for the liberating of the energy of half the country will give the necessary impetus for the regeneration of the country and if the women's point of view finds its rightful place in the management of the public life, then we may have fewer wars, fewer quarrels. Therefore to the candidate, irrespective of his or her political party who will stand for the condition laid down in our manifesto will have the votes of the women.

(*Source*: *Stri-Dharma*, Sept. 1934, p. 494-95).

APPENDIX - IV

Ambujammal S (1898-1984)

Born 1898 - in an aristocratic family in Mylapore - met Gandhi and Kasturibai in the 1920s - their simple life inspired her - became white clad devotee of Gandhi - dedicated her life to the women's welfare - participated in the foreign cloth boycott movement - 1930 and 1932 - it was she who set the pace for the conservative women folk in the south to join the freedom movement - active member Women's India Association - started the Srinivasa Gandhi Nilayam in 1948 - chair person of the reception committee - Congress session 1955 - chair person of the State Social Welfare Board, 1961 - 64 - awarded the presidential award of 'Padmasri' in 1964 - author of several books - her autobiography was titled *nankanda bharatham*.

Ammu Swaminathan

Born 1894 in Malabar - married to Dr. Swaminadhan, a lawyer of the Madras Bar - started her Public career as a member of the Women's India Association - later became a Vice - President and President, one of the founder members of the AIWC - in 1930 entered the freedom movement - elected to Madras Corporation 1934 -39 - went to USA as a guest delegate of the International Women's Conference, 1939 participated in the QIM arrested and imprisoned - elected to central assembly from Madras city constituency 1945 - in 1946 member of the constituent assembly from the Madras - elected to Rajya Sabha-travelled widely.

Anchalai Ammal

Born 1890 - Cuddalore, South Arcot district - studied upto VIII standard - married to R.Murugesapadayachi, a freedom fighter - had four daughters and two sons - travelled throughout India - joined the Congress in 1920 - participated in the Neill statue Satyagraha in 1927 - sentenced to imprisonment till the rising of the court and a fine of Rs. 25/- or in default one week severe imprisonment - her daughter Amma kannu Ammal of 11 years - participated in the Neill statue Satyagraha and was sent to the children's home - Anjalai Ammal look part in the toddy shop picketing and the boycott of foreign cloth shops, 1932 and Individual Satyagraha of 1941 and Quit India movement 1942 - imprisoned in 1932 for six months 1933 for three months, 1941 for eighteen months and 1943 for eight months and two weeks - called as Velu Nachiar of South Arcot district.

Duragabai Amma (Duragabai Deshmukh)

At the age of 12 left school - took up Gandhi's constructive work - 1930, led the Salt Sathyagraha in Madras - became Madras city Dictator - imprisoned - private study -M.A degree from Andhra University in 1940 - bachelor of law - Madras Bar in 1942 -she along with others started the Andhra Mahila Sabha - developed into tutorial school coaching given particularly to widows and deserted women - member Social Services Planning Commission in New Delhi 1952 - married Deshmukh in 1953, the then Finance Minister of India - 1953 to 1962 chairperson - Central Social Welfare Board.

Manjubhashini

Born Madras in 1906 d/o Narasimha Iyer - one of the leading lawyers of Madras - S.S.L.C - married at the age of 13 to Subramaniam - public career began in 1932 with the setting up of the Madras Swadeshi Emporium, a shop run by the women to sell swadeshi articles in support of the Congress khadi movement - 1942 - took part in the Quit India Movement - arrested - imprisoned for one year - kept in Vellore jail - as a member of the INA she helped in the rehabilitation of the INA personnel. From 1940 to 1949 she served as a commissioner for Bharat Scouts and Guides, Madras Presidency as was responsible for encouraging large number of young people to join the movement - in 1949 - set up the Bala Mandir (Children's hospital) of which she was the honorary general secretary- convener of the women's section of the Congress in 1947-

continued till 1967 - became the state convener for the Bharath Sevak Samaj from 1952 for about ten years - nominated to the Madras Legislative Council in 1952 continued till 1972. As a member of the parliamentary delegation she visited U.K. in 1964 as a guest of the British Govt - member of the State Social Welfare Board for two years.

Muthulakshmi Reddy (1886-1968)

Born 1886 - Pudukottai - first woman student to join Maharajah Men's College Pudukottai - with the aid of a State scholarship she joined the Madras Medical College in 1907 - passed M.B.C.M exam 1912 - in 1914 married Dr. T. Sundara Reddi - in 1925 with the aid of the Govt. of India scholarship she went to England to specialise in the diseases of women and children for a year - active member Women's India Association from 1917 - became a nominated member Madras Legislative Council - in 1927 became its Deputy president the first woman to hold such position - brought legislations to abolish *devadasi* system, immoral traffic on women and children and child marriage-worked for compulsory primary education-founded the Auvai home in 1930-founded Cancer Institute awarded 'Padma Bushan'-she was a member of the Hartog-Education Commission - travelled all over.

Radhabai Subbarayan (1988-1955)

Born 1888 - married to Subbarayan an advocate Kumaramagalam - M.A in the Presidency College, Madras - joined the Congress in 1922 - participated in the II R.T.C in London - member Franchise Sub Committee - advocated special representation for women - took part in the Individual Satyagraha in 1941 - arrested and imprisoned for six months - Minister for Health in the Rajaji Ministry.

Rukmini Lakshmipathi (1891-1951)

Born Madras, 1891 - ed. B.A - connected with the Congress since 1928 -led the Vedaranyam Salt Satyagraha in 1930 - arrested and imprisoned for one year - first woman in India to be arrested during C.D.M - founder president of the Madras Youth League - member Women's India Association - President TNCC, 1930, Vice President 1935 - 36 - MLA 1937 - Deputy speaker MLA 1937 - 39 - bye election 1934 - elected to the Central Legislative Assembly - Minister of Health 1946.

Sister Subbulakshmi (1886-1969)

Born 1886 - Tanjore - at the age of 11 married to a boy whom she had never seen - a few weeks later he died continued her studies - passed her B.A in 1911 winning first class, first Hindu woman and a first widow to pass that examination - founded widows home, Sarada home and Sarada Vidyalaya with its own training sectors and model school - she educated a lot of widows - in recognition of her services to the women and girls of Madras Presidency, she was awarded *Kaiser-i-Hindu* gold modal. Her motto had always been, 'to give and not count the cost to achieve through suffering and sacrifice. Her biography entitled 'A child widow's story' was written by Dr. Monica Felton, published in London.

Dr. Soundaram Ramachandran (1905-1984)

Born Madurai - joined Lady Hardinge Medical College - New Delhi and graduated in 1935, standing first in the University - interested in the harijans and women welfare - married G. Ramachandran, a well known Gandhian doing Harijan uplift work - took part in the Quit India Movement 1942 - founded Avvai Rural Mahila Service with the help of Muthulakshmi Reddy and Prathinidhi Kasturba Gandhi National Memorial Trust in Tamil Nadu - founded the Gandhigram in 1947 - elected to the Madras Assembly in 1952- also founded the Siva Sailam Ashram in 1962 - Deputy Minister for Education Govt. of India - travelled widely.

Selected Glossary

charka	- spinning wheel
deeparadhana	- waving of lighted lamp
devadasi	- woman dedicated to Hindu temple
dharmayutha	- war of justice
garbhadan	- consummation
hartal	- strike, closing of shops and suspension of work as a mark of protest or sorrow
inams	- lands given to the devadasis in recognition of their services
kaimpen	- widow
karpu	- chastity
khadi, khaddar	- hand spin hand woven cloth
kumkum	- a mark put in the forehead by the Hindu women
kudumba vizhakku	- lamp of the home
lathi	- stick used as weapon
mufassal	- up country, interior, rural localities
parathaiyar	- prostitutes
patta	- official document given recognising the ownership of the land
pativrata	- absolute obedient wife
pennkalvi	- women education
pottugattu	- the ceremony of the dedication of devadasis
purnaswaraj	- complete independence
satyagraha	- non-violent resistance
satyagrahi	- non-violent agitator

sruti	- a music
swaraj	- self-rule, a movement for India's Independence
swadeshi	- indegenous, one's own country
tali	- sacred chain or thread worn by the married woman as a symbol of marriage
toddy	- country liquor
vande mataram	- salutation to the mother land

Bibliography

I. Primary Sources

(A) Government Orders and Secret, Under Secretary's Safe Files.

(B) Freedom movement - type scripts (TNA).

(C) Reports, Memorandas and Proceedings.

(D) Interviews.

(E) Ancient Tamil Literature.

II. Secondary Sources

(A) Periodicals

(B) Journals

(C) Articles

(D) Books

(a) English

(b) Vernacular

I. Primary Sources

(A) (1) Government Orders pertaining to the Departments of Education, Educational and Public Health, Home, Judicial, Law, Local and Municipal, Local Self Government, Public, Public Works, Revenue.

(2) Secret, Under Secretary's Safe Files, 1924 - 1933.

(B) Freedom Movement - Type Scripts (TNA)

Anti War and Quit India Movement, 1939-1945.

Civil Disobedience Movement (Confidential) 1930-1932, 1934-1935.

Civil Disobedience Movement, (Secret Reports Retained File).

Diary of Important Events, 1910-1947.

District Magistrates Accounts on Civil Disobedience Movement.

Extracts from Secret Files relating to Civil Disobedience Movement, 1929-1932, 1931-1932, 1934-1935.

Extracts from the *New India*, 1914-1918.

Extracts from *The Hindu*, 1910, 1912 1921-1936.

Extracts from the Report on English and Vernacular News papers owned by Indians relating to the role of the Press in the Home Rule Movement, 1915-1918.

Extracts from G.O's relating to Home Rule Movement in the Madras Presidency, (Rowlatt Act, 1914-1920).

Extracts from Secret Reports relating to Home Rule movement, 1914-1920.

Extracts from G.Os Relating to Provincial Autonomy, Elections, Ministry, Prohibition, 1935-1940.

Extracts taken from Govt. of Madras Secret Book : District Calendar of Events of Civil Disobedience Movement, August-December 1942.

Personal Statements of Political Personalities 1955 (TNA).

(C) Reports, Memorandas and Proceedings

Annuals, Reports on the Administration of the Madras Presidency, 1916-1917 to 1946-47 (30 volumes) (Madras: Govt.press, 1918-1948).

Annuals, Reports of the Women's India Association, 1922-23 to 1936-37, (Madras : WIA., 1924 to 1938).

Annuals, Reports of the Indian National Congress, 1887, 1888, 1916, 1919, 1927.

Annuals and Quinquennium Reports, Reports on the Public Instruction of the Madras Presidency 1870-71 to 1945-46 (Madras: Govt. press 1882 to 1947).

All India Spinners Association Report 1925-26.

Asylum Press Almanac, 1897, 1898.

Bamford, B.C. *Histories of Non Cooperation and Khilafat Movements* (Confl.) (Delhi, 1925).

Census of India, 1891, Vol. XIII, *Madras*, (Madras: Govt. Press, 1892).

Census of India, 1911, Vol. XII, *Madras*, Part I (Madras: Govt. Press, 1912).

Census of India, 1961, *Handlooms in Madras State*, Vol. IX, Part XI-A (Madras: Govt. Press, 1965).

Census of India, 1961, *General Report, Madras*, IX, Part- IA (II), (Madras : Govt. Press, 1960).

Demi - Official Fortnightly Reports from the Government of Madras to the Government of India 1914-1937.

Govt. of Madras, Proceedings of the Madras Legislative Council, 1921-1937 (Many volumes).

Govt. of India's Despatch on Proposals for Constitutional Reform (Calcutta: Govt. Press, 1930).

Handbook of Information on the Administration of the Presidency of Madras, 1929 and 1939 (Madras: Govt. Press, 1929, 1941).

Indian Statutory Commission: Interim Report (Calcutta: Govt. Press, 1929).

Indian Statutory Commission Report, Vol. I, Survey (London: His Majesty's Stationary Office, 1930).

Joint Committee on Indian Constitutional Reform 1933-1934 Vol. II, part-I, Report (London: His Majesty's Stationary Office, 1934).

Joint Committee on Indian Constitutional Reform, Vol. II-C, Minutes of Evidence given before the Joint Committee on Indian Constitutional Reform (London: His Majesty's Stationary Office, 1934).

Madras Year Book, 1923 (Madras : Govt. Press, 1923).

Madras in 1940 (Madras : Govt. Press, 1941).

Madras in 1945 (Outline of the Administration) part-I (Madras: Govt.Press, 1946).

Madras Native Newspaper Reports, 1885-1935.

Manual of the Administration of the Madras Presidency (Madras : Govt. Press, 1885).

Memoranda of the Administration of the Madras Presidency (Madras: Govt. Press, 1930).

Memoranda of the Madras Government on the working of the Reformed Government : Submitted to Indian Statutory Commission (Madras: Govt. Press, 1930).

Progress of Education in India 1897-1902 (Calcutta : Govt. Press, 1903).

Report of the Age of Consent Committee 1929 (Calcutta: Govt. Press, 1930).

Report of the Indian Central Committee, 1929 (Calcutta : Govt. Press, 1929).

Report of the Indian Franchise Committee, Vols. I-IV (Calcutta: Govt. press, 1932).

Report of the Indian Education Commission, 1882, Part II (Calcutta: Govt. Press, 1883).

Report of the Madras Abkari Department, 1918-19 to 1938-39 (Madras : Govt. Press, 1919 to 1939), 21 volumes.

Review of Education in India in 1886 with special reference to the report of the Education Commission (Calcutta : Govt. Press, 1888).

Selections from Educational Records, Vol. I Educational Reports, 1859-71 (Delhi: Govt. 1960).

Status of Women in India: A Synopsis of the Report of the National Committee on the Status of Women, 1971 - 1974 (New Delhi: ICSSR, 1975).

The Civil Disobedience Movement, 1930-31 (Confidential) (Madras: Govt. press, 1932).

(D) Interviews

Interview with Mrs. Meena Krishnaswamy, veteran freedom fighter, 12 August 1993, Madras.

Interview with Mr. Dalavai, a veteran freedom fighter, 12 August 1993, Madras.

Interview with Mr. Srinivasan, husband of Sonabai, veteran freedom fighter, 10 October 1993, Coimbatore.

(E) Ancient Tamil Literature

Kalithokai
Nanmanikkadikai
Purananuru
Thirukkural

II. Secondary Sources

(A) Periodicals

(a) Vernacular (Tamil)

Ananda Vikadan
Kudi Arasu
Navasakti (1920 - 1932)
Sutandira Sangu, 1931-1935

(b) English

Harijan
Indian Annual Register
Indian Quarterly Register
Indian Ladies Magazine
New India
Shri-Dharma
Young India

(B) Journals

Economic and Political Weekly
Indo-British Review
Journal of the Institute of Asian Studies
Journal of the Mythic Society
Manushi
Social Change
Social Welfare

(C) Articles

Ali, Aruna Asaf "Women's Suffrage in India" in Shyam Kumari Nehru (ed.) *Our Cause : A Symposium of Indian Women* (Allahabad : Kitabistan, 1938).

Ambujammal, S. "Manjubhashini" in Butchi Arumugam, et. al (ed.) *Some Illustrious Women of India : With special reference to Tamilnadu* (Madras : Asian Books, 1975).

Amrit Kaur, Rajkumari "Women : Their role in the Reconstruction of India" *Congress Golden Jubilee Brochur*, NO.9 (Allahabad : AICC, 1935).

Bahadurji, G.J. "Women and Political Struggle" in Shyam Kumari Nehru (ed.) *Our Cause : A Symposium of Indian Women* (Allahabad : Kitabistan, 1938).

Basu, Aparna "The Role of Women in the Indian's Struggle for Freedom" in B.R. Nanda (ed.) *Indian Women : From Purdah to Modernity* (rpt., New Delhi: Radiant pub., 1990).

Baig, Tari Ali "Durgabai As I See Her" *Social Welfare*, August-September 1978.

Caplan, Patricia, "Women's Organizations in Madras city, India" in Patricia Caplan and Janet M. Burja (eds.) *Women United Women Divided : Cross Cultural Perspectives on Female Solidarity* (London : Tavilstock pub., 1978).

Chakravarthy, P. "Emergence of Justice Party" *Journal of Indian History*, April and August, 1977, part-II, Vol. LV.

Chandra Sekhar, Lalitha "Sister Subbulakshmi" in *Women's India Association Golden Jubilee Souvernir 1917-1967* (Madras: WIA, 1969).

Chattopadhyaya, Kamaladevi "Future of Indian Women's Movement" in Shyam Kumari Nehru (ed.) *Our Cause : A Symposium of Indian Women* (Allahabad : Kitabistan, 1938).

Chitnis, Suma "Women's movement : Indian Ethos and Indian Convictions" in Rehana Ghadially (ed.) *Women in Indian Society : A Reader* (New Delhi: Sage pub., 1988).

Forber, Geraldine, "The Women's Movement in India, Traditional Symbols and New Role" in M.S.A. Rao (ed.), *Social Movements in India* (New Delhi: Manohar pub., 1979).

__________ "Votes for Women : The Demand for Women's Franchise in India 1917-1937" in Vina Mazumdar (ed.) *Symbols of power : Studies in the Political Status of Women in India* (Bombay : Allied pub., 1975).

Jayalakshmi, S. "Women Poets and Musicians of Tamil Nadu", *Journal of the Institute of Asian Studies,* Madras, Vol. 4, September, 1986.

Iyer, Seshagiri T.V. "The Devdasis in India" *The Journal of Mythic Society,* Bangalore, Vol. XIII, October 1922, No. I.

Kalpagam, U " Women in the 21st Century" in Sebasti L.Raj (ed.) *Quest for Gender Justice : A Critique of the Status of Women in India* (Madras : T.R. pub., 1991).

Kaur, Amrit, "Women Under the New Constitution" in Shyam Kumari Nehru (ed.) *Our Cause* : *A Symposium of Indian Women* (Allahabad: Kitabistan, 1938).

Krishna, Sushila, "Ammu Swaminitham" in Butchi Arumugam et. al (ed.) *Some Illustrious Women of India: With special preference to Tamilnadu.* (Madras : Asian Books, 1975).

Mazumdar, Vina "Women in the Political Process" in Maithreyi Krishna Raj (ed.) *Women's Studies in India : Some Perspectives* (Bombay : Popular Prakasan, 1986).

________ "The Social Reform Movement in India : Ranade to Nehru" in B.R. Nanda (ed.) *Indian Women : From Purdah to Modernity* (rpt., New Delhi: Radiant pub., 1990).

Mehta, Hansa "Political status of the Indian Women" in Shyam Kumari Nehru (ed.) *Our Cause : A Symposium of Indian Women* (Allahabad: Kitabistan, 1938).

Mehta, Rama "From Purdah to Modernity" in B.R. Nanda (ed.) *Indian Women: From Purdah to Modernity* (rpt., New Delhi : Radiant pub., 1990).

Menon, Lakshmi Nandan "Traffic in Women and Children" in Shyam Kumari Nehru (ed.) Our Cause : *A Symposium of Indian Women* (Allahabad : Kitabistan, 1938).

Nagaraja, Yamini "Women and Social Change" in Yashoda Bhat (ed.) *Beyond the threshold:Indian Women on the Move* (Delhi: B.R. pub, 1995).

Neelakandan, Seetha "Margaret E. Cousin" in Butchi Arumugam et.al (ed.) *Some Illustrious Women of India : With special reference to Tamil Nadu* (Madras : Asian Books, 1975).

Nehru, Uma "Whither Women" in Shyam Kumari Nehru (ed.) *Our Cause : A Symposium of Indian Women* (Allahabad : Kitabistan, 1938).

Paul, P.C. "Colonialism and Women's Education in India" in *Social Change*, Vol. 19, No.2, June, 1980.

Ramaswami, Vasumathi "Padmashri S., Ambujammal" in Butchi Arumugam, et al (ed); *Some Illustrious Women of India : With special reference to Tamil Nadu* (Madras : Asian Books, 1975).

Rani, Prabhu "In the name of Humanity" in Aparna Basu (ed.) *Dr. Muthulakshmi Reddy : The Path finder* (AIWC pub., 1978).

Sadasivan, D. "Social reform movement in Tamil Nadu with particular reference to women" in S.P. Sen (ed.) *Social and Religious reform Movements in the nineteeth century* (Calcutta: Institute of Historical Studies, 1979).

Sathianadhan, V. "History of Education in the Madras Presidency" in V.Kalyana Ram Iyer, *The Madras Journal of Education*, vol.V, New Series, January-December, 1891.

Sathyarani, G.A.L. "Women's Education, Attitudes of Indian Intelligentsia, and the British Government" in K.R. Hanumanthan (ed.) *Proceedings of the Tamil Nadu History Congress, I session*, 1994 (Madras, 1995).

Sivaraman, Mythily " Remarkable political Activist, *The Hindu*, 29 March 1992.

Somasekhar, Renuka " Ida Sophia Scudder" in Butchi Arumugam, et, al (ed.) *Some Illustrious Women of India : With Special Reference to Tamil Nadu* (Madras : Asian Books, 1975).

Subramanian "The Home Rule League and Mrs. Annie Besant" in N.R. Ray (ed.) *Public Associations in India* (Calcutta, 1989).

Sundari, Shantha "Sister Subbulakshmi" in Butchi Arumugam, et. al (ed.) *Some Illustrious Women of India : With Special Reference to Tamil Nadu* (Madras : Asian Bookes, 1975).

Viswanathan, E. Sa. "E.V. Ramaswami Naicker and the Tamil Nadu Congress" *Journal of Indian History*, April 1976, Part-1, Vol. LIV, p. 178.

Vijayalakshmi, S. "Healing the Breach and the Home Rule Movement" in B.N. Pande (ed.) *A Centenary History of the Indian National Congress*, 1885-1919, Vol. I, (New Delhi : Vikas, 1885).

(D) Books

(a) English

Agnew, Vijay *Elite Women in Indian Politics* (Delhi : Shakti Pub., 1986).

Agarwal S.P. and J.C. Aggrawal *Women's Education in India : Historical Review, Present Status Perspective Plan with Statistical indicators* (New Delhi : Concept pub., 1992).

Ahluwalia, B.K. and Shashi Akluwalia, *Rajaji and Gandhi* (New Delhi : Allora pub., 1978).

Altekar, A.S. *The Position of Women in Hindu civilization : From Prehistoric Times to the Present day,* (rpt., Delhi: Motilal Banarsidass, 1983).

Aiyangar, P.J. Srinivasa *Pre Aryan Tamil Culture* (rpt., New Delhi : Asian Educational services, 1985).

Arnold, David *The Congress in Tamil Nadu : The Nationalist politics of South India* (1919-1937), (New Delhi : Manohar, 1977).

Arumugam, Butchi, et al. (ed.) *Some Illustrious Women of India: With Special Reference to Tamil Nadu* (Madras : Asian Books, 1975).

Arunachalam, A. *Khadi Economics : A few Aspects*, (Madurai, 1977).

Baig, Tara Ali, (ed.) *Women of India* (rpt., New Delhi : Govt. of India, 1990).

Baker, Christopher John *The Politics of South India*, 1920-1937 (New Delhi: Cambridge, 1976).

Bakshi, S.R. *Gandhi and Ideology of Swadeshi* (New Delhi : Reliance Pub., 1987).

__________ *Gandhi and Status of Women* (New Delhi : Criterian Pub., 1987).

_____________ *Gandhi and Civil Disobedience Movement* (New Delhi : Criterian pub., 1986).

Balasubramanian, C. *The Status of Women in Tamil Nadu during the Sangam age* (Madras, 1976).

Bala, Usha and Anshu Sharma, *Indian Women Freedom Fighters 1857 - 1947* (New Delhi : Manohar pub., 1986).

Baliga, B.S. *Gazetteers of India, Madras, Madurai* (Madras : Govt. Press, 1960).

_________ *Studies in Madras Administration,* Vol. II (Madras : Govt. Press, 1960).

________ *Compendium on Temperance and Prohibition in Madras* (Madras: Govt. Press, 1960).

_______ *Compendium on History of Handloom Industry in Madras* (Madras: Govt. Press, 1960).

________ *Tanjore District Handbook* (Madras: Govt. Press, 1957).

Banerji, Projesh *Art of Indian Dancing* (New Delhi : Sterling pub., 1985).

Basu, Aparna (ed.) *Dr. Muthulakshmi Reddy : The Path finder* (AIWC pub., 1987).

Bebi, Renu *Progress of Education in Assam* (Guwahati : Omsons pub., 1987).

Besant, Annie *Women and Politics : the Way out of the Present Difficulty, pamphlet* (London, 1916).

________, *The Political Status of Women* (II ed., London, 1885).

_________, *Birth of New India* (Madras : Theosophical Society, 1917).

_________, *The Future of Indian politics* (Madras; Theosophical Society, 1922).

_________, *National Home Rule League : Why Founded and How? (Madras :* Theosohical Society, 1919).

Bharati, C.Subramanya *Agni and other Poems and Translations and Essays and other Prose Fragments* (Madras : N. Natarajan, 1980).

Bhat, Yashoda (ed.) *Beyond the Threshold : Indian women on the move* (Delhi : B.T. pub., 1995).

Bhasin, Kmala and Nighat Said Khan, *Some Questions on Women's movement and its Relevance in South Asia* (New Delhi: Kali for Women, 1986).

Brophy, Julia and Carol Smart (eds) *Women in Law : Explorations in Law : Family and Sexuality* (London : Routledge and Regan Paul, 1985).

Caplan, Patricia and Janet M. Bujra (eds) *Women United Women Divided : Cross Cultural Perceptions on female solidarity* (London : Tavistock pub., 1978).

Caplan, Patricia *Class and Gender in India : Women and their organisations in a South Indian city* (London : Tavistock pub., 1985).

Chandrababu, B.S. *Social Protests in Tamilnadu* (Madras : Emerald pub., 1993).

Chapman, E.F. *Notable Indian women of the 19th century* (rpt., New Delhi: Inter - India pub., 1984).

Chatterjee, Santosh *Devadasi* (Temple Dancer) (Calcutta : The Book house, 1945).

Chattopadhyaya, Kamaladevi *The Awakening of Indian Women* (Madras : Everyman's press, 1939).

____________ *Indian Women's Battle for Freedom* (New Delhi : Abhinay pub., 1983).

Chintamani, Yajesvara *Indian Social Reform,* Vol. V, in four parts (Madras : Thomson & Co., 1901).

Chopra, P.N. et al. *History of South India,* Vol. III, *Modern Period* (New Delhi: Chand & Co, 1979).

Coatman, J, *India in 1927-1928 to 1937-1938. Social Political and Economic Developments* (10 volumes) (rpt., Delhi : Anmol pub., 1985).

Cousins, E. Margaret *What Women have gained by the Reforms,* the national conference leaflet series (Madras : The General secretary's office, n.d.).

Debi, Renu *Progress of Education in Assam* (Gauhati : Omsons pub., 1987).

Desai, Neera *Women in Modern India* (IIed, Bombay : Vora & Co., 1977).

Devandra, Kiran *Status and Position of Women in India* (New Delhi: Shakti Books, 1985).

Diana L. Eck and Devaki Jain (ed.) *Speaking of Faith : Cross - Cultural Perspectives on Women, Religion and Social Change* (New Delhi : Kali for women, 1986).

Dwarkardar, Jamnadar *Political Memoirs* (Bombay, 1929).

Encyclopaedia of Social Work in India, Vols. I-III (Freedom 40 Commemoration work) (New Delhi : Govt. of India, 1987).

Everett, Jana Matson *Women and Social Change in India* (rpt., New Delhi: Heritage, 1981).

Forbes, Geraldine *The New Cambridge History of India,* IV-2 *Women in Modern India* (New Delhi: Cambridge University Press, 1996).

Gandhi, M.K. *To the Women* : Gandhi series, Vol. II (III ed. Karachi : Anand T. Hingorani, 1946).

Gandhi, M.K. *The Collected Works of Mahatma Gandhi,* Vols. 1-59 (New Delhi: Govt. of India, 1953-73).

Gandhi, Nandita and Nandita Shah *The issues at stake : Theory and pratice in the Contemporary Women's Movement in India* (New Delhi : Kali for women, 1991).

Ghardially, Rehana (ed.) *Women in Indian Society : A Reader* (New Delhi : Sage pub., 1988).

Ghosh, S.K. *Women in a Changing Society* (New Delhi : Ashish pub., 1984).

Gore, M.S. *Education and Modernization in India* (Jaipur : Rawat pub., 1982).

Gupta, Shai Ved Prakash, *Franchise in India* (Bombay: All India Institute of Local Self Govt., 1965).

Gulati, Saroj *Women and Society : Northern India in the 11th & 12th centuries* (Delhi : Chanakya pub., 1985).

Hanumanthan, K.R. (ed.) *Proceedings of the Tamil Nadu History Congress,* 1994 (Madras, 1995).

Hartog, Philip *Some Aspects of Indian Education : Past and Present* (London: Oxford Press, 1939).

Hazel, D. Lima *Women in Local Government : A Study of Maharashtra* (New Delhi : Concept pub., 1993).

Hemingway, T.R. Madras District Gazetteers, Trichinopoly (Madras, Govt. Press, 1907).

History of Higher Education in South India, Vol. II : *Madras University,* 1857 to 1957 (Madras : Associated printers, 1957).

Hunter, W.W. *The Imperial Gazetteer of India*, Vol. XXIII (Oxford: Henry Froidable pub., 1908).

Indian Women: Marriage and Social Status, Report of the Age of Consent Committee 1928-29 (Calcutta : USA, 1984).

Indian Womanhood through the Ages (Madras : Vivekananda Prakashen Kendra, 1975).

Irschick, F. Eugene *Tamil Revivalism in the 1930s* (Madras : Cre A, 1988).

____________ , *Politics and Social Conflict in South India*: *The non Brahmin movement and Tamil Separatism, 1926 - 1939* (Berkeley : California University Press, 1969).

Jayawarduna, Kumari *Feminism and Nationalism in the Third World* (New Delhi : Kali for women, 1986).

Justice party Golden Jubilee Souvenir (Madras, 1968).

Kanakasabha, V. *The Tamils Eighteen Hundred Years Ago* (Tirnevelly, 1956).

Kalidos, Raju *History and Culture of the Tamils : From Pre Historic Times to the President's rule* (Dindigul : Vijay pub., 1976).

Kaur, Manmohan *Women in India's Freedom Struggle* (II ed., New Delhi : Sterling, 1992).

Kesavanarayana, B. *Political and Social Factors in Andhra, 1900-1956* (Vijayavada : Navodaya pub., 1976).

Krishnamurthy, J. (ed.) *Women in Colonial India : Essays on Survival, Work and the State* (Delhi : Oxford University, 1981).

Krishna Raj, Maithreyi, (ed.) *Women's Studies in India : Some Perspectives* (Bombay : Popular Prakasan, 1986).

Krishnaswamy, S. *The Role of Madras Legislature in the Freedom struggle* 1861 - 1947 (New Delhi : ICHR, 1989).

Krishnaswami, *Rural Problems in Madras,* Monograph (Madras, 1947).

Kumar, Radha *The History of Doing : An Illustrated Account of Movements for Women's Rights and Women's Movement in India 1800-1990* (New Delhi : Kali for Women, 1993).

Kumar, Ravindra *The Selected Works of Subhas Chandra Bose - (1936-1946)* Vol. II (New Delhi : Atlantic pub., 1992).

Lahkar, Bina *Development in Women Education.* (Guwahati : Omsons pub., 1987).

Lakshmi, C.S. *The Face Behind the Mask : Women in Tamil Literature* (New Delhi : Sakti Books, 1984).

Liddle, Joanna and Rama Joshi, *Daughters of Independence : Gender, Caste and Class in India* (New Delhi : Kali for women, 1986).

Maharani of Baroda and S.M. Mitra *The Position of Women in Indian Life* (II rpt., Delhi : Neeraj pub., 1984).

Mahalingam, T.V. *South Indian Polity* (Madras : University of Madras, 1955).

Mandal, Naik Maratha *Dedication of Girls to Gods : Plea for Prohibition by Law* (Bombay, 1929).

Markovits, Claude, *Indian Business and Nationalist Politics : The Indegenous Capitalist Class and the rise of the Congress Party* (Bombay: Orient Longman, 1985).

Marcus Fuller, B. *The Wrongs of Indian Womenhood* (rpt., New Delhi : Inter India pub., 1984).

Mathew, P.M. and M.S. Nair, *Women's Organisations and Women's Interests* (New Delhi : Ashish pub., 1981).

Mazumdar, Vina (ed.) *Symbols of Power: Studies on the Political Status of Women in India* (Bombay : Allied pub., 1979).

Mehta, Rama *Socio - Legal Status of Women in India* (New Delhi: Metro Politan Book, 1982).

Menon,G., Karunakara *G. Subramania Iyer : His Life and Carriers* (Madurai: Ganesh & Co., n.d).

Mies, Maria, et. al *Women : The Last Colony* (New Delhi : Kali for Women, 1988).

Naidu, T. Varadarajulu, *The Justice Movement,* 1917 (Madras, 1932).

Natesan, G.A. and Co-(ed.) *Congress Resolution* (Madras : Natesan & Co., 1917).

Nanda, B.R. (ed.) *Indian Women : From Purdah to Modernity* (rpt., New Delhi: Radiant pub., 1990).

________ *Builders of Modern India : Motilal Nehru* (New Delhi : Govt. Press, 1970).

Nehru, Shyam Kumari (ed.) *Our Cause : A Symposium of Indian Women* (Allahabad : Kitabistan, 1938).

Nora Brockway, K. *A Larger way for Women : Aspects of Christian Education for Girls in South India, 1712-1948* (Geoffrey Cumberlege : Oxford Univ. Press).

Omvedt, Gail *Feminism and the Women's Movement in India, Pamphlet,* (Bombay : SNDT University, 1987).

Pande, B.N. (ed.) *A Centenary History of the Indian National Congress* (three volumes) (New Delhi : Vikas, 1985).

Pandit, H.N. *Fragments of History, India's Freedom Movement and After* (New Delhi, 1982).

Paramarthalingam,C. *Social Reform Movement in Tamilnadu in the Nineteenth Century.With special reference to St. Ramalinga* (Madurai : Rajkumari pub., 1995).

Pillay, K.K. *A Social History of the Tamils,* Vol. I (II ed. Madras: 1975).

Pope, Gill et.al. (Trans) *Tirukkural* (Tirunelveli : The South Indian Saiva Siddhantha Work, 1982).

Pratima, Asthana *Women's Movement in India* (Delhi : Vikas, 1974).

Premalatha, P.N. *The Congress Party in Tamilnadu,* 1905-1937 (Unpublished Ph.D. Thesis) Madurai University, 1990.

Parthasarathy, Rangaswami, *A Hundred years of the Hindu : The Epic Story of Indian Nationalism* (Madras: Kasturi and son, 1978).

Pate, H.R. *Madras District Gazetteers, Tirunelveli,* Vol. I (Madras: Govt. Press, 1917).

Pujari, Premlata, Vijay Kumari Kaushik, *Women Power in India,* (Delhi : Kanishka pub., 1994).

Pruthi Raj, Bela Rani Sharma, *Encyclopaedia of Women, Society and Culture*, Vol. II, *Women and Social Charge* (New Delhi Anmol pub., 1994).

Rajalakshmi, R., *The Political Behaviour of Women in Tamilnadu* (Bombay : Inter India pub., 1985).

Raj, S.J. Sebasti (ed.) *Quest for Gender Justice : A critique of the status of Women in India* (Madras : T.R. Publications, 1991).

Rajayyan, K. *History of Madurai 1736-1801* (Madurai : Madurai University, 1974).

____________ *History of Tamilnadu*, 1562 - 1982 (Madurai: Raj pub., 1982).

Ramaswami, A. *Gazetteer of India, Tamil Nadu State, Ramanathapuram District* (Madras : Govt. Press, 1972).

Ramachander, M. and K. Lakshmi *Women and Politics : A Study in Political Participation* (Hyderabad : Book links Corporation, 1993).

Rao, M.S.A. (ed.) *Social Movements in India* (New Delhi : Manohar, 1979).

Reddy, S. Muthulakshmi *My Experience as a Legislator* (Madras: Recurrent Thought Press, 1930).

_______, _______ *Autobiography* (Madras, 1964).

Sadasivan, D. *Growth of Public opinion in the Madras Presidency*, 1858-1909 (Madras : University, 1964).

Sangari, Kumkum, Sudesh Vaid (eds.) *Recasting Women : Essays in Colonial History* (New Delhi : Kali for Women, 1989).

Sanger, William, W. *The History of Prostitution, its extent causes and effects throughout the world* (New Delhi : Inter India pub., 1986).

Sapiro, Virginia *The Political Integration of Women: Roles, Socialization and Politics* (Urbana : University of Illinois Press, 1984).

Sastri, Nilakanta, K.A. *The Colas* (Madras University, 1984).

Sathianadhan, S. *History of Education in the Madras Presidency* (Madras : Srinivasa Varadachari & Co., 1894).

Saxena, Vinod Kumar *Indian Reaction to British Policies*, 1898-1911 (Delhi : Sundeep Prakashan, 1978).

Schmitt Pantel, Pauline (ed.) Arthur Gold Hammer, (Trans) *A History of Women : From Ancient Goddesses to Christian Saints* (London : The Belknap Press of Harvard University, 1990).

Sen, S.P. (ed.) *Social and Religious Reform Movements in the Nineteenth and Twentieth Centuries* (Calcutta : Institute of Historical Studies, 1979).

________, *Dictionary of National Biography,* Vols. I-IV (Calcutta: Institute of Historical Studies, 1973).

Sen Gupata, Padmini *The Story of the Women of India* (New Delhi, 1974).

Shah, Ghanshyam *Social Movements in India : A Review of the Literature* (New Delhi : Sage pub., 1990).

Shah, Giri Raj *The Encyclopaedia of Women's Studies* (in two volumes) (New Delhi : Gyan pub. 1995).

Sharma, Radha Krishna *Nationalism Social Reform and Indian Women : A study of the Interaction between our National movement and the movement of social reform among Indian Women, 1921-1951* (Patna : Janaki Prakashan pub., 1981).

Sharma, Tripat, *Women in Ancient India from 320 A.D. to 1200 A.D.,* (New Delhi : ESS ESS pub., 1987).

Shridevi, S. *A Century of Indian Womanhood* (Mysore : Rao & Raghavan, 1965).

Shukla, D.M. *Political Socialization and Women Voters : A case study of Kodarma constituency* (New Delhi : Anmol pub., 1987).

Sinha, B.S. *Law and Social Change in India* (New Delhi : Deep and Deep, 1983).

Siromoney, Gift et al. *Tirukkural an Ancient Script* (Thambaram: Madras Christian College, 1980).

Srinivasachari, C.S. *History of the City of Madras* (Madras, 1939).

Subbarayan, Radhabai *The Political Status of Women under the New Constitution*, Pamphlet (Madras, n.d).

Subramanian, N. *History of Tamil Nadu (to AD 1565),* (III ed. Madurai : Koodal pub., 1978).

__________, *Social and Cultural History of Tamil Nadu (to AD 1336)* (Madurai : Koodal pub.).

Sumati, G. *Women Awakened* (Madras : Swarajya, 1928).

Sundaram, P.S., (Trans.) *Poems of Subramania Bharati* (Delhi : Vikas pub., 1982).

Sundara Raj, M. *Prostitution in Madras : A Study in Historical Perspective* (Delhi : Konarch pub., 1993).

Sundararajan, Saroja *March to Freedom in Madras Presidency, 1916-1947* (Madras : Lalitha pub., 1989).

Sundararajan, S. *Ancient Tamil Society : Its Social and Economic Structure* (New Delhi : Navraj, 1991).

Tata, A. Herabai *A Short Sketch of Indian Women's Franchise Work* (1920, n.d).

Tharu, Susie and K. Lalitha (eds.) *Women Writing in India : 600 BC to the Present,* Vol. I-II, (Delhi : Oxford University Press, 1993).

The Official Guide to The Christian Medical College and Hospital, Vellore 1900 - 2000, (Vellore : C.M.C. publication, 2001).

The Women's India Association Golden Jubilee Souvenir, 1917-1967 (Madras, 1967).

The Women of India and What can be done for them (Madras : The Christian Vernacular Education Society, 1888).

The Awakening : Demand for Devadasi Legislation, Pamphlet (Madras, 1928).

TNA, *Select Document series, 1900-1947* : Neill Statue Satyagraha (Madras : Tamilnadu Archives, 1986).

Thompson, Edward *Suttee:A Historical and Philosophical Enquiry into the Hindu Rite of Widow Burning,* (London: George Allen and Unwin, 1928).

Thurston, Edgar *Castes and Tribes of Southern India* (rpt. Delhi : Cosmo pub., 1975).

Tuttle, Lisa, *Encyclopedia of Women's movement,* (London : Longman, 1986).

Venkataraman,S. *A Treatise on Hindu Law* (II ed., New Delhi : Orient Longman, 1980).

Venkatarangaiya, M. (ed.) *Freedom Struggle in Andhra Pradesh, 1906-1920,* Vols. I-III (Hyderabad : Andhra Pradesh State Committee, 1969).

Venkatasubramanian, K., *Issues in Education* (Madras : Macmillan, 1982).

Veeramani K. and R. Sundara Raju *Periyar on Women's Rights* (Madras : Emerald pub., 1992).

Verma, G.C. *Modern Education : Its growth and development in Rajasthan* (1818 to 1983) (Jaipur : Publication Scheme, 1984).

Viswanathan, E.Sa. *The Political Career of E.V. Ramaswamy Naicker* (Madras: Ravi and Vasanth pub., 1983).

Wake up India (A series of lectures delivered in Madras in 1913 to mark the beginning of a movement for uplifting of India organised by Annie Besant, n.d.).

Zaidi, Moin A and Zaidi Shaheda, *The Encyclopaedia of the Indian National Congress,* Vols. I-XI (New Delhi: S. Chand & Co., 1977-1980).

(b) Vernacular (Tamil)

Ambujamal, S. ***naan kanda bharatham*** (Bharath which I have seen) (Madras, 1973).

Dalavai, R.R. ***oru thyahiyin chila ninaivugal*** (A few memories of a martyr) (Chennai : Tamilnadu Gandhian Association, 1984).

Eraiyan, A. ***suyamariyathai chudarozhikal*** (Great self respecters) (Chennai : Suyamariyathai pub., 1981).

Illango, cha-chu ***bharatidasan padaippukal*** (Works of Bharatidasan) (Sivagangai, 1983).

Kaliyana Sundaranar, Thiru.Vi. ***pennin perumai allathu vazhkai thunai*** (Prestige of women or life partner) (Chennai: Poompuhar pub. 1959).

____________, ***thiru vi.ka. vazhkai kurippukkal*** (Notes on Thiru.Vi. Ka) (rpt. Thirunelveli : Saivasiddantha pub., 1982).

Madurai jilla thiyahigal malar (Madurai District Martyrs' issue) (Suthandira prasuralayam, 1983).

Mani, Pa.Chi ***bharatiyarum samooga ceerthiruthamum*** (Bharati and Social Reform) (IIed. Chennai : Thirumagal pub., 1982).

Manikkanar, A. ***pathinen keezhkanaku noolkal : moolamum, thezhlivuraiyum*** (Eighteen Anthologies: Original and Explanation) Part-III (Chennai: Varthamanan pub., 1991).

Padmanabhan, R.A.(ed) ***bharathi puthaiyal perunthirahu*** (Great works of Bharathi) (Vedaranyam: Gurukulam pub., 1982).

Pavendar bharathidasan noorandu vizhamalar, 1991 (Bharatidasan Centenary Celebration Souvenir) (Thiruchi: Bharadidasan University, 1991).

Premalatha, P.N. *india pennkal : pandaya kaalam muthal 1947 varai,* (Indian Women: From ancient period to 1947) (Kodaikanal : MTWU, 1997).

________, "indiya suthandiraporil tamilagapenngal" (Women of Tamilnadu in Freedom struggle) in R. Kabaliswaran (ed.) *Tamilaha pengal nilai* (Status of Tamil Women) (New York : Federation of Tamil Sangam, 1990).

Ragami *Vidulhalai Veerankunai hukumini Lakshmipathi* (woman Freedom Fighter Rukmini Lakshmipathi) Chennai, 1995.

Rajagopal, Sarala ***tamil thenralum pennmaiyam*** (Tamil thenral and women) (Chennai: Alaigal press, 1988).

________ ***puratchi kavingnarum pennmaiyum*** (Revolutionary poet and women) (Chennai, 1990).

Rajendran, ***magalir manam kavarntha muthulakshmi*** (Muthulakshmi, the favourite of Women) (Chennai, 1984).

Santha, N. Apthe "thiru.vi.ka.karuthiyalil pennmai" (Women according to Thiru.Vi.Ka) in Rama Shanmugam et.al(ed), ***thiru.vi.ka. oru palkalai kazhagam*** (Thiru Vi. Ka, an University) (Chidambaram: Manivasagam pub, 1983).

Shanmugam, Rama et.al ***thiru.vi.ka oru palkalai kazhagam*** (Thiru Vi. Ka. an University) (Chidambaram : Manivasagam pub., 1983).

Sivakami Sundari, Chu "pavendar parvaiyil pennmai" (Women in the eye's of Pavendar) in ***Bharatidasan noorrandu vizhamalar*** (Bharatidasan Centenary Celebration Souvenir) (Thiruchi: Bharatidasan University, 1991).

Somala ***madurai mavattam*** (Madurai District) (Vedaranyam: K.G. and K.G. pub., 1980).

Vachiravelu, ***thiru.vi.kavin pennin perumai oarayvu*** (An analysis of Thiru.vi.ka's women's fame) (Dharmapuri, 1988).

Vedanayagam pillai, kuzhathur ***penkallvi, penmanan, penmathimalai*** (Women's Education, Women's Mind and Women's Knowledge) (Thirunelveli : Saiva Siddantha Press, 1978).

Velupillai, Narayanan, N. *navayuga nava manigal* (Nine Women) (Madras, 1982).

Visvanathan, E. Sa., *"thiru.vi.ka.vin karuthoyalil pennmai"* (Women according to Thiru. Vi. Ka.) Rama Shanmugam, et.al. *thiru.vi.ka. oru palkalai kazhagam* (Chidambaram : Manivasagan pub., 1983).

Abbreviations used in the References

AIWC	-	All India Women's Conference
CDM	-	Civil Disobedience Movement
CWMG	-	Collected Works of Mahatma Gandhi
CONFL.	-	Confidential
Cr.PC	-	Criminal Procedure Code
EINC	-	Encyclopaedia of Indian National Congress
FMF	-	Freedom Movement File
FR	-	Demi Official, Fortnightly Reports from the Government of Madras to the Government of India
GO	-	Government Order
HRM	-	Home Rule Movement
IFC	-	Indian Franchise Committee
IPC	-	Indian Penal Code
JUD	-	Judicial
MNR	-	Madras Native Newspaper Report
MPCC	-	Madras Provincial Congress Committee
PMLC	-	Proceedings of the Madras Legislative Council
PUB	-	Public
PSPP	-	Personal Statements of Political Personalities
RAMP	-	Report on the Administration of the Madras Presidency
REV	-	Revenue
RIEC	-	Report of Indian Education Commission
RPIMP	-	Report on the Public Instruction of the Madras Presidency
RINC	-	Report of the Indian National Congress
SRRF	-	Secret Report Retained File
TNA	-	Tamilnadu Archives
USSF	-	Under Secretary's Safe File (Secret)
WIA	-	Women's India Association

Index